IMAGES
of America

THOMASVILLE

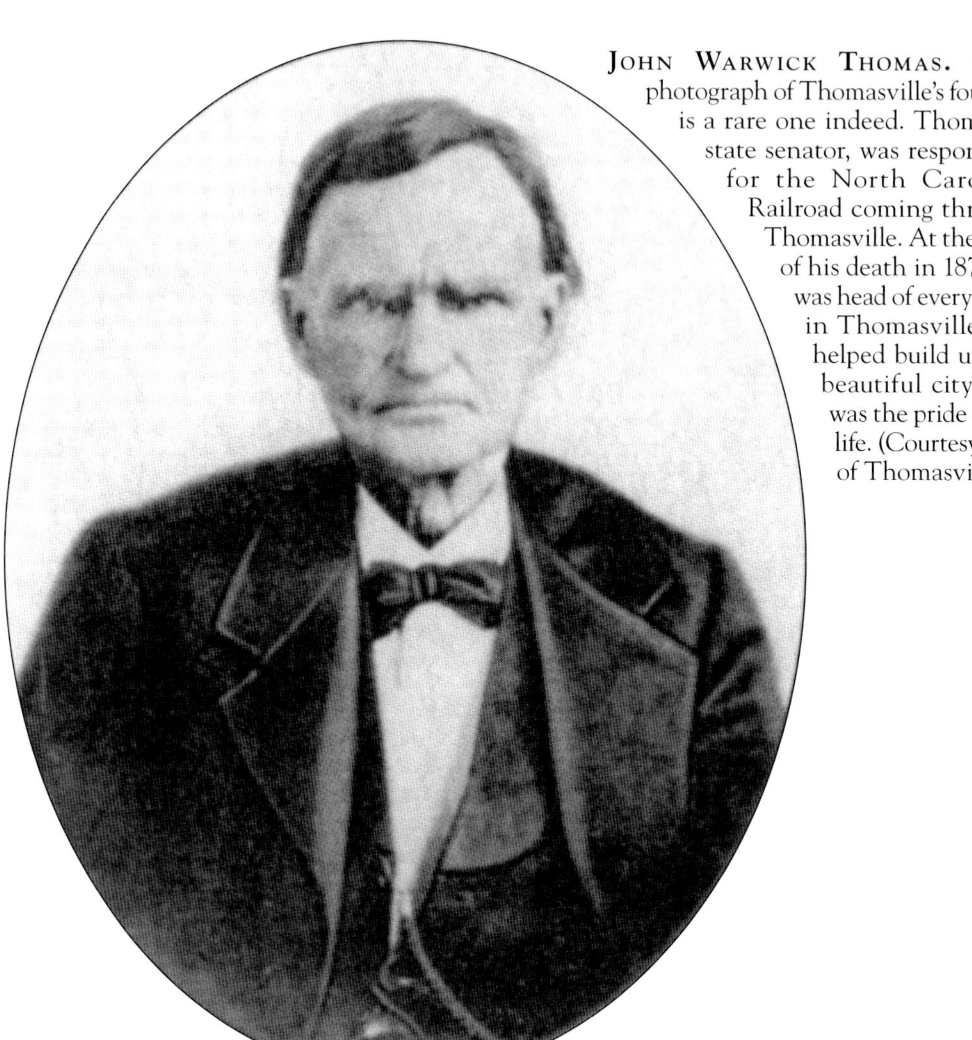

John Warwick Thomas. This photograph of Thomasville's founder is a rare one indeed. Thomas, a state senator, was responsible for the North Carolina Railroad coming through Thomasville. At the time of his death in 1871, he was head of everything in Thomasville and helped build up the beautiful city that was the pride of his life. (Courtesy City of Thomasville.)

On the Cover: Quail Capital of the South. Everett Shelton Swaim Sr. (left) was the hunting guide and dog trainer for the Thomasville Shooting Club. There were only 25 members allowed in the club, and they were all prominent Yankees. Quail can be seen on the car's fender and in the hands of the man at right. Swaim was a great-great-grandfather of the author of this book. (Courtesy Tommy Swaim.)

IMAGES
of America

THOMASVILLE

Austin J. Hill

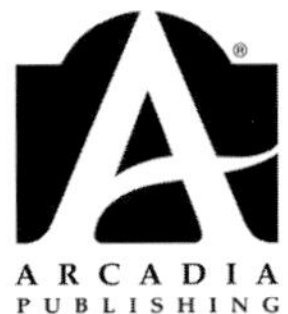

ARCADIA
PUBLISHING

ISBN 978-1-4671-0787-7

Published by Arcadia Publishing
Charleston, South Carolina

Printed in the United States of America

Library of Congress Control Number: 2021946304

For all general information, please contact Arcadia Publishing:
Telephone 843-853-2070
Fax 843-853-0044
E-mail sales@arcadiapublishing.com
For customer service and orders:
Toll-Free 1-888-313-2665

Visit us on the Internet at www.arcadiapublishing.com

For Mom-Mom.

Contents

ACKNOWLEDGMENTS

I would like to thank the following people for making this book possible: my parents, Mark and Caroline, for being my rock; all four of my grandparents, whom I love and admire deeply; my other two sets of parents, Todd and Lorie Sechrist and Maurice and Lori Rayburn, for your love and support; Mark and Jane Cox Leonard for your depth of knowledge on this fine place; Luke Hunsucker and Renee Hayes for making me the man I am today; Danny Ward, Andrew Clement, and Paxton Taylor for loving our city so well; Jay Hartsfield, Kylie Nguyen, and Eddie Nickens for inspiring the writer inside of me; Katelyn Jenkins and Angel Prohaska with Arcadia Publishing for being as passionate about this as I am; and the citizens of Thomasville—what a wonderful place we have to call home.

Unless otherwise noted, all images are from the collection of the author and his family.

INTRODUCTION

Thomasville is a city that grew up along the tracks. The community was founded in 1852, and its initial growth paralleled the construction of the North Carolina Railroad. John W. Thomas, the founder of Thomasville, was born in 1800 and left his native Caswell County around 1816 to settle in the area known as Fair Grove; according to Mary Green Matthews and M. Jewell Sink in *Wheels of Faith and Courage*, "At that time, the future founder of Thomasville had a blind horse, a gun . . . and a little more."

Thomas went on to be elected to the North Carolina legislature, and as a state senator, he was instrumental in the decision to build the North Carolina Railroad. Around 1838, when Thomas found out the railroad would be located a few miles north of his homestead, he acquired 1,500 acres of land that the proposed railroad would cross, paying for the tract with a four-horse load of bacon. This means that the property that would become the city of Thomasville was bought with bacon.

With less than 300 residents, the town was officially incorporated in 1857. Thomasville was named for John Thomas and Dr. Henry E. Rounsaville. Dr. Rounsaville was the community's first physician and served as postmaster from 1854 to 1865. Thomas, with a pioneer spirit, was not content with just establishing a town—he also wanted to see it develop.

According to *Wheels of Faith and Courage*, Thomas was ahead of his time when it came to public improvements: "When the railroad was finished, he turned his attention to improving the roads leading out from the town and to assisting all comers who were interested in any kind of business."

Early Thomasville industry included steam-powered mills, the first of which was located where the old Thomasville Furniture Industries main office now stands. That early mill used water from Hamby's Creek to produce flour and lumber for the first residents of Thomasville. Shoe-manufacturing was another early industry, and the sole suppliers were credited with making major contributions to both the Union and the Confederacy during the Civil War.

Following the war, the community's growth slowed. Thomas died in 1871, and by 1900, Thomasville's population numbered 752. But the industrial surge Thomas had hoped for—in the form of furniture manufacturing—was just beyond the horizon at the dawning of the 20th century.

When John Walter Lambeth Jr., born in Thomasville in 1896, retired from the US House of Representatives in 1939, the citizens of Thomasville honored him with a banquet. Lambeth's speech that night summarizes Thomasville best:

> I owe a personal debt to every person of whatever creed, color or walk of life in Thomasville, not only of the present but of the past. Somehow I felt the urge to come back to renew my faith—to be near those who sleep at Fair Grove and out there by the old factory, to see more of friends old and young, to be closer to the soil from which I have sprung. I am thinking tonight of many who have influenced my life, not only those who are here in person or may be listening in the invisible audience but of many who have gone on. . . . And so I

am a part of Thomasville and Thomasville is a part of me. I do not know where the future may lead, for 'There's a divinity that shapes our ends/Rough-hew them how we will.' But I can tell you that my heart will always be here with you. I have visited cities more beautiful than Thomasville where culture is more highly developed and one can drink of beauty and knowledge. But after seeing a good part of the world, new and old, I would not trade it for any place I have known. Whether measured by climate, soil, people, or any other yardstick, when you put it all together, where is another place more desirable to live, if one can find one's work here and find in it the music of life? I must remind you how fortune and providence have smiled upon us. Not in my lifetime has a major catastrophe of nature visited Thomasville in the way of earthquake, cyclone, tornado, flood or famine. We have not had to burrow in the ground like most moles to save ourselves from air raids. When the ground was giving way and the skies were falling in 1932 and 1933, Thomasville stood firm because it was founded upon a rock, and there was not a single major failure in our business community. Thomasville is a throbbing little city of great energy and vitality. Payrolls are its lifeblood, and somehow there have always been men with the courage, enterprise, initiative, thrift, and fortitude to keep the bloodstream flowing. But it takes more than payrolls to build a city. It takes community spirit, which is the family spirit, to give a city a soul. I charge you here tonight that just as a farmer should guard his land against soil erosion, we should guard our city against the insidious processes of soil erosion, economic, political, and social erosion.

Lambeth concluded his speech by quoting poet Emilie Daniels:

> Yes, I live in Goshen, this little town of little streets and little ways, of little men and great. I eat, sleep, and work here; but mostly I *live* and laugh and weep and agonize and pray. I dream in Greece and Rome, and I try to bring my dreams to Goshen; and sometimes I do, but mostly I fail; but here I meet my friends—my living, breathing fellows, and we walk and think and do, and bless and hurt each other every day. Here I see great men sometimes small and small men sometimes great; and out of all Goshen's ugliness I see great beauty grow, and so I live in paradise *right here.*

This book aims to give readers an idea of what Thomasville was like before the 1950s. Carts pulled by horses and oxen creaked along the dirt paths in town. Steam locomotives hissed to a stop as passengers disembarked at the depot. Citizens built homes for themselves and their families, as many still do today.

One

Downtown

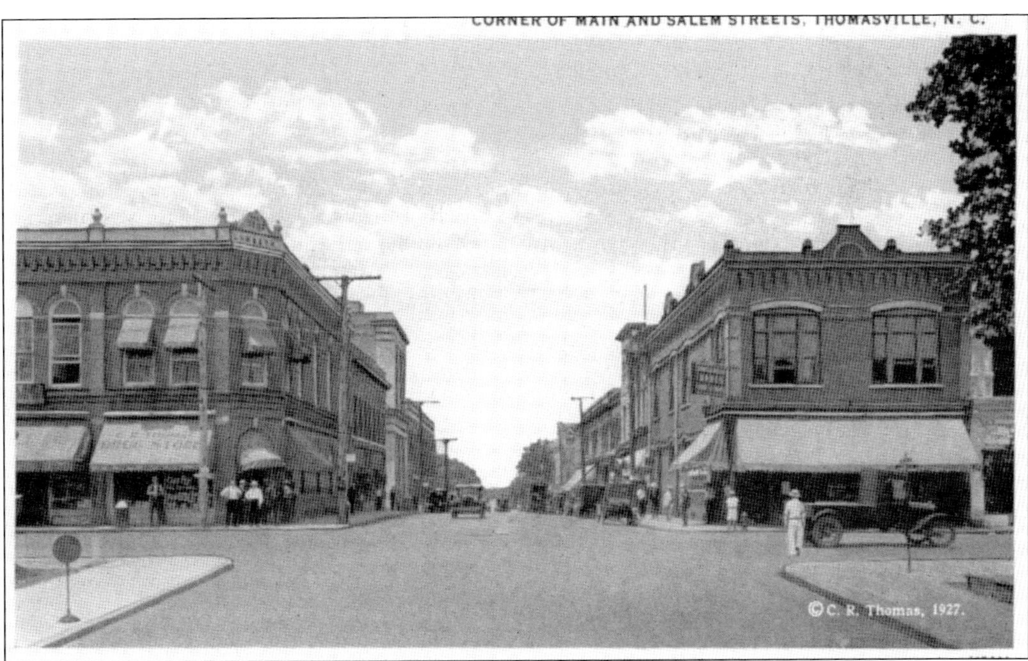

Corner of Main and Salem Streets, 1927. Although this street scene has evolved, it is still a familiar view to many. The heart of downtown Thomasville, once known as the town square, has changed much since this postcard was created. Drugstores dominated these corners, with C.R. Thomas Drug Store on the left and Harville Drug Company on the right.

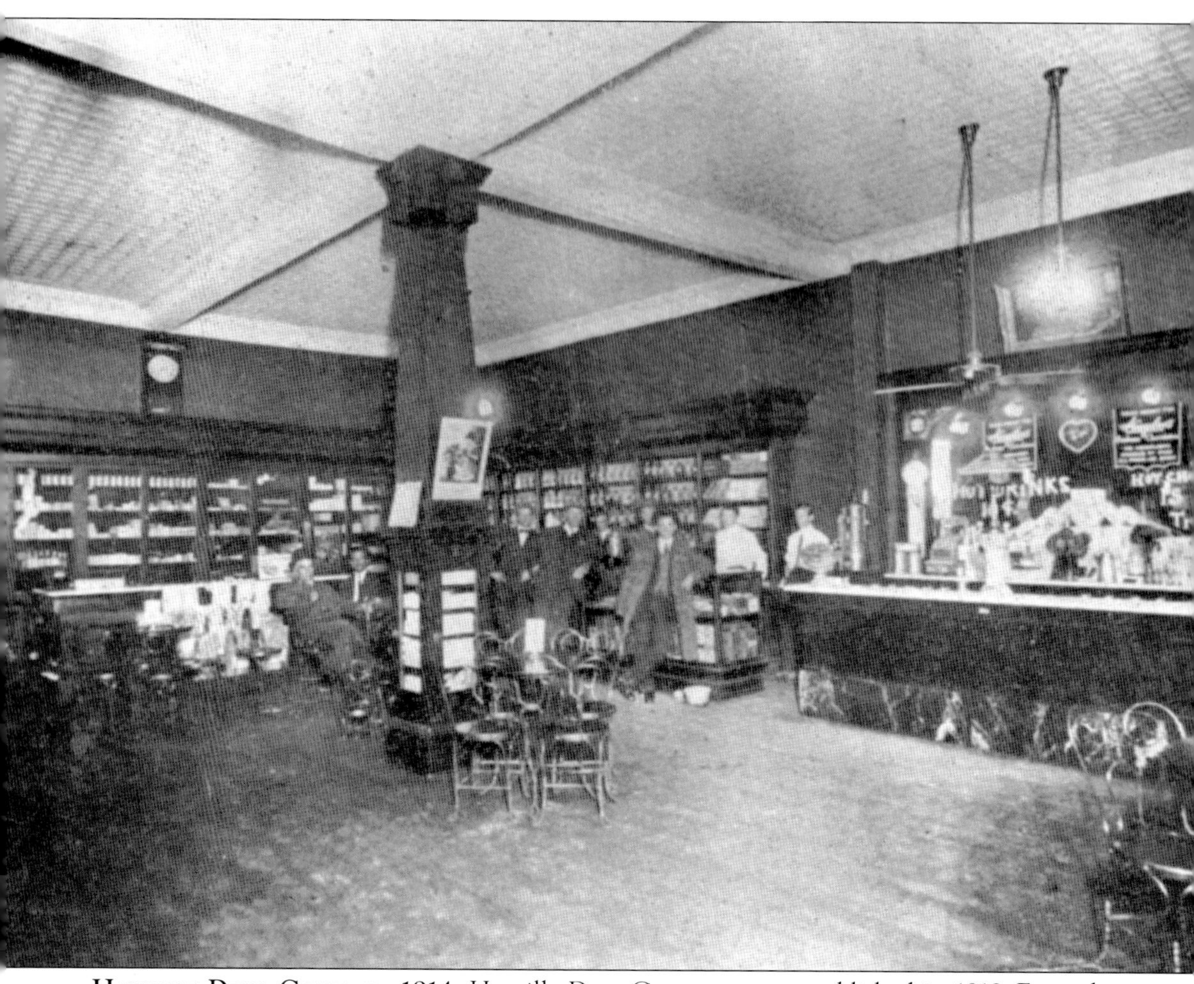

Harville Drug Company, 1914. Harville Drug Company was established in 1910. From the time its doors were opened to trade, it maintained steady growth. The business grew so rapidly that the building did not have enough floor space to meet demands, and by 1912, the store had doubled in size.

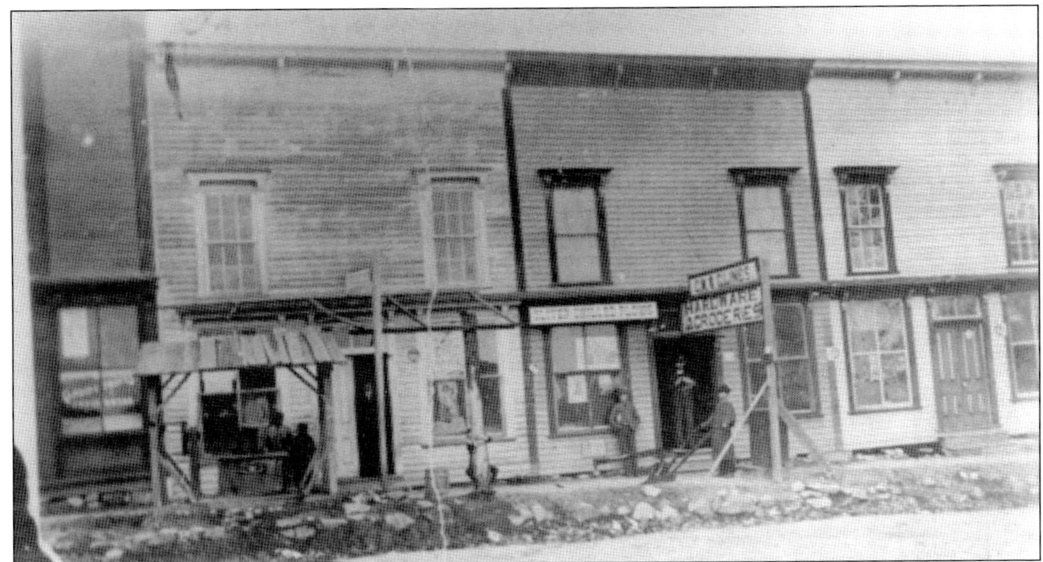

Salem Street, 1892. The CM&G Lines company once sold shoes on the same lot where its shoe factory was located. It later moved the retail operation, managed by John Tyler, to this block on Salem Street. A line of stables was built on the lot behind this block to provide a convenient place for rural customers to feed and water their horses.

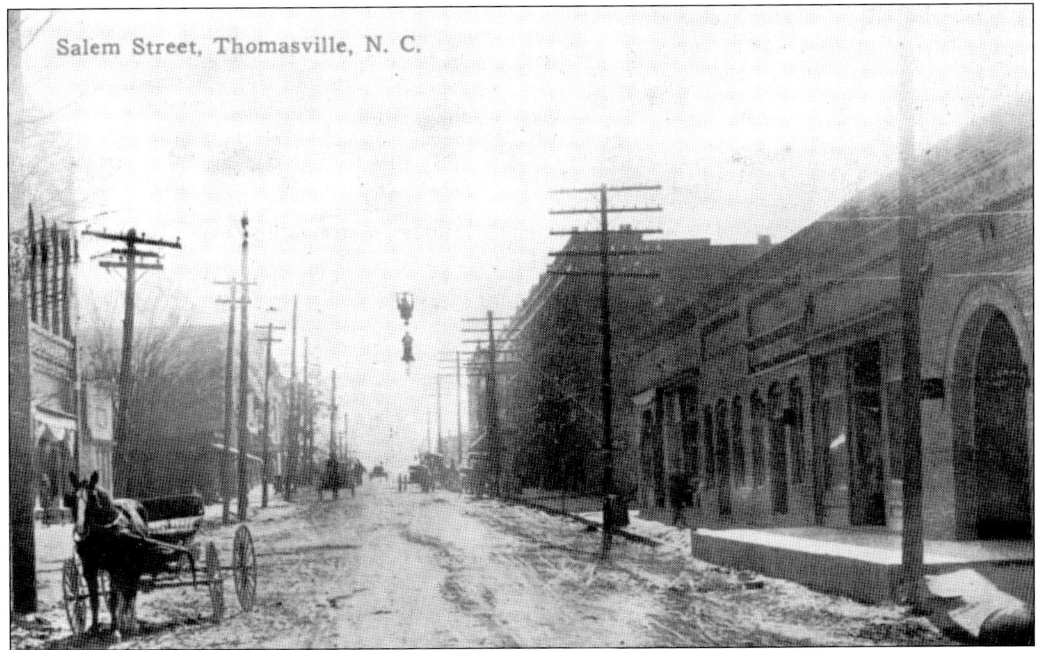

Salem Street, c. 1912. According to Wint Capel in his book *In Words & Pictures: Thomasville in the Nineteen Twenties,* "Salem Street was still a muddy passageway when the photograph for this postcard was made. The camera was pointed southward, toward the Town Square. Only horses and buggies were about. In April 1918, Thomasville issued bonds in the sum of $8,000 to finance a street-paving program that got under way soon thereafter."

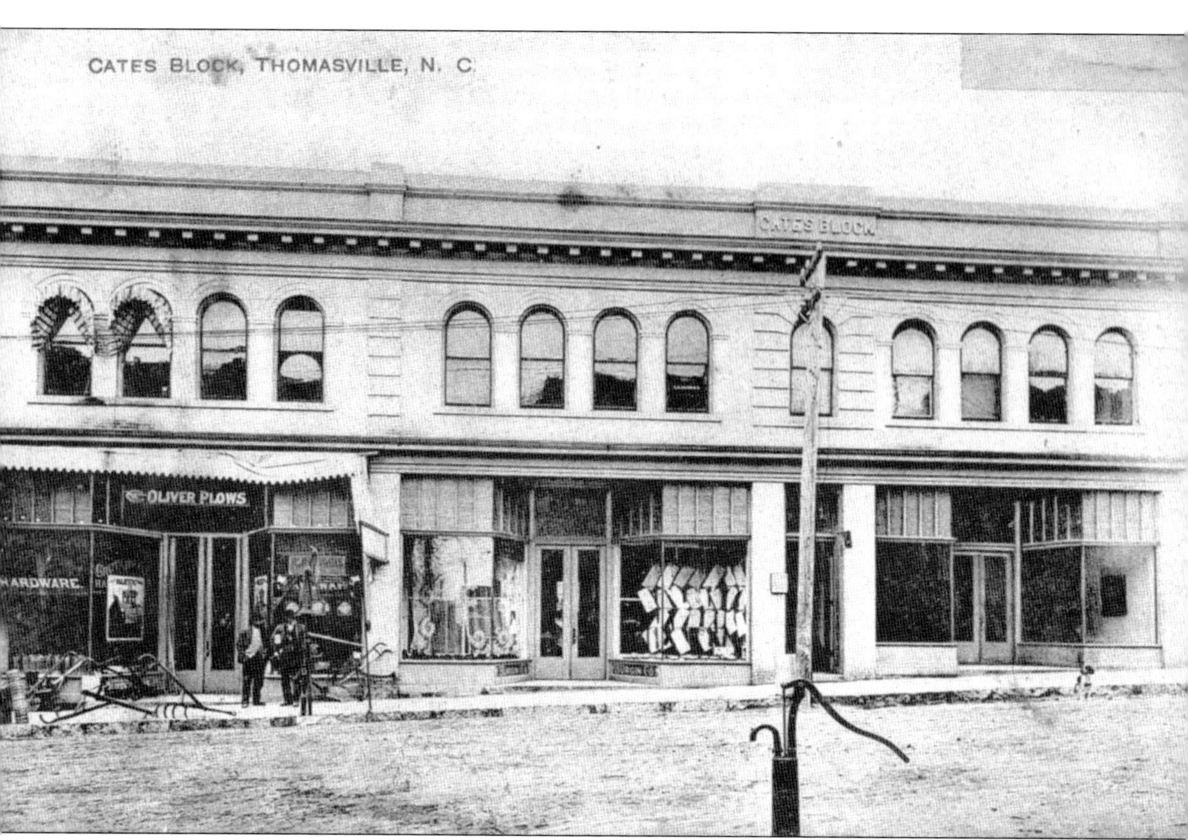

Cates Block, c. 1912. The Cates Block was built in 1911 on the east side of the first block of Salem Street. It housed Crutchfield Hardware (left) and the Burgin Company (center). The vacant space at right later housed the post office for a brief period. Note one of the town's water pumps in the foreground.

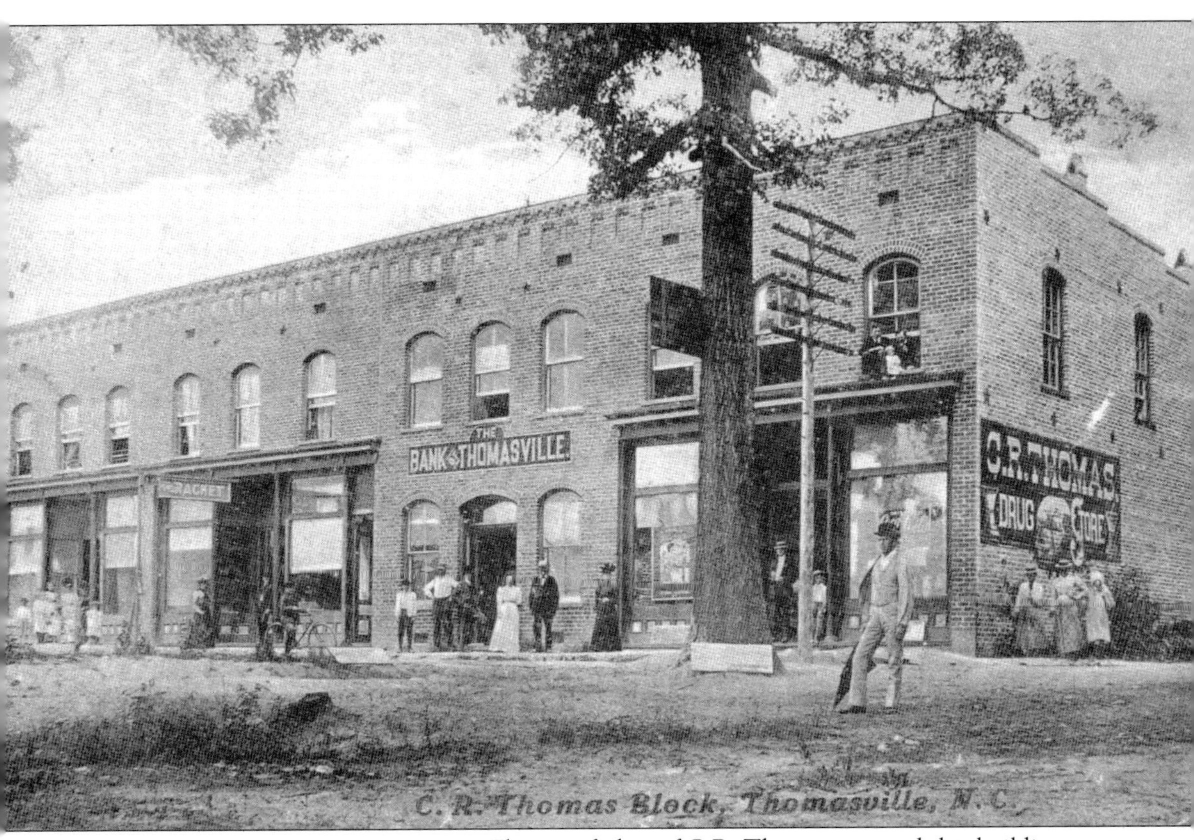

C.R. Thomas Block, 1905. Dr. R.W. Thomas, father of C.R. Thomas, erected this building on the first block of West Main Street. The C.R. Thomas block housed the Bank of Thomasville and C.R. Thomas Drug Store. A large, illustrated C.R. Thomas Drug Store sign—featuring a mortar and pestle—is visible on the east side of the building.

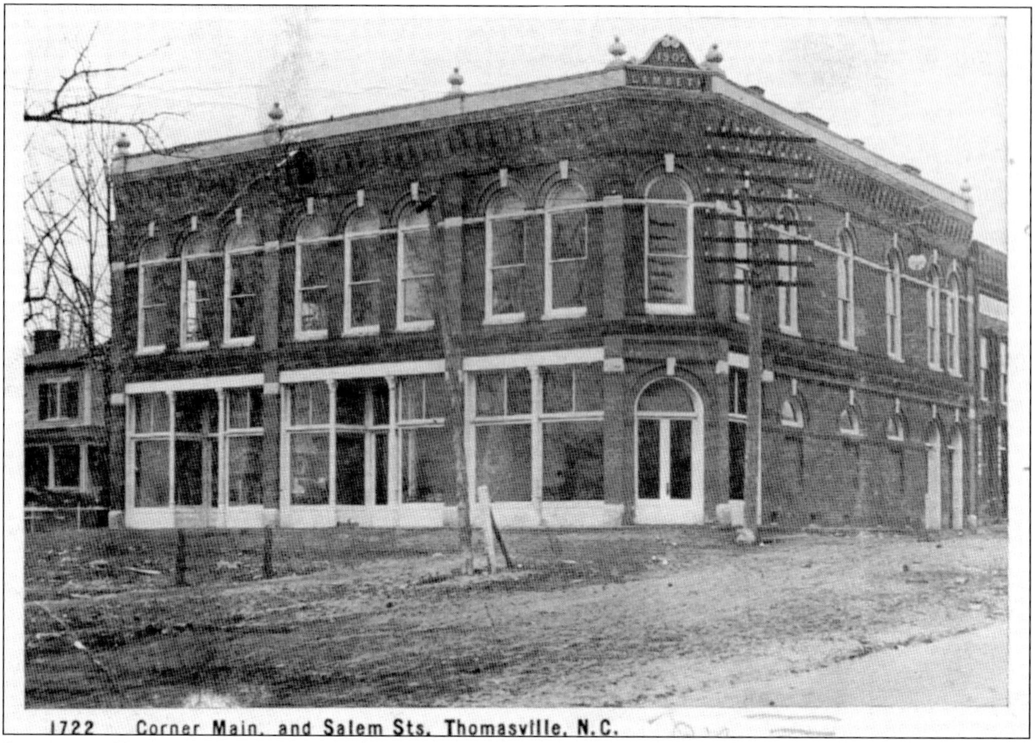

1722 Corner Main. and Salem Sts. Thomasville, N.C.

Lambeth Building, 1902. As shown on this postcard, the Lambeth Building was yet to be occupied after being completed in the year this photograph was taken. The first business to occupy the corner of the ground floor was Thomasville Drug Store (later known as C.R. Thomas Drug Store). The John W. Thomas residence is visible on the left.

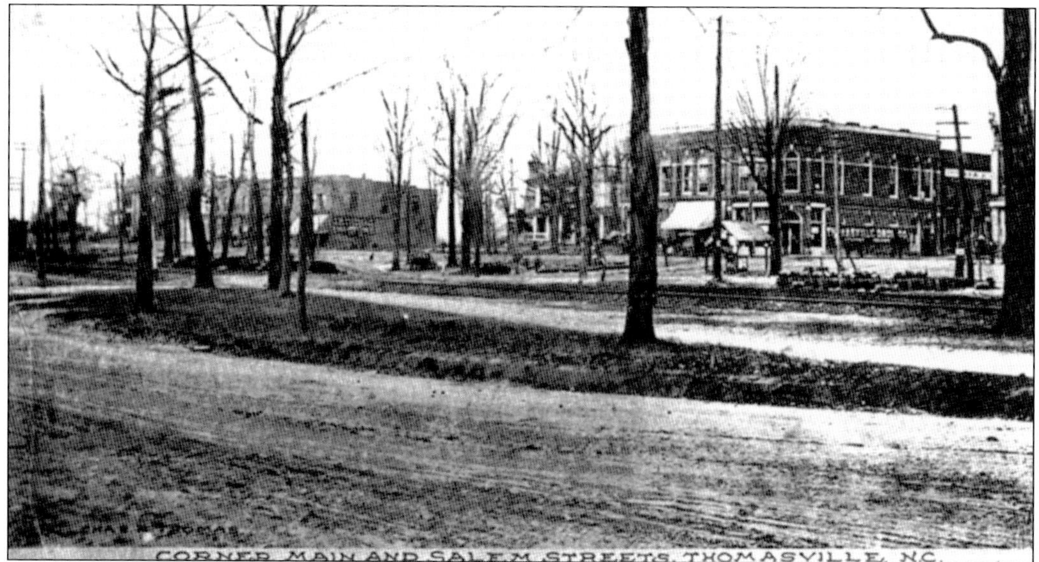

Corner of Main and Salem Streets, 1910. This C.R. Thomas postcard displays a view across the railroad tracks toward the town square. From left to right are the C.R. Thomas block, the John W. Thomas residence, and the Lambeth Building. The Thomasville Shooting Club mansion was out of frame to the left.

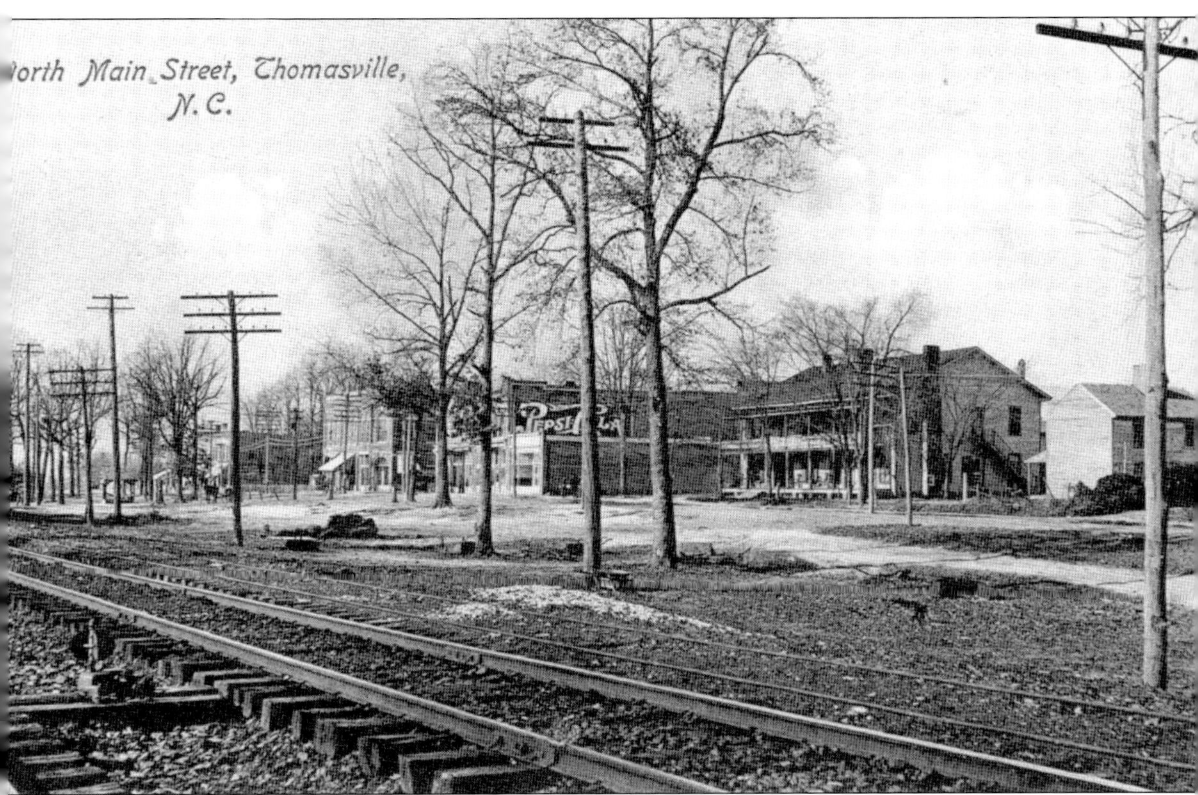

North Main Street. By 1890, there were a few kerosene oil lamps on posts about six feet high to light the streets of Thomasville. Electric streetlights were obtained thanks to an arrangement with the Lambeth Furniture Company in 1902 powered by a dynamo in its factory. This continued until 1908, when a contract was made with the Thomasville Power and Lighting Company (later absorbed by Southern Power Company, then Duke Power Company).

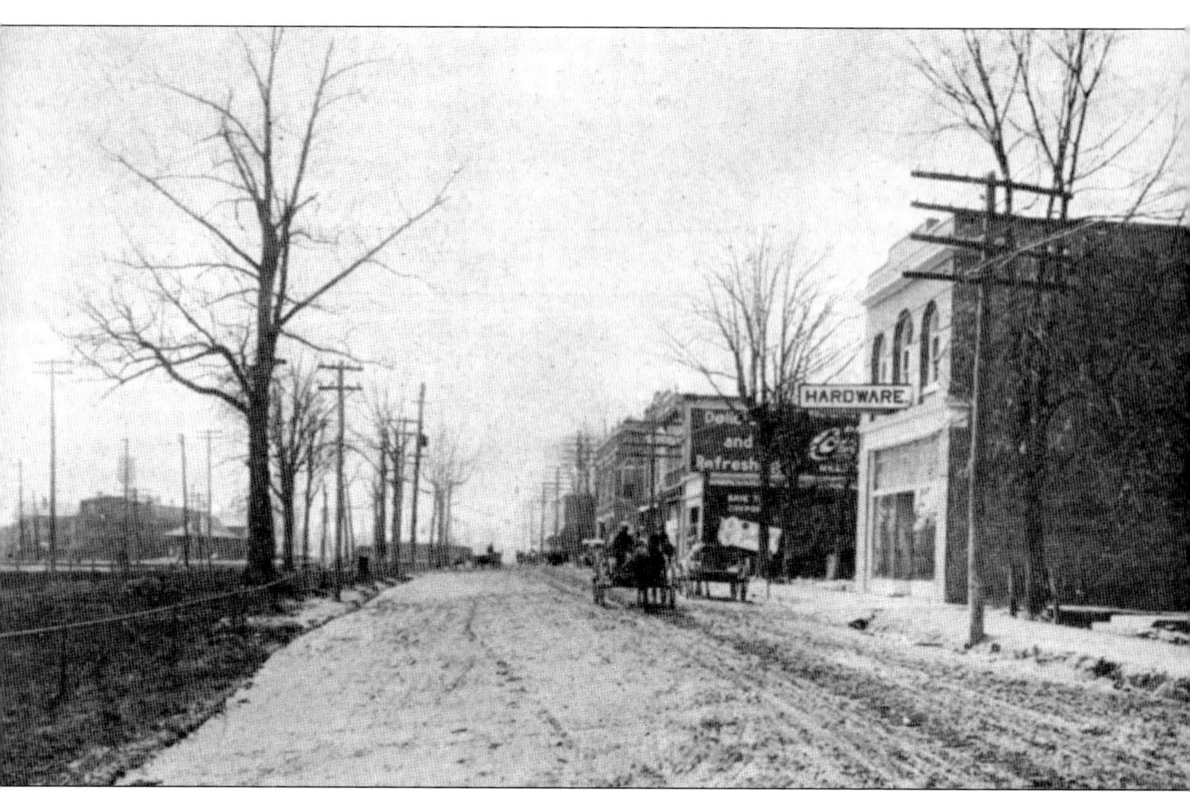

East Main Street, 1914. This rare photograph looks west down East Main Street toward the town commons. Notable landmarks include the Mock Hotel and Southern Railway passenger station at far left, and the corner of the Lambeth Building at center, above the buggy rider's head.

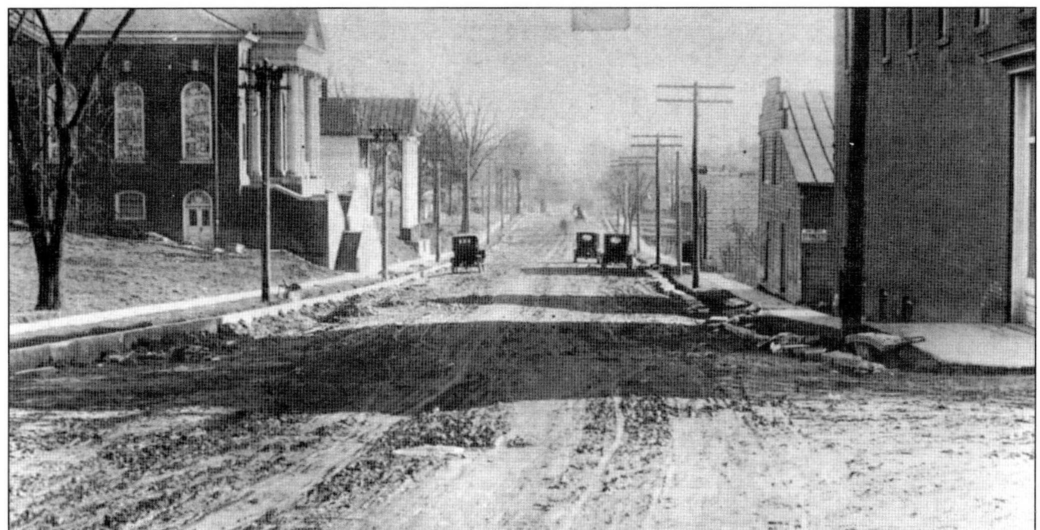

Randolph Street, Late 1910s. A giveaway that this view looks south down Randolph Street is the First Baptist Church on the left. Note that the concrete for the curbs and sidewalks has been poured, although the road is still dirt. The businesses that once stood here are visible in the image on page 37.

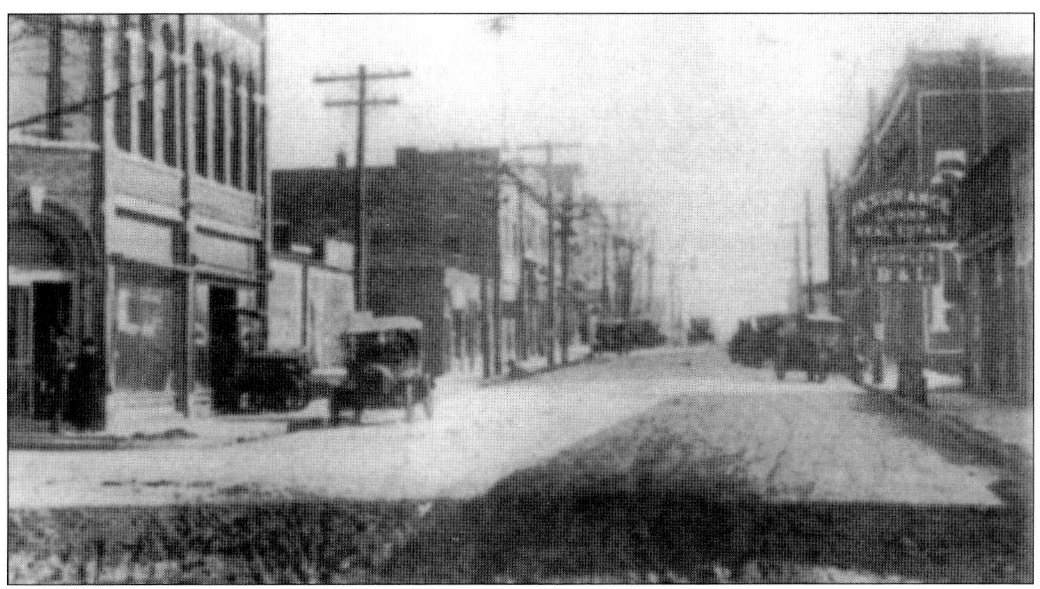

Corner of East Guilford and Salem Streets. This is an early street scene looking south. Barely visible on the right is the Pepsi-Cola wall sign that is still painted on the side of 30 Salem Street today. The sign runs parallel with present-day J.W. Thomas Way.

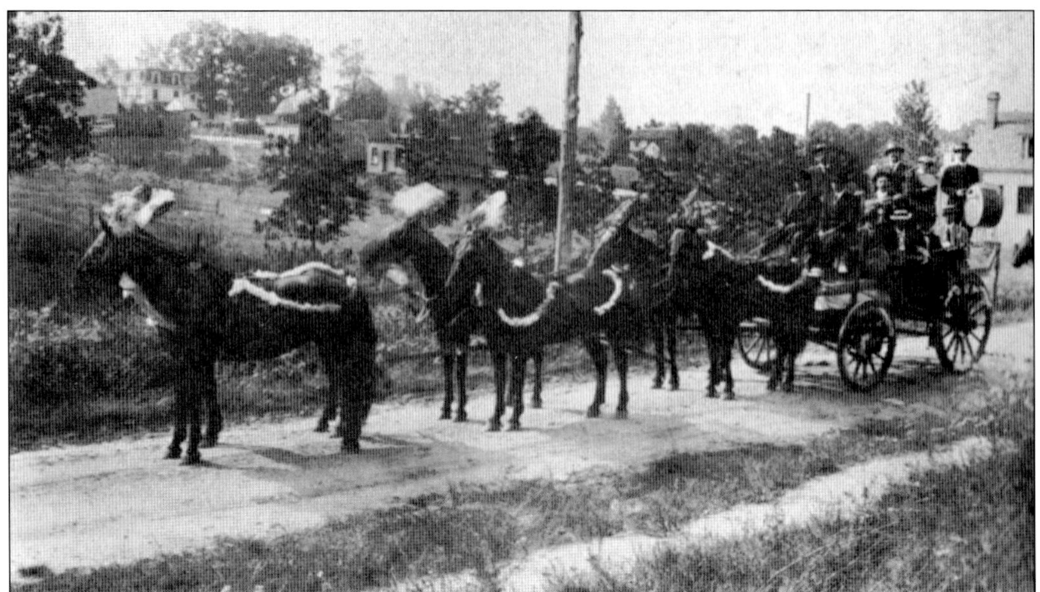

Everybody's Day, 1913 and 1914. In 1908, Mayor W.O. Burgin promoted a celebration on the first Saturday in October as a kind of local fair with the purpose of bringing great numbers of people to Thomasville. A parade, games, exhibits (featuring produce, home-canned goods, and women's handiwork), and rides and other entertainment filled the streets and stores on October 3 of that year. The next year, a larger celebration was planned and named Everybody's Day. After the 1909 parade, a riding tournament was held on the Graded School playground in which Mr. Hite, Mr. Lantz, Dr. Mock, and other horsemen competed to catch suspended rings on their lances as they rode at top speed. Each year thereafter, the crowds increased and new features were added. From an initial attendance around 5,000, the numbers grew to 10,000 and beyond. Everybody's Day continues to hold the title of North Carolina's oldest street festival. (Above, courtesy City of Thomasville.)

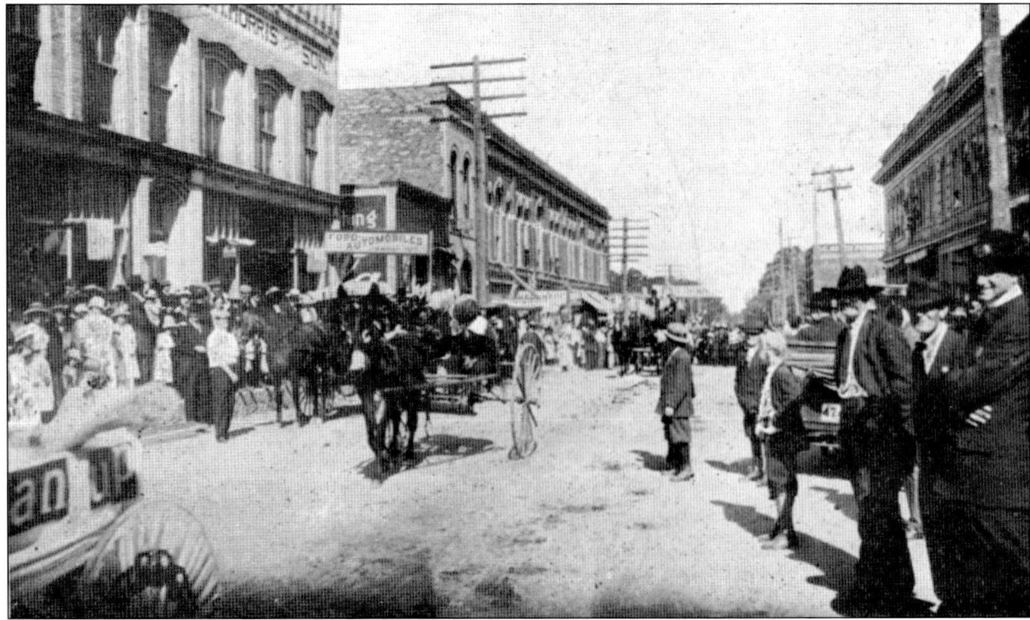

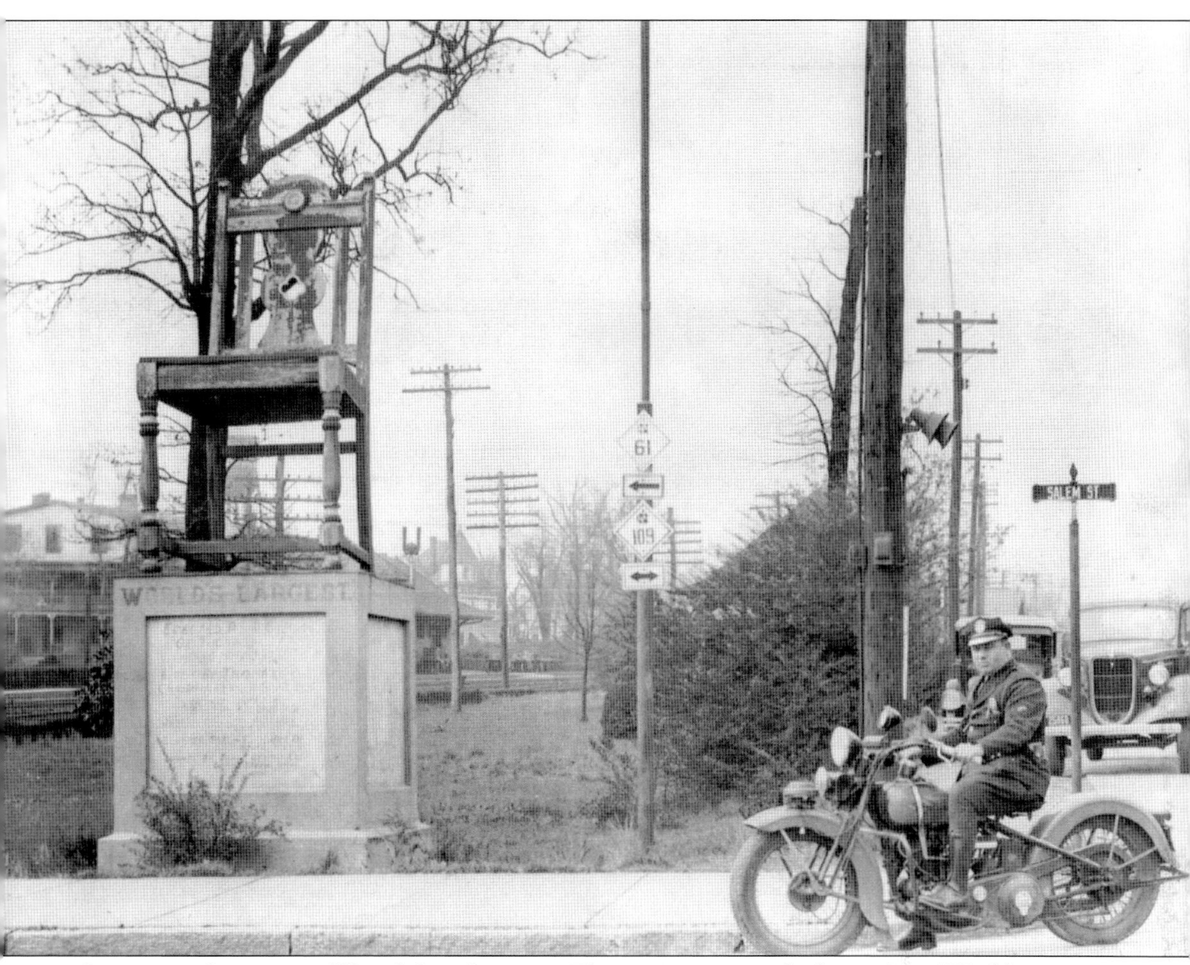

Corner of Salem and West Main Streets. The inscription on the base of the "World's Largest Chair" reads that it was "Erected as a Symbol of Thomasville's Leading Industry." The chair was designed by Otto A. Jiranek of Grand Rapids, Michigan, and built by Thomasville Chairmakers in September 1922. It was 13 feet, 6 inches high, with a leather seat measuring 6 feet by 5 feet, 6 inches.

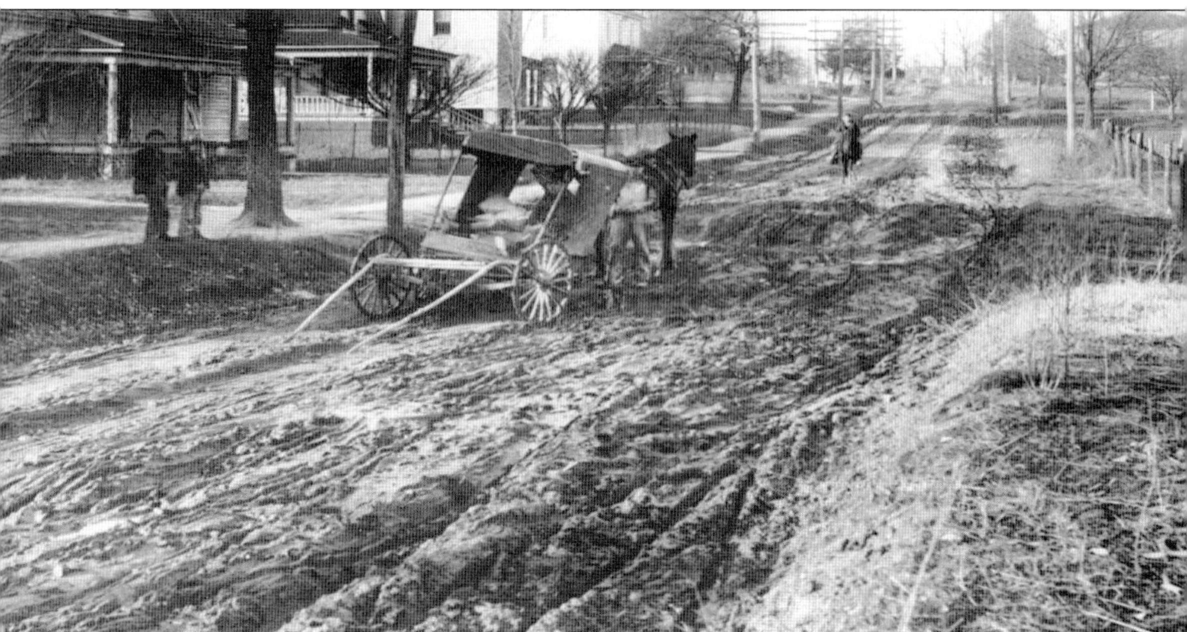

FISHER FERRY STREET, FEBRUARY 16, 1920. For several years, the condition of the town's streets was very bad; as traffic became heavier around the start of the 20th century, complaints about the mud became more frequent. D.A. Long Grocery's horse-drawn delivery wagon is shown here. Charles File is seated in the wagon, and Neil Peterson is using the horse to get the rear axle free.

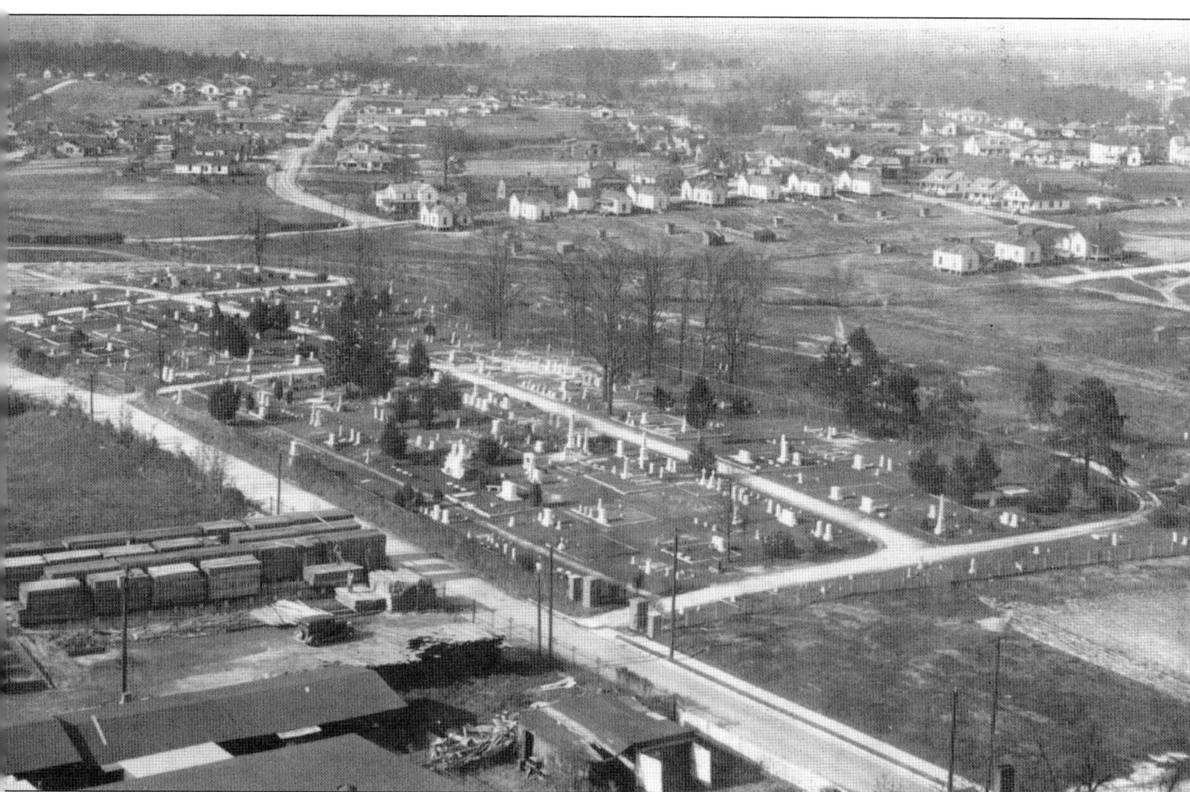

Thomasville City Cemetery from the Water Tower, 1935. The 34 Civil War soldiers who died after the war in makeshift Thomasville hospitals—among them 26 Confederates, 4 Federals, and 4 unknowns—were buried in the common plot of Thomasville City Cemetery. In 1908, a Georgian who had served in the hospital depot provided headstones for those who died. This is the only known place where Confederate and Union soldiers are buried side by side.

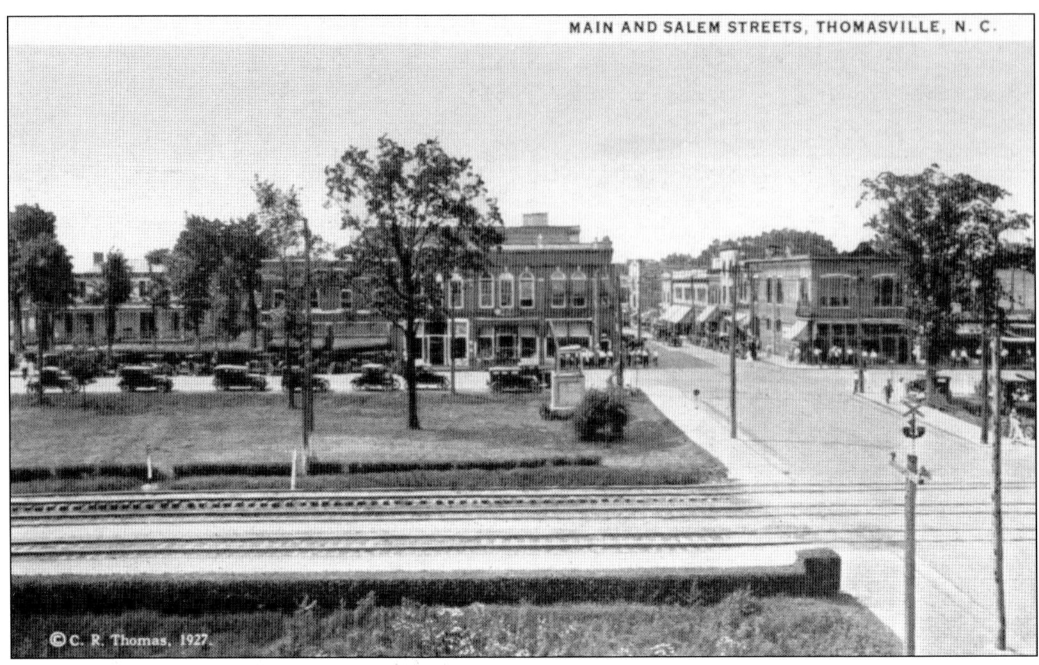

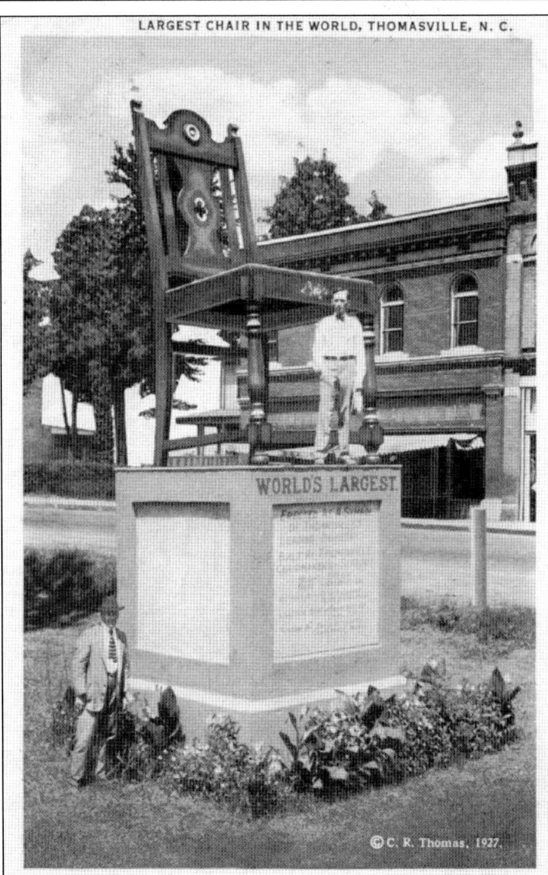

TOWN COMMONS, 1927. Druggist C.R. Thomas, grandson of the city's founder John Thomas, produced and issued postcards of Thomasville in 1927. This photograph looks north up Salem Street. Notable landmarks are the original "Big Chair" in the center and the John W. Thomas home on the left.

WORLD'S LARGEST CHAIR, 1927. The first Big Chair stood from 1922 until 1936, by which time weather had made it unsightly. By 1921, Thomasville was making more chairs than any other city in the world. That year, *Chairtown News* editor Charles Sturkey proudly boasted that Thomasville was planning to build the world's largest chair. This news quickly spread across the United States, and Sturkey presented the Rotary Club with the idea after it had gained national attention.

BIG CHAIR, 1922. Sadie Blair Fouts sits atop the original Big Chair before it was mounted on its pedestal. There was enough lumber in the Big Chair to build 100 regular-size dining room chairs. Harvey Crews, Ray Yarbrough, and Walter Loftin crafted the chair together, working on weekends. It was made of pine, and the seat was covered with hide from a Swiss steer.

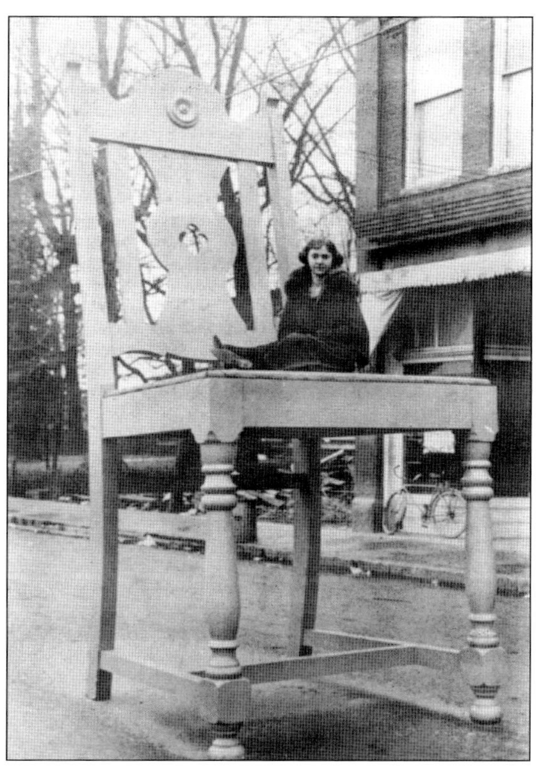

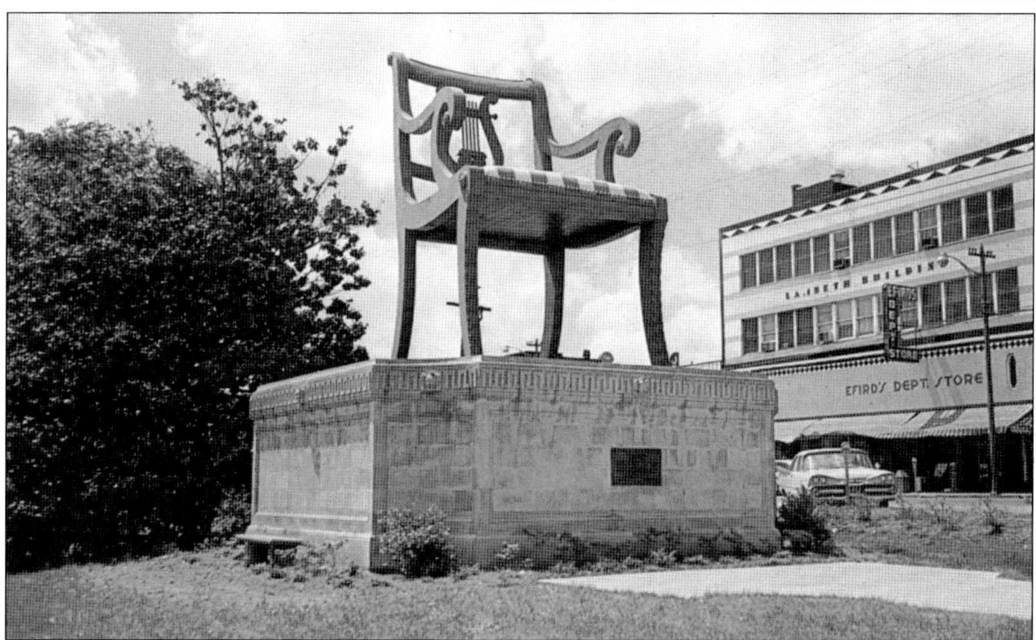

BIG CHAIR, 1950S. The second and current Big Chair was built in 1950 of Salem steel and concrete on a base of Indiana limestone. Designers Tom Johnson and C.L. White Jr. modeled the chair after the Duncan Phyfe dining-room chair in the Smithsonian Institution—the Big Chair is exactly six times larger. It remains a great symbol of the achievements of Thomasville's early generations and contains a time capsule to be opened in 2051.

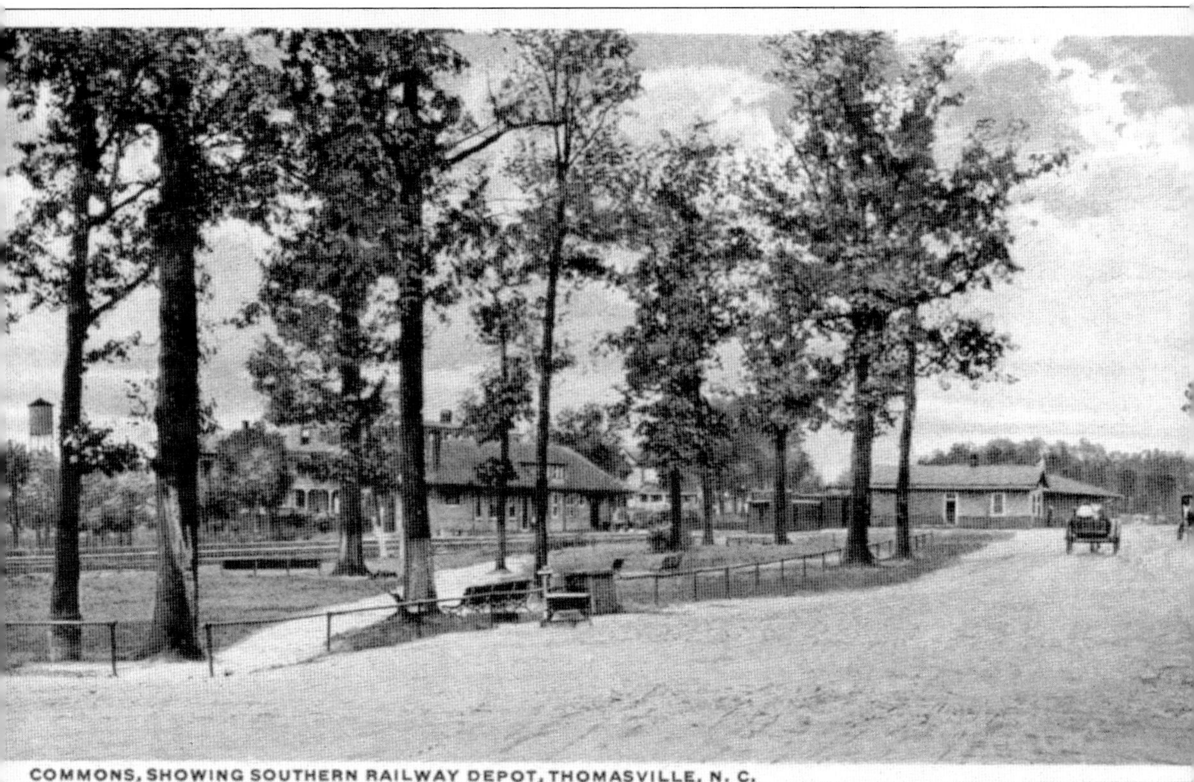

CORNER OF SALEM AND WEST MAIN STREETS, 1912. This postcard, published by R.G. Brooks 5 & 25¢ Store, is the best surviving image that features both the Southern Railway passenger station (left) and the freight depot (right). The most visible part of the freight depot is the office, which now serves as Thomasville's visitor center.

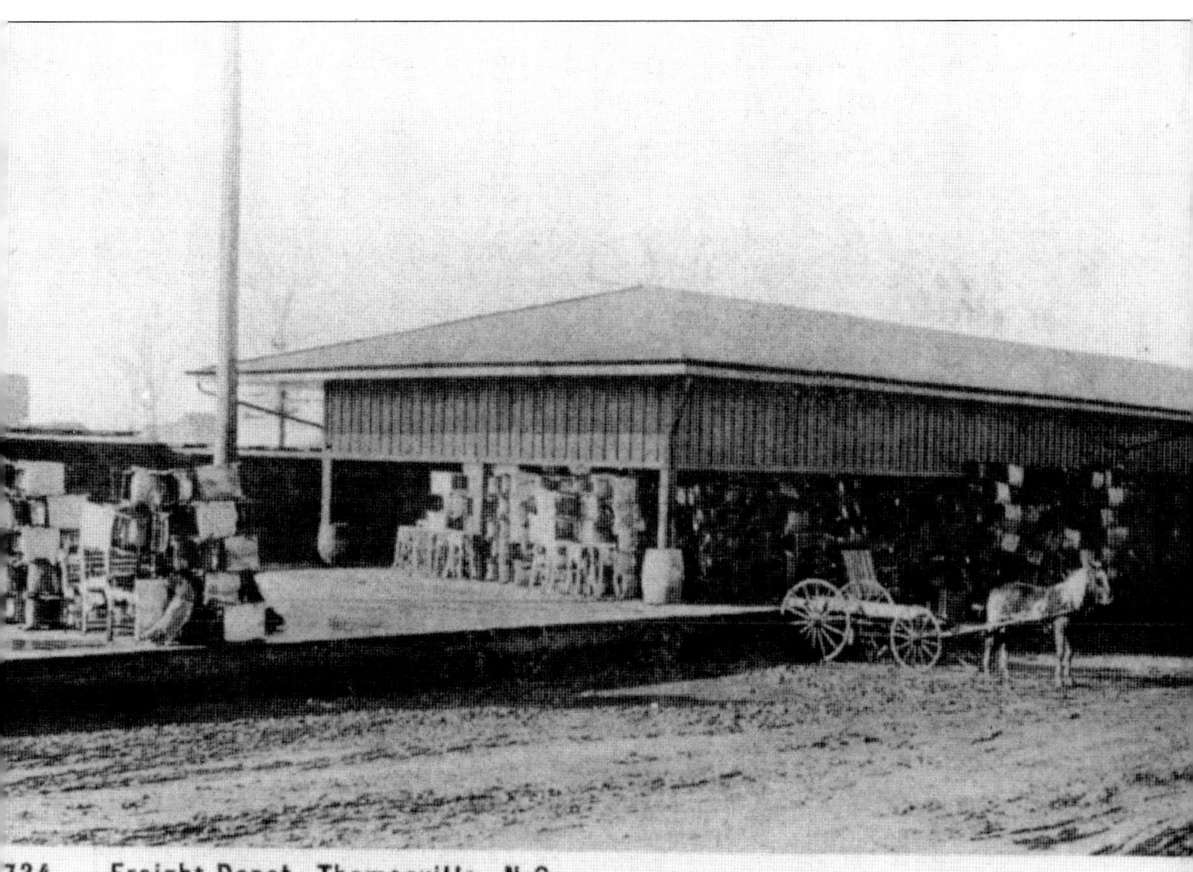

Southern Railway Freight Depot. An example of the local furniture factories' first transportation departments is shown backed up to the depot platform. Local manufacturers used horses and wagons to haul goods to the Southern Railway's freight depot on West Main Street. A large quantity of chairs are shown overflowing onto the platforms outside the covered area, as hundreds of chairs were ready to be shipped.

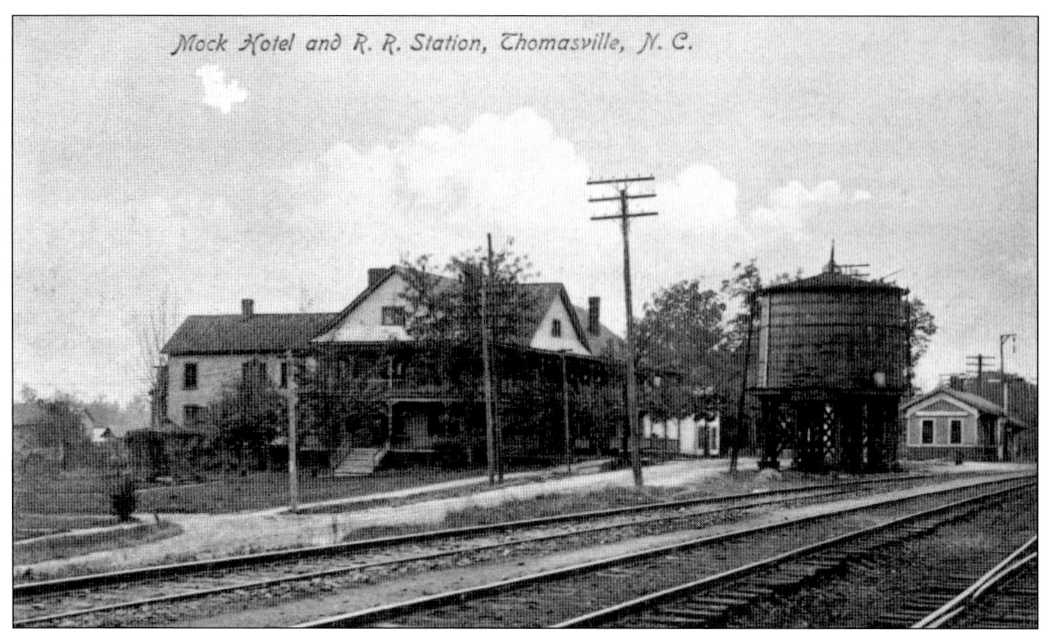

MOCK HOTEL AND SOUTHERN RAILWAY STATION. The original Mock Hotel, which burned in 1892, is shown in its full grandeur in this image. J.W. Gray, a successful businessman and woodworker, operated the Southern Railway water pump standpipe. The water was pumped from Hamby's Creek to the tank on the main line of the railway, and steam engines used the tank to take on water.

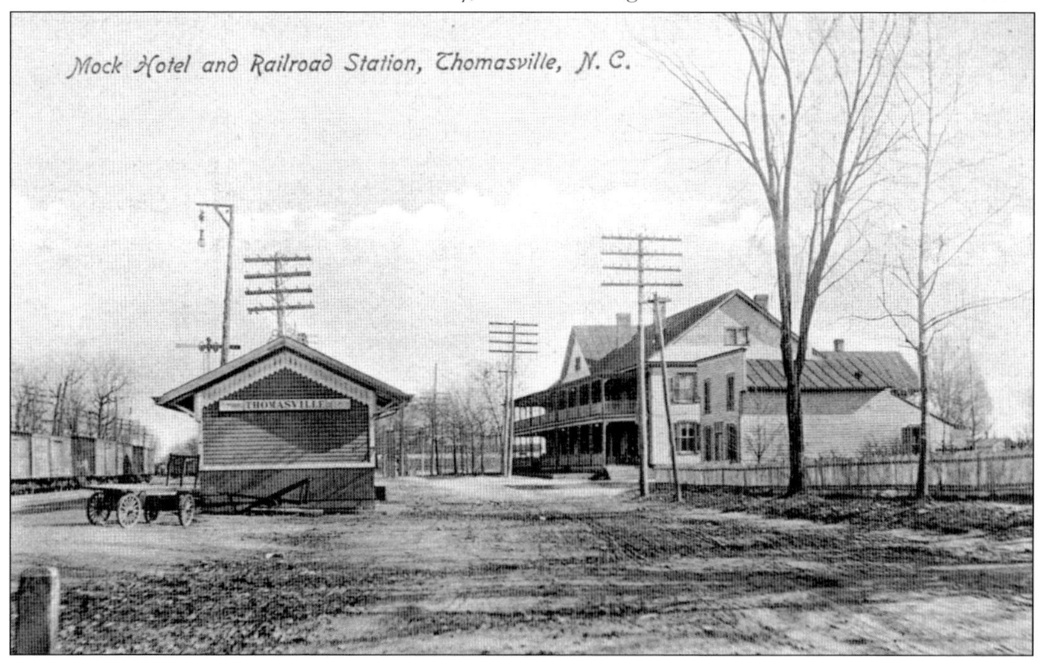

MOCK HOTEL AND RAILROAD STATION. This view looks east down West Main Street just south of the railroad tracks. Thomasville's first passenger depot, built in 1870, is prominent. The depot was moved across the tracks in 1912 and used as the office portion of the freight depot until it was moved in 1978 to its current location at 44 West Main Street, where it serves as Thomasville's visitor center. It is the oldest passenger depot in North Carolina.

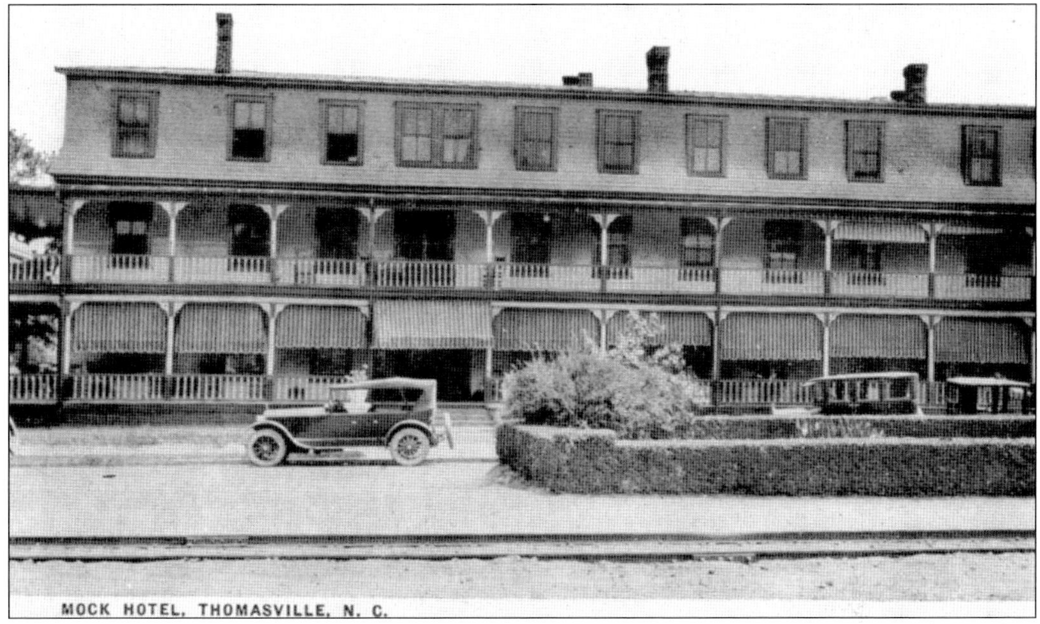

MOCK HOTEL. On January 11, 1879, John A. Mock purchased Cynthia P. Clouse's residence that she was running as a hotel. A few months after the purchase, Mock started building an addition to convert the residence into a real hotel. While helping a guest board a train, Mock fell under it and was killed. His widow was left with two small children and an unfinished hotel that she completed with unusual determination. This image shows the second Mock Hotel, which was built in 1892.

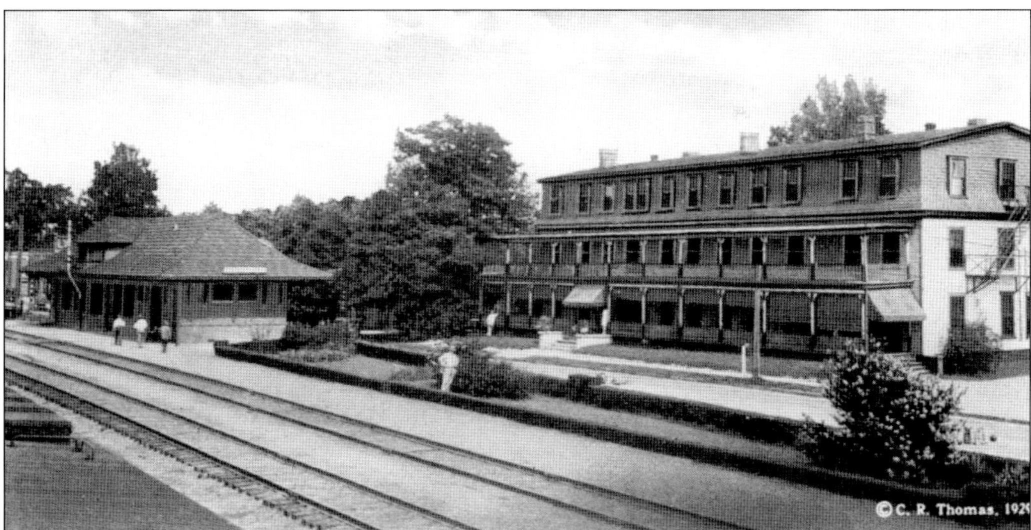

MOCK HOTEL AND PASSENGER STATION, 1927. With over 40 rooms, the Mock Hotel offered every accommodation possible to guests. Mrs. M. McIntyre (formerly Mrs. John A. Mock) owned and operated the hotel, personally attending to the needs of those who stayed there. It was a Thomasville social center for quite a long time, as clubs held luncheons and dinner meetings there. For visitors who arrived by train, hotel accommodations were just a few steps away from the railroad stations. In 1939, just 10 years after the death of Mrs. McIntyre, the hotel burned down. Tragically, a guest lost his life in the fire.

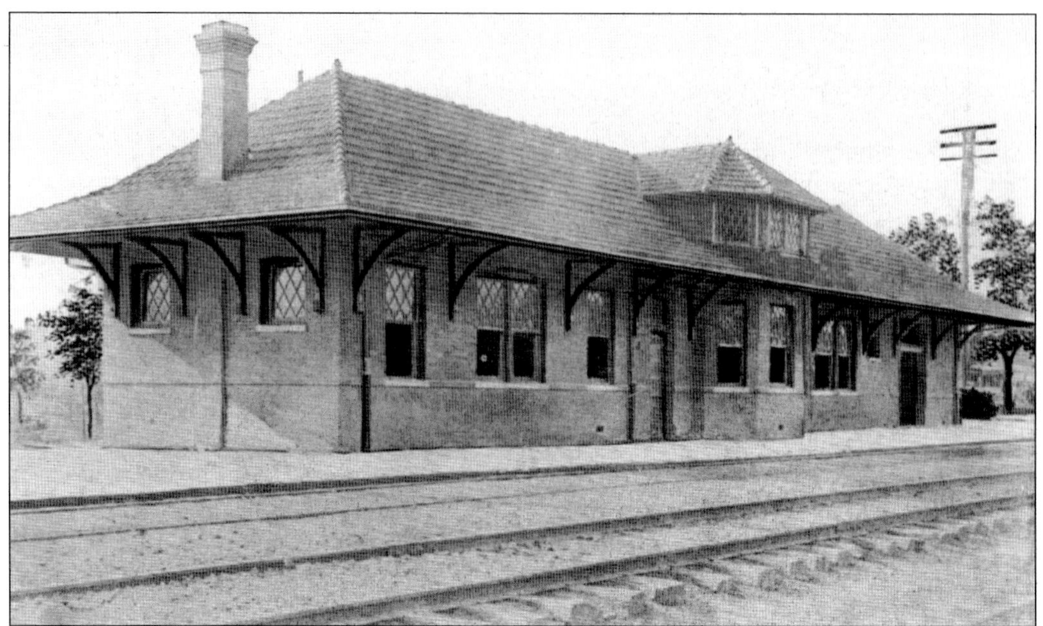

SOUTHERN RAILWAY PASSENGER STATION, 1912. Boarding or debarking from a train is no longer possible in Thomasville. The failure of efforts to turn this passenger station into a museum resulted in it being demolished in 1975. The train tracks through town still take passengers and freight to their destinations, but Thomasville is no longer a stop on the railroad.

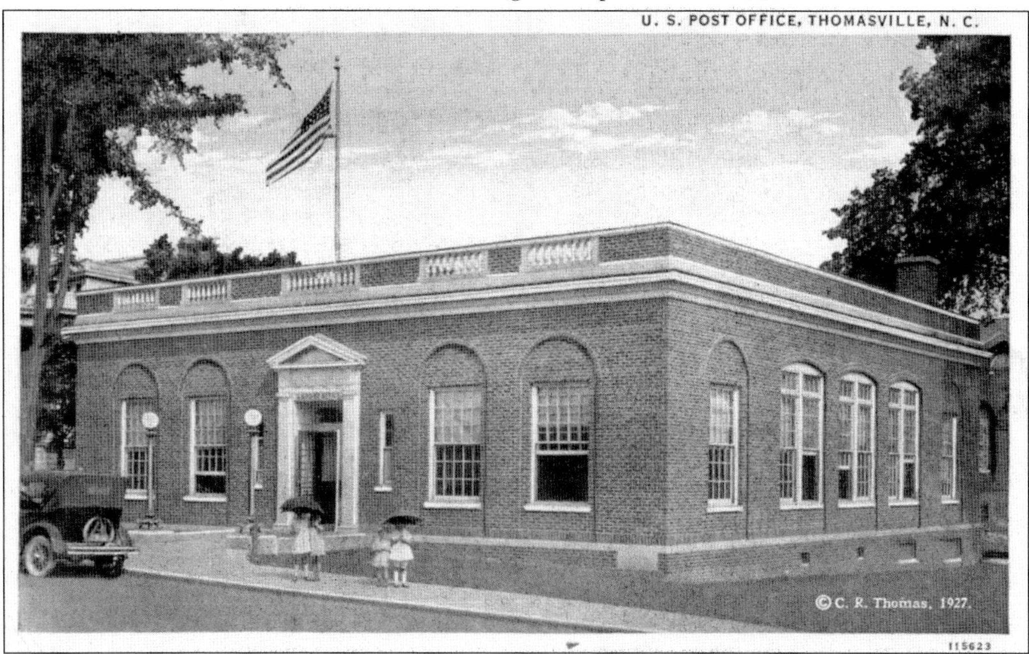

US POST OFFICE, 1927. In 1925, ground was broken for Thomasville's first federal building: the post office. This one-story brick building was designed by architect James Wetmore and completed in 1926. In 1963, the post office moved to its present location at 101 West Main Street. The old post office building occupies the site where Leach Shoe Factory once stood and currently houses the city's parks and recreation department.

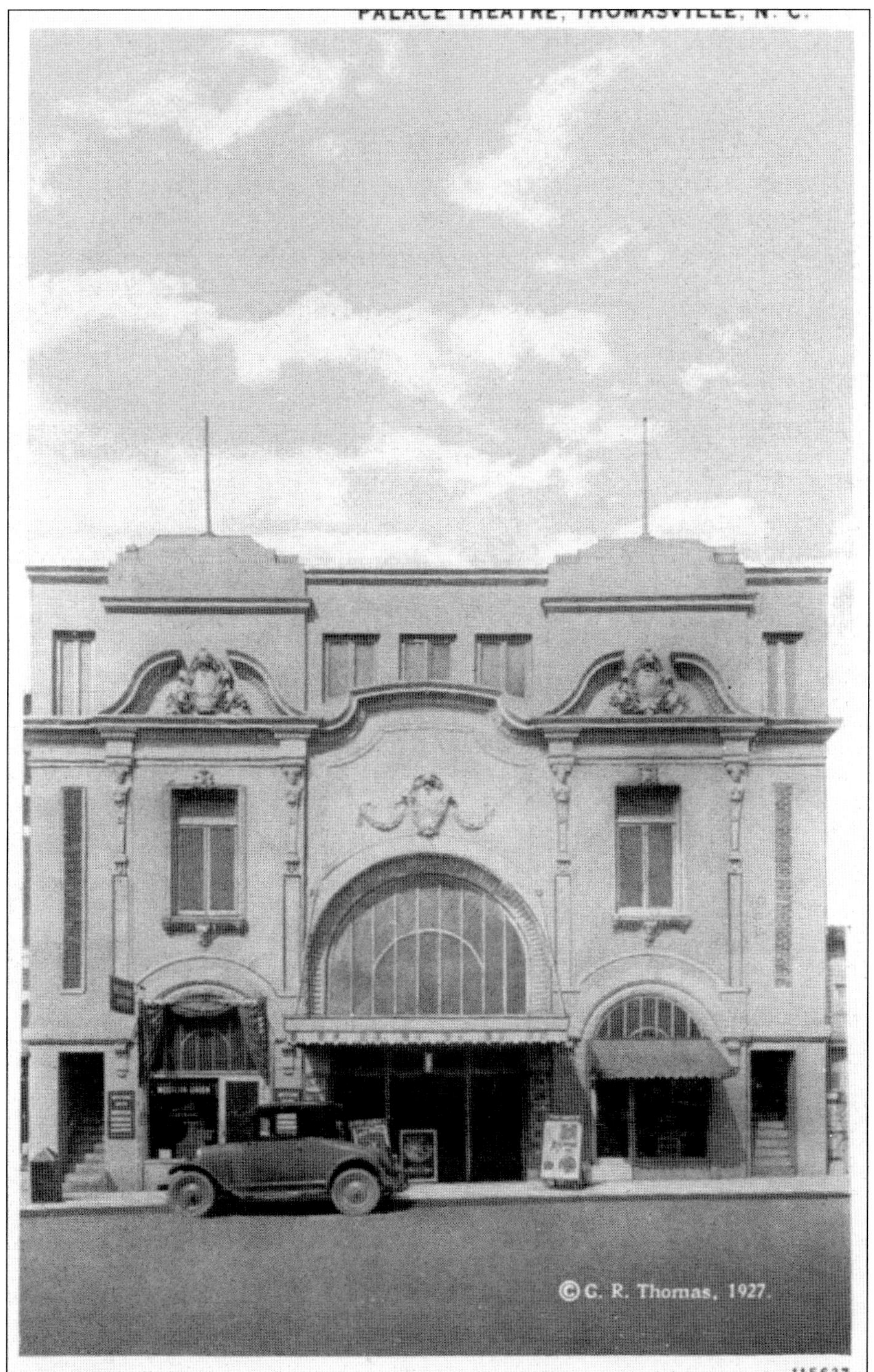

PALACE THEATER, 1927. Crowds gathered to watch *Her Temporary Husband* on the opening night of the Palace Theater in February 1924. Thomasville banker R.L. Pope preferred to characterize the Salem Street spectacle as a "temple of pleasure." The Palace was Thomasville's main theater until it closed in January 1959.

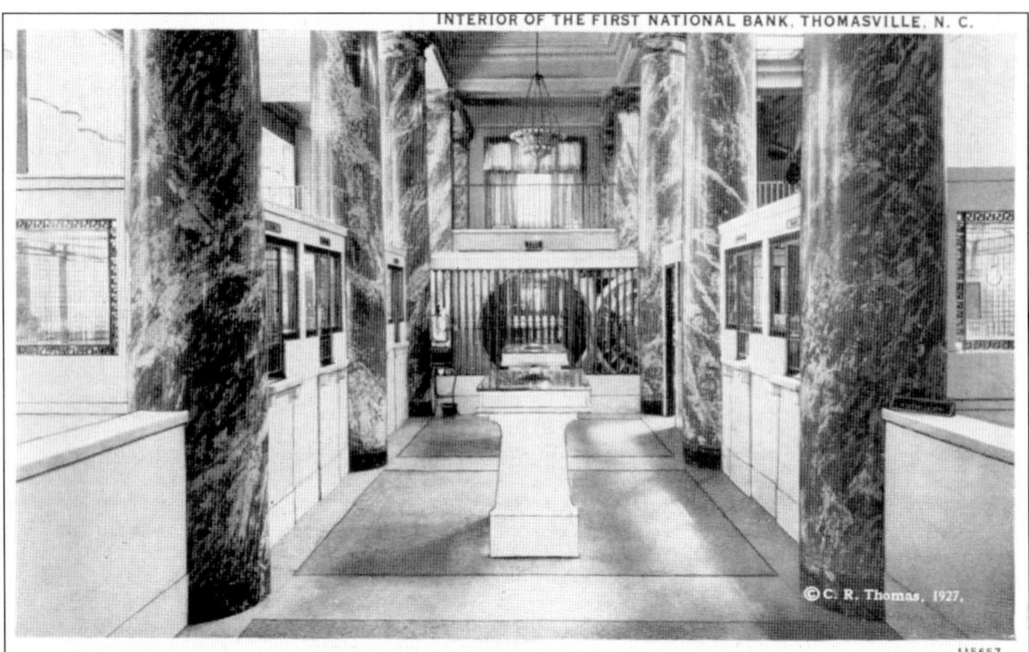

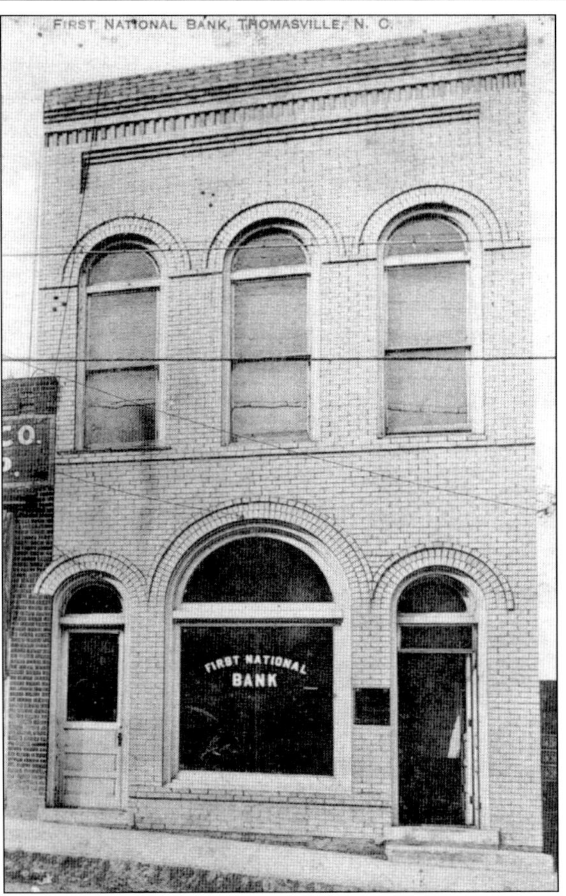

FIRST NATIONAL BANK, 1927. Believe it or not, this lobby still sees a lot of activity today. Most folks do not recognize this as the current Thomasville city hall on Salem Street. Large marbled columns and a second-story balcony no longer characterize the building that was once First National Bank, but the bones are still there.

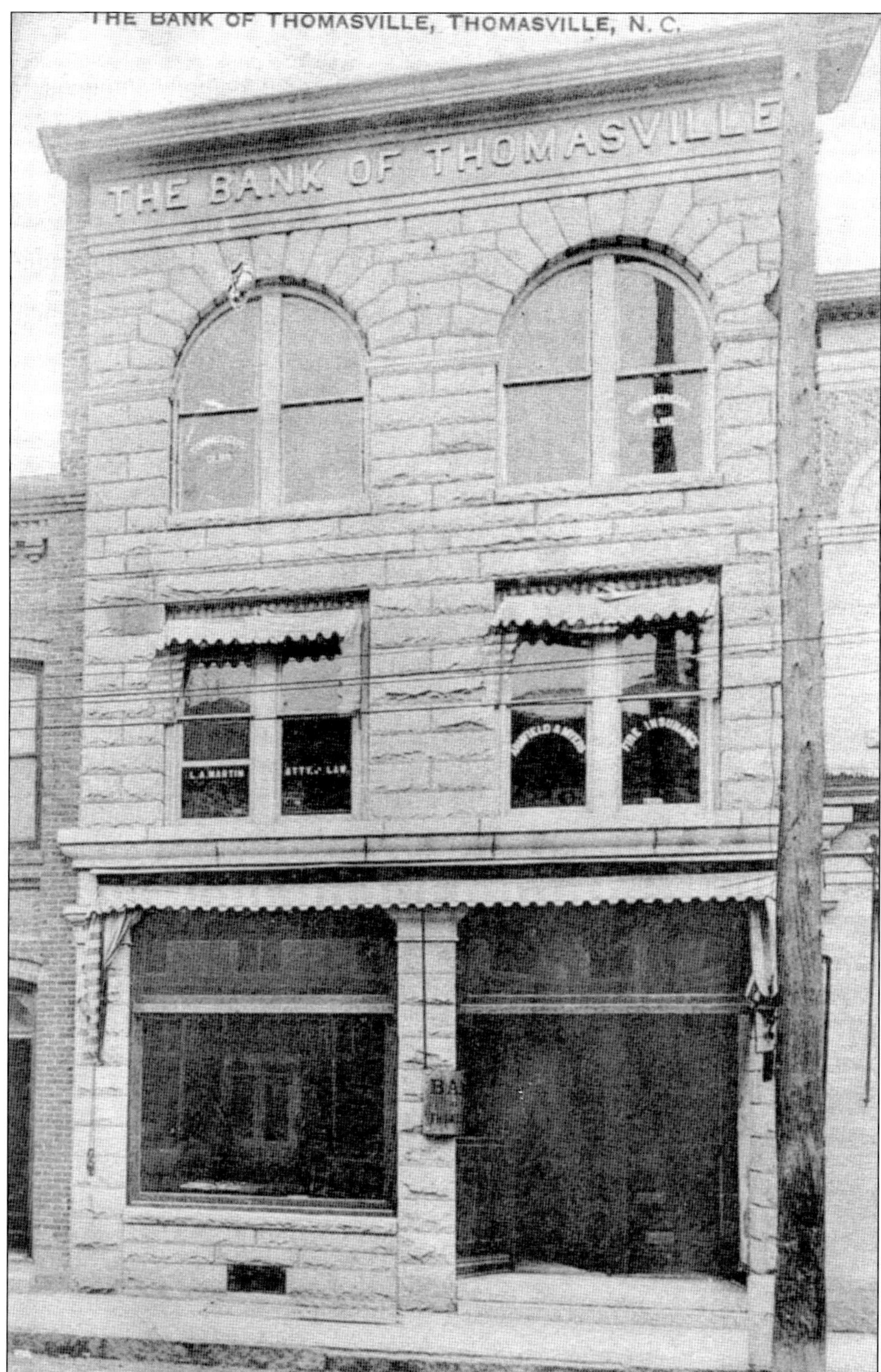

The Bank of Thomasville. In the 1914 book *Thomasville: The Chair Town of the South*, the Bank of Thomasville is characterized as an "institution fully equipped to take care of the present and future banking business of Thomasville and the community." It was organized in 1899 with a capital stock of $25,000. A recession in 1921 led to the end of its run.

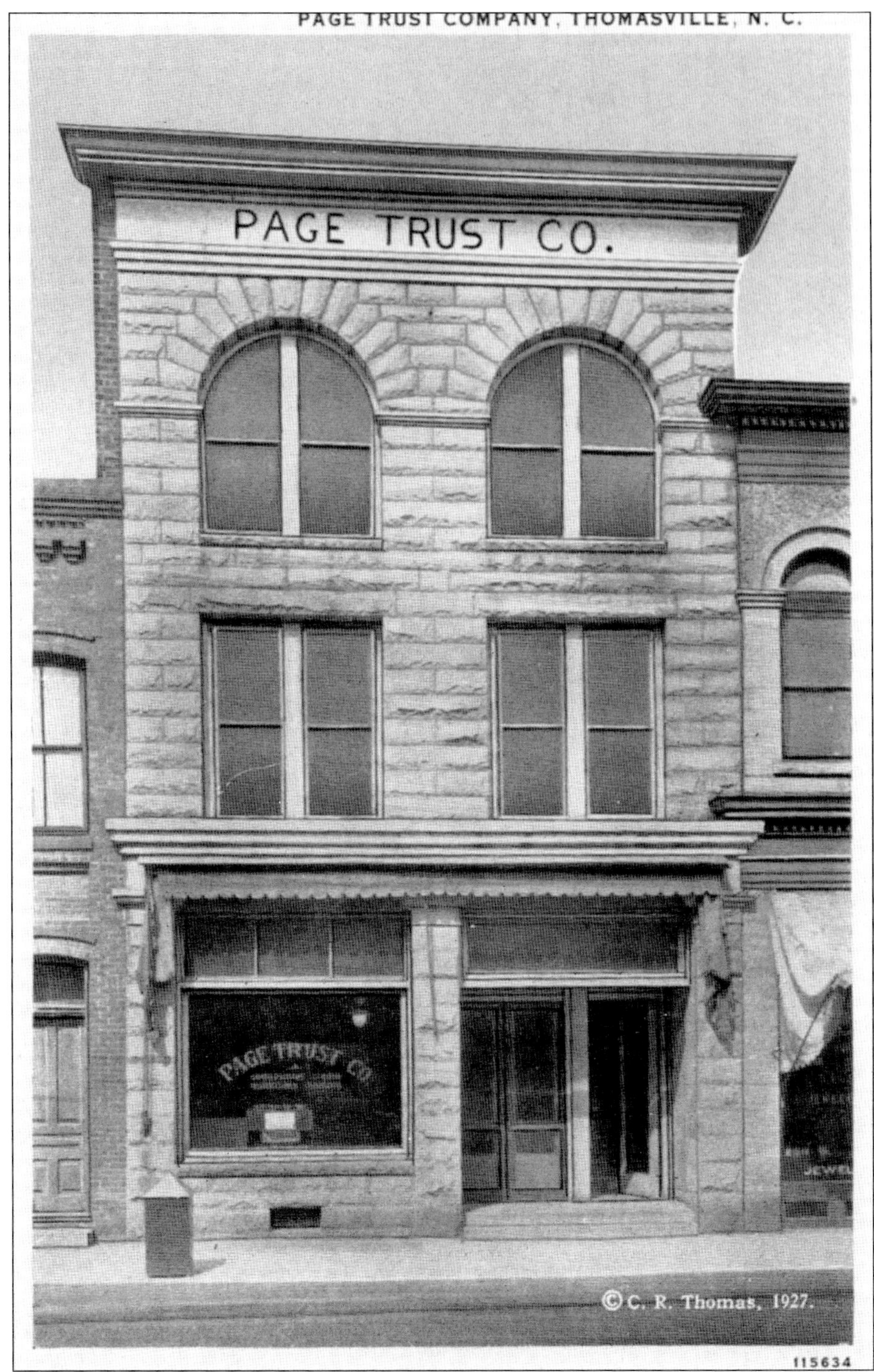

Page Trust Company, 1927. Located in the old Bank of Thomasville building, Page Trust Company of Aberdeen opened a branch in Thomasville on November 1, 1923. The trust's first officers were J.R. Page, president; H.A. Page Jr., treasurer; and E.H. Mahone, cashier of the local branch. When the bank holiday was declared in March 1933, this bank was closed and did not reopen.

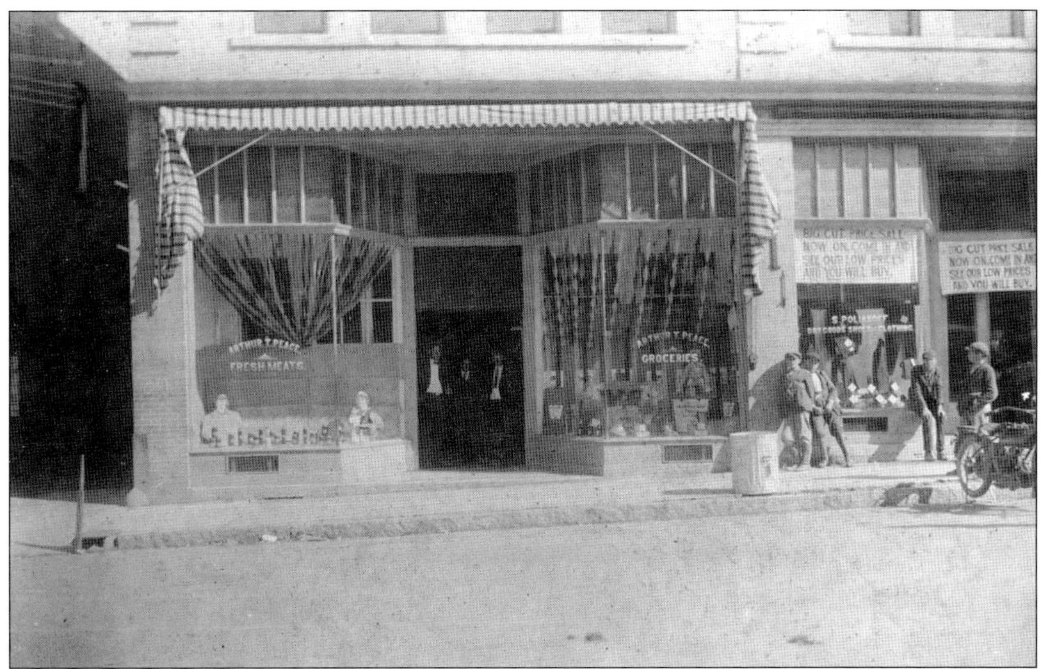

A.T. Peace Grocery Store. Arthur T. Peace is shown above standing at left in the doorway of his Salem Street grocery store. It was in this store that Dr. J.W. Peacock killed police chief John Edgar Taylor with four rounds of a 9-millimeter Luger after shooting him twice on the street with a shotgun on April 16, 1921. Bystander Henry Shaver was shot in the abdomen, to which Peacock remarked, "Tell him I'm sorry, but I couldn't help it. Tell him to go see a good doctor."

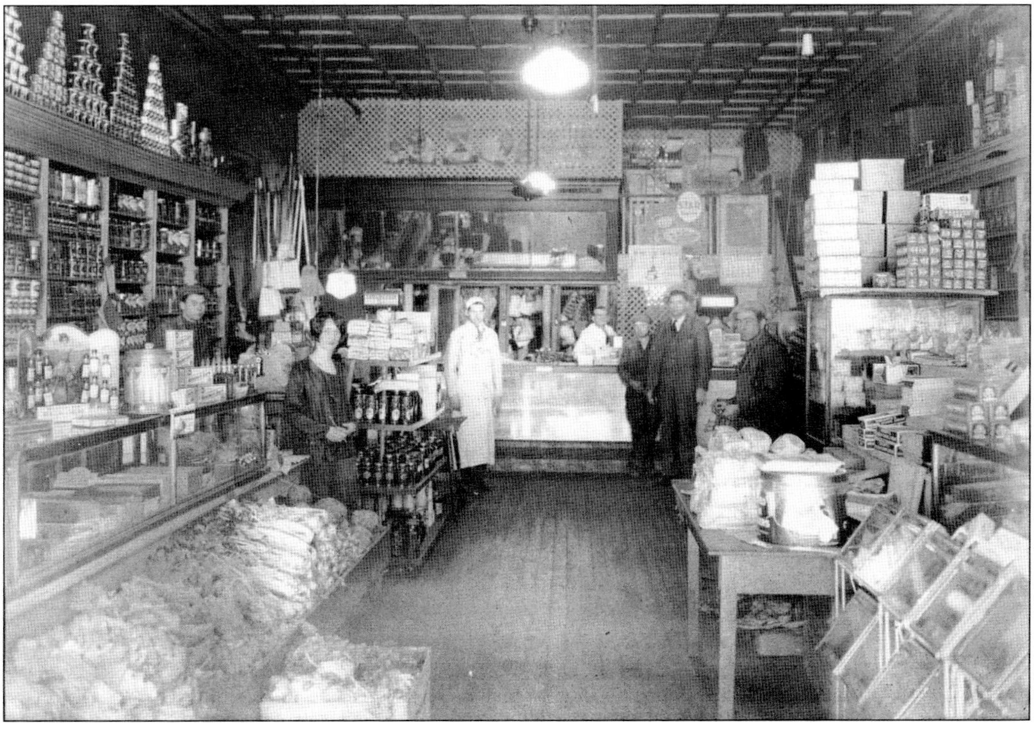

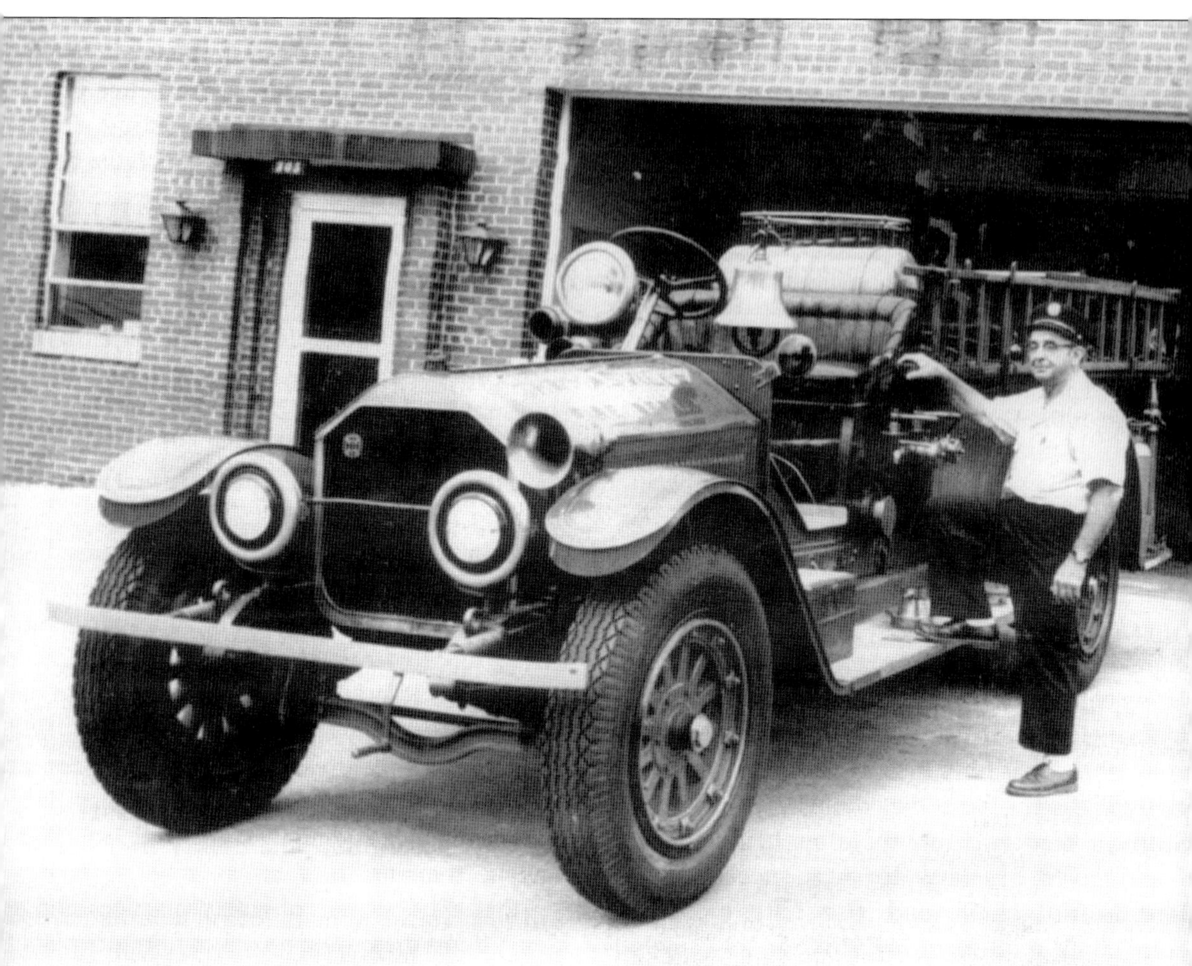

First Fire Truck, 1964. Thomasville's first fire engine was a 1922 American LaFrance 750-gallon pumper that cost $12,500. It first saw action on September 13, 1922, when a tobacco barn on Lexington Road caught fire. As police chief George Wimberly drove, fire chief Charles White and firefighters clung to the side of the vehicle. Everyone gave the big truck the right of way, but in a moment, a large number of cars were speeding in its wake, filled with eager people wanting to see the fire. The barn was reduced to ashes before the truck arrived. The Thomasville Fire Department was organized in 1908 by A.H. Ragan and several young men.

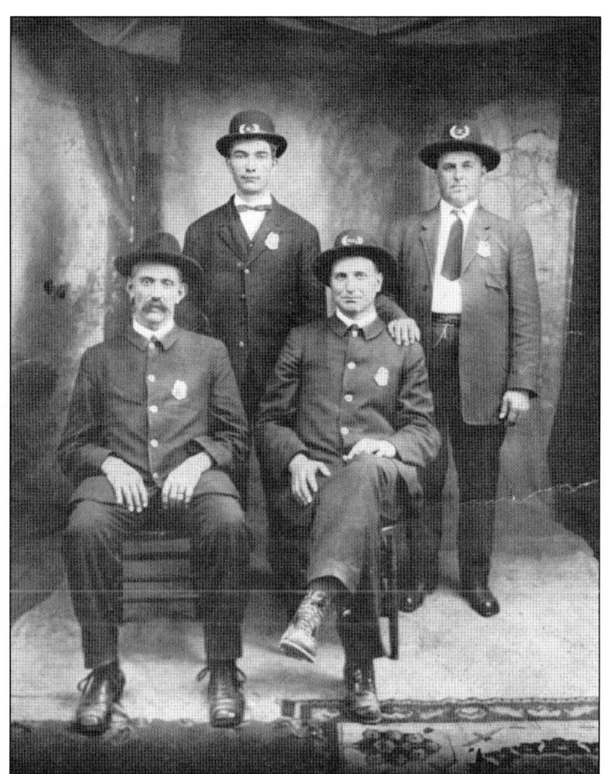

THOMASVILLE POLICE FORCE, 1914. Pictured here are, from left to right, (seated) W.M. Reid and chief John R. May; (standing) W.B. Warren and "Bud" Lookabill. An example of a law enforced in those days was "That any person who shall disturb any municipal concert, tableaux, theatrical performance, or any place of public amusement within the town by loud talking, hissing, snoring, whistling, or by loud and boisterous or unnecessary cheering shall be fined $5."

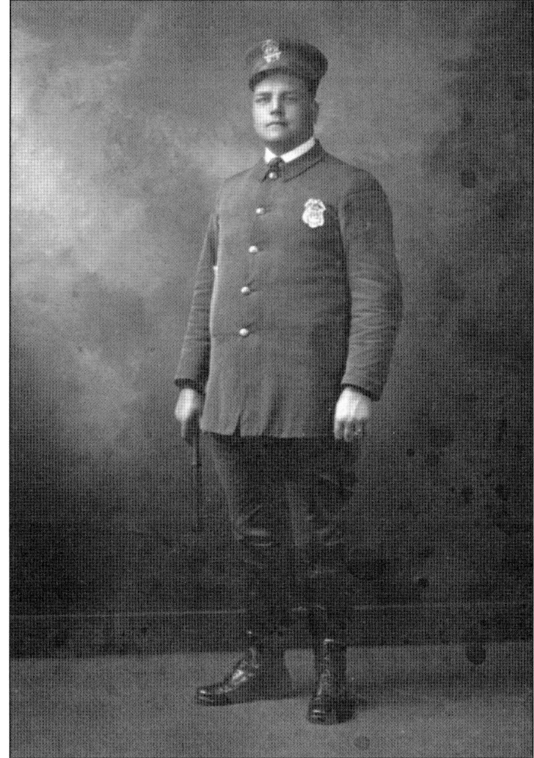

POLICE CHIEF J.E. TAYLOR. John Edgar Taylor was killed by town physician Dr. J.W. Peacock on Saturday, April 16, 1921—the day after the doctor's barn burned down. An ongoing Prohibition-related dispute between the two men led Peacock to shoot Taylor twice from his second-story office window with No. 4 buckshot. As Taylor sought shelter in A.T. Peace's grocery store, Peacock came in to finish him off with two shots to the chest and two to the head.

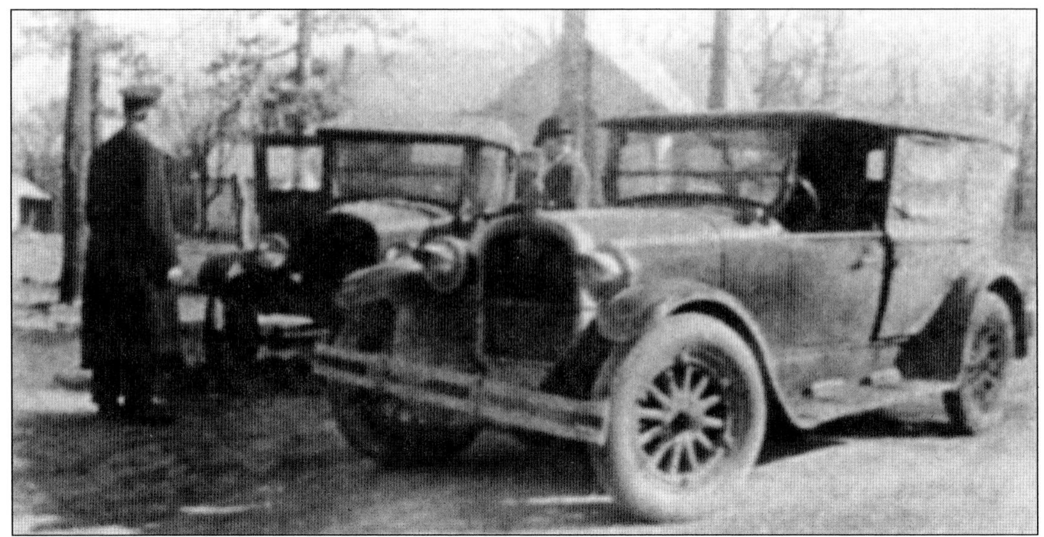

Reenactment of a Fatal Encounter, 1928. The 1927 automobile in the foreground is a Dodge touring car—the second vehicle owned by the city's police department. Officer T.L. Reddick and sheriff's deputy C.D. Morgan were using the patrol car when Riddick was shot to death and Morgan sustained serious chest wounds. This photograph is a reenactment of the February day when Reddick and Morgan pulled over a Ford roadster.

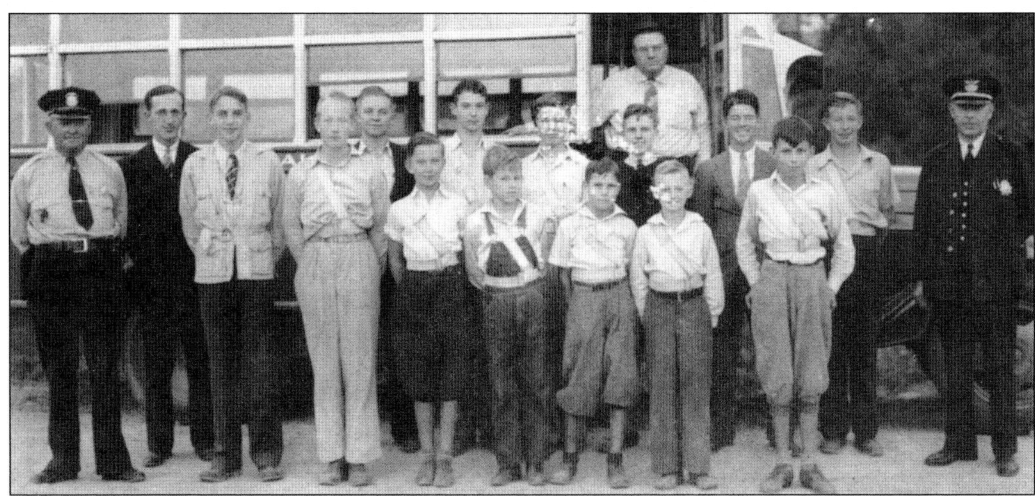

Schoolboy Patrol, 1930s. Police chief F.C. Smith (far right), officer Tommy Russell (far left), and attorney Carl Wilson (second from left) are shown with the schoolboy patrol. This patrol was comprised of young men who acted as safety officers for street and railroad crossings both before and after school.

Two

Industry

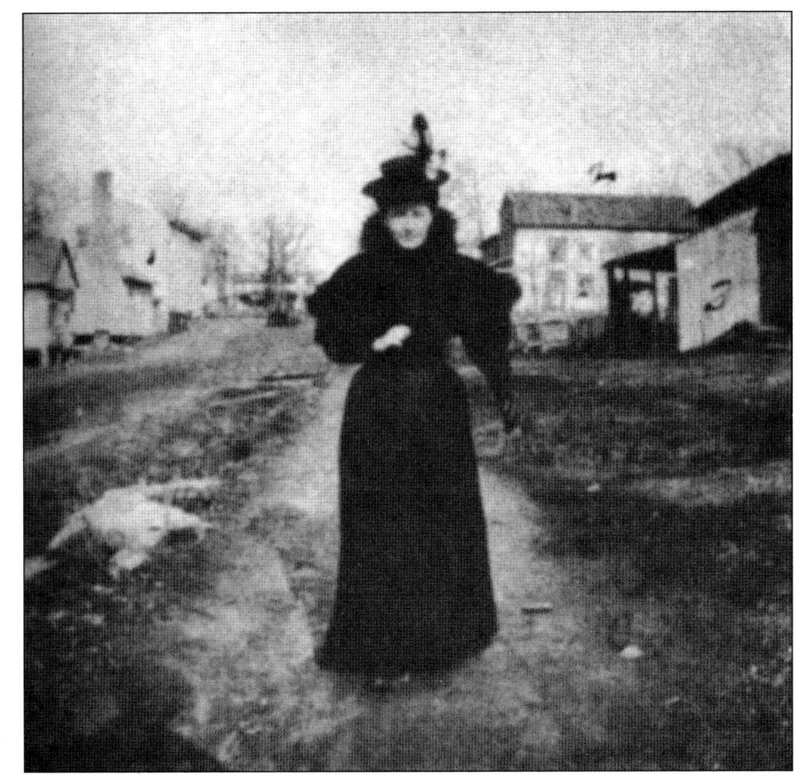

Randolph Street, 1897. Marilla Kinney, who later married J.Q. Miller, is pictured as she faces south down Randolph Street. The building in the right foreground is Kelly Welborn's blacksmith shop, and the two-story building on the right is the J.A. Leach Shoe Factory. The two-story building on the left is Elliot's Store. (Courtesy City of Thomasville.)

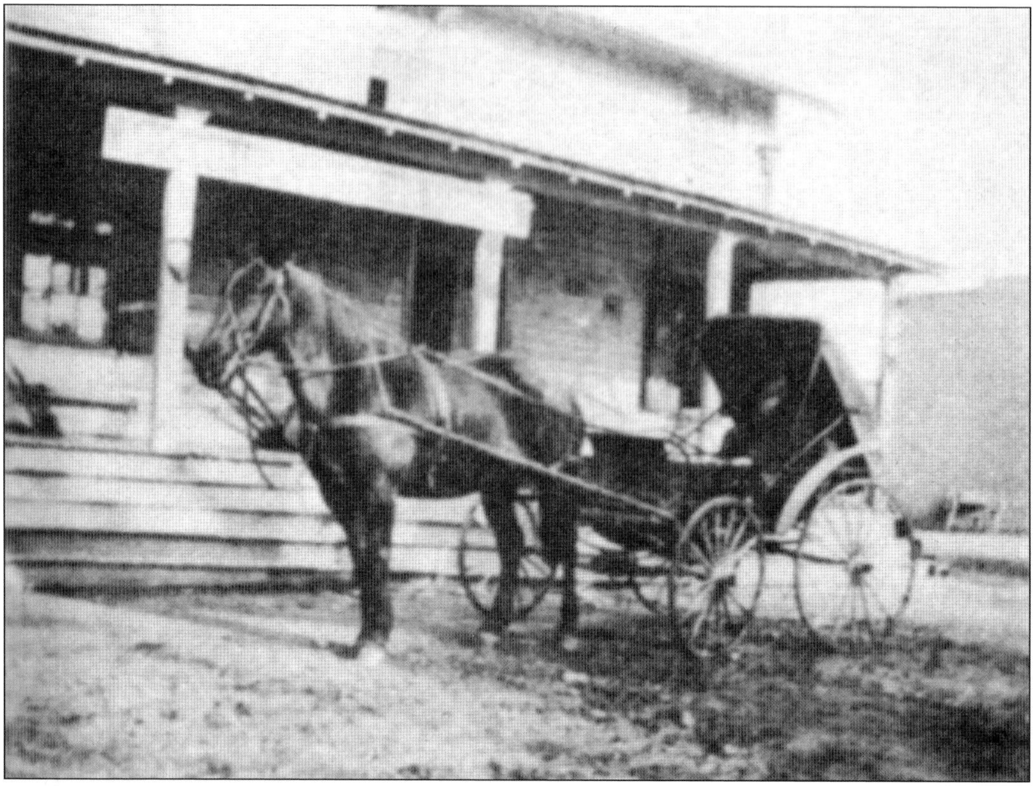

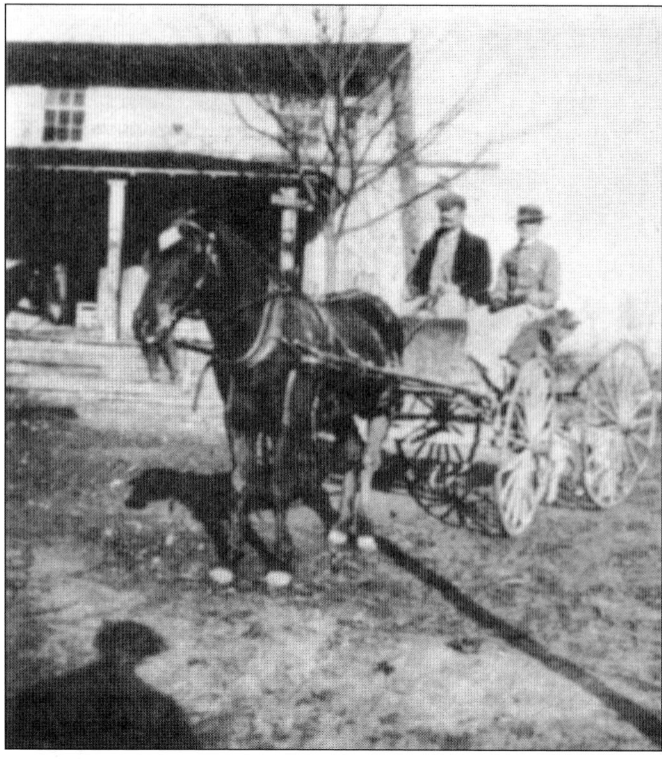

First Store in Thomasville, 1897. The store built by John W. Thomas in 1852 on the corner of Main and Salem Streets was destined to be the hub of trading in Thomasville for 46 years. To the country people, it represented the romance and adventure of town. Even though the lighting was poor due to its small windows, and the line of merchandise was meager, people could obtain goods ranging from sugar to castor oil to fans to flaxcloth and ticking. The store was sold to John A. Mock in 1870, who in turn sold it to D.T. Lambeth in 1878 after purchasing the old Mock Hotel. Lambeth advertised, "When in town, call in and we will make it your interest to trade with us." The store burned down in 1898. (Both, courtesy City of Thomasville.)

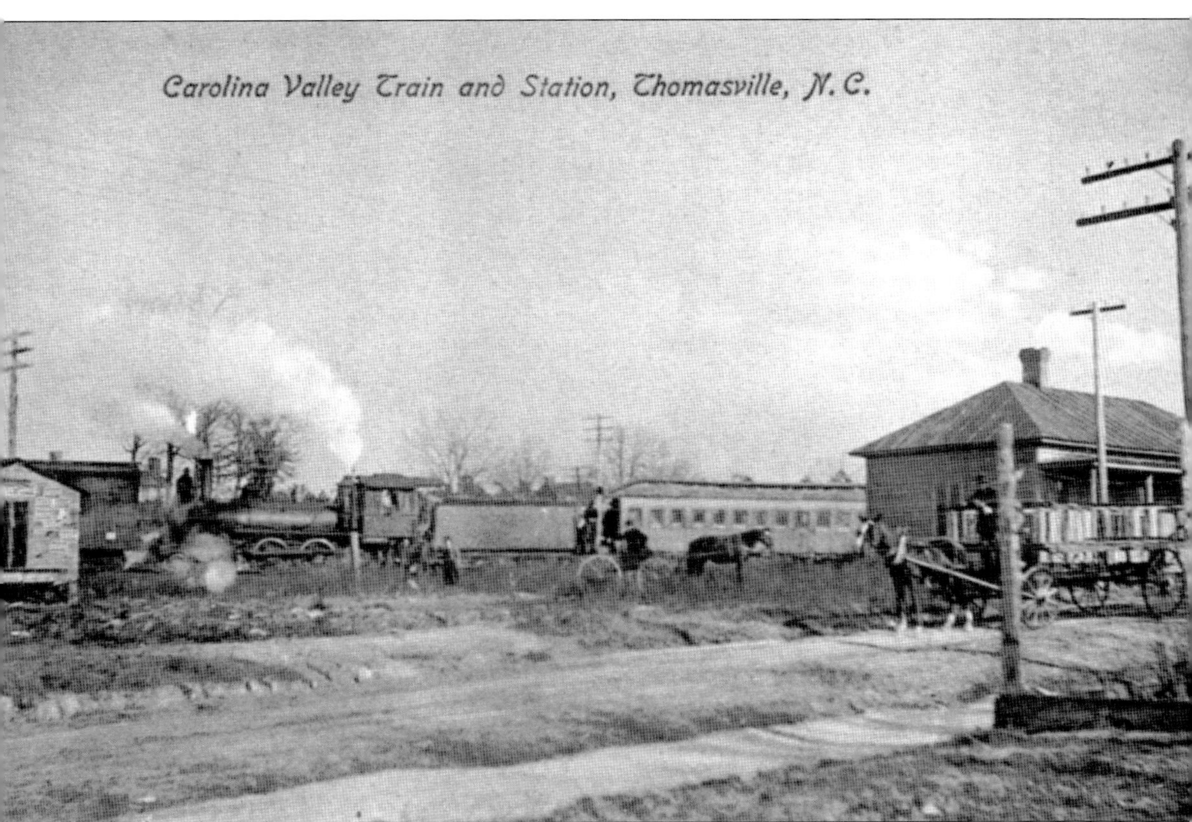

CAROLINA VALLEY TRAIN STATION, C. 1907. The railroad was a success from the moment the tracks were completed in Thomasville. Transportation service gave vigor to community business and keen capitalists. The Carolina Valley Railroad was the predecessor of the High Point, Thomasville & Denton Railroad. The station sat south of Hamby's Creek, where the old Hill's Farm and Garden sits vacant.

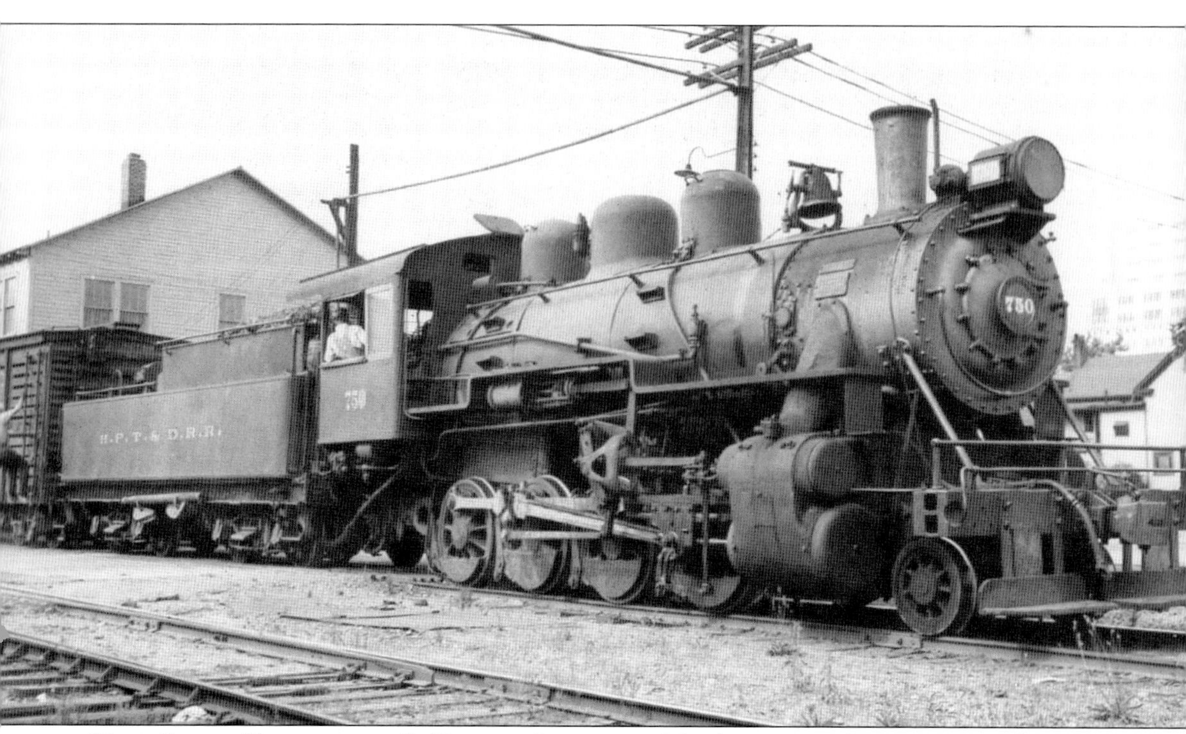

High Point, Thomasville & Denton Railroad. The last piece of equipment to leave the High Point, Thomasville & Denton Railroad property was engine No. 750. The engine was sold in 1947 for $6,000 and went on to serve the Tuskegee Railroad in Alabama. This sale marked the end of steam engine days and the beginning of diesel locomotives. The acronym of the railroad—HPT&DRR—led to it sometimes being referred to as "High Priced Tickets and a Damn Rough Ride."

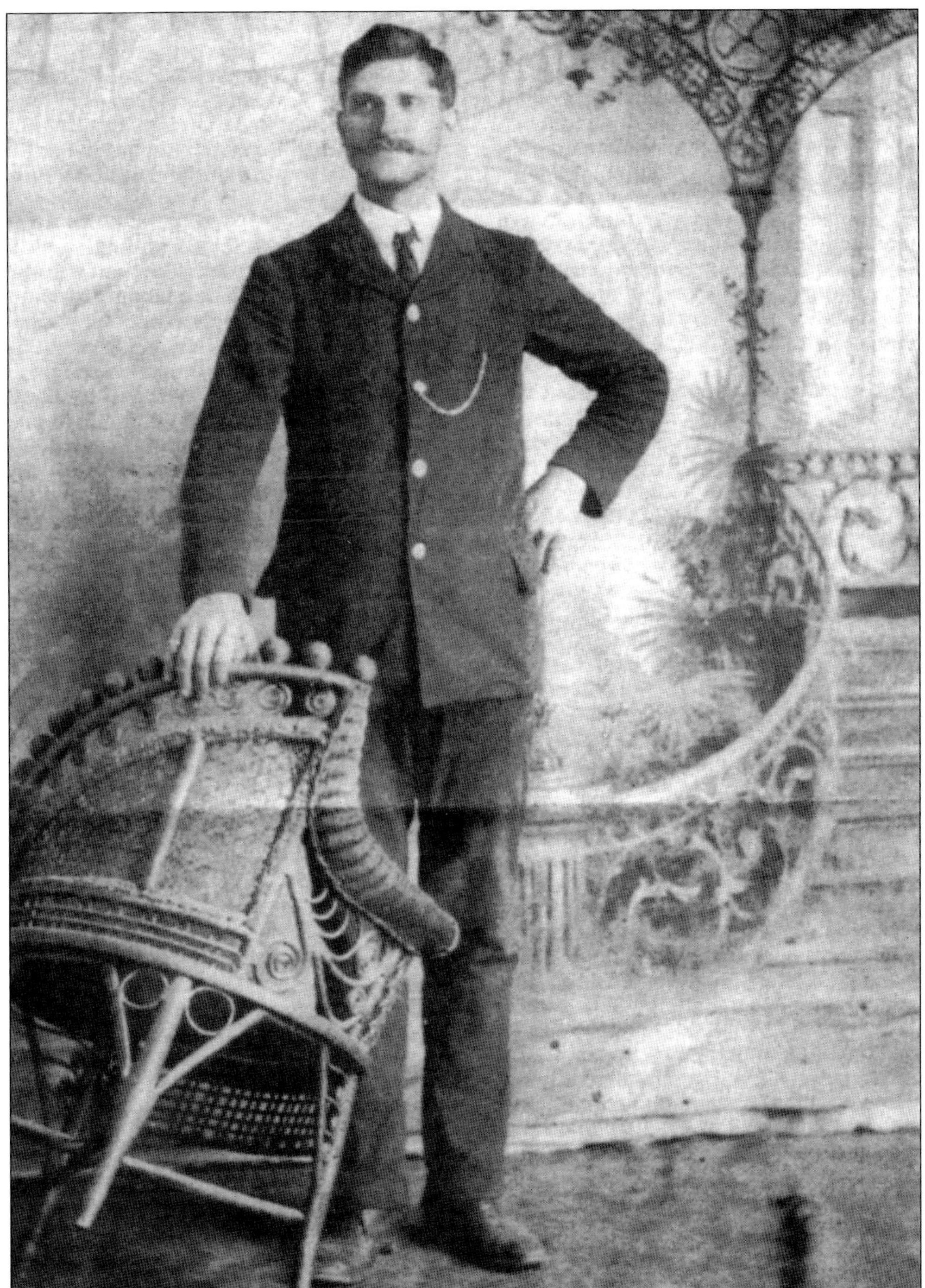

CAPT. M.L. JONES. According to Cecil Hiatt in his book *High Point, Thomasville, & Denton Railroad Company*, Capt. Milton Jones "began construction without any help or financing and laid two ribbons of steel through what had been a virgin wilderness between Thomasville and Denton. He saw firsthand the need for a railroad and his goal was to break away the chains of isolation which were binding the townships of lower Davidson County."

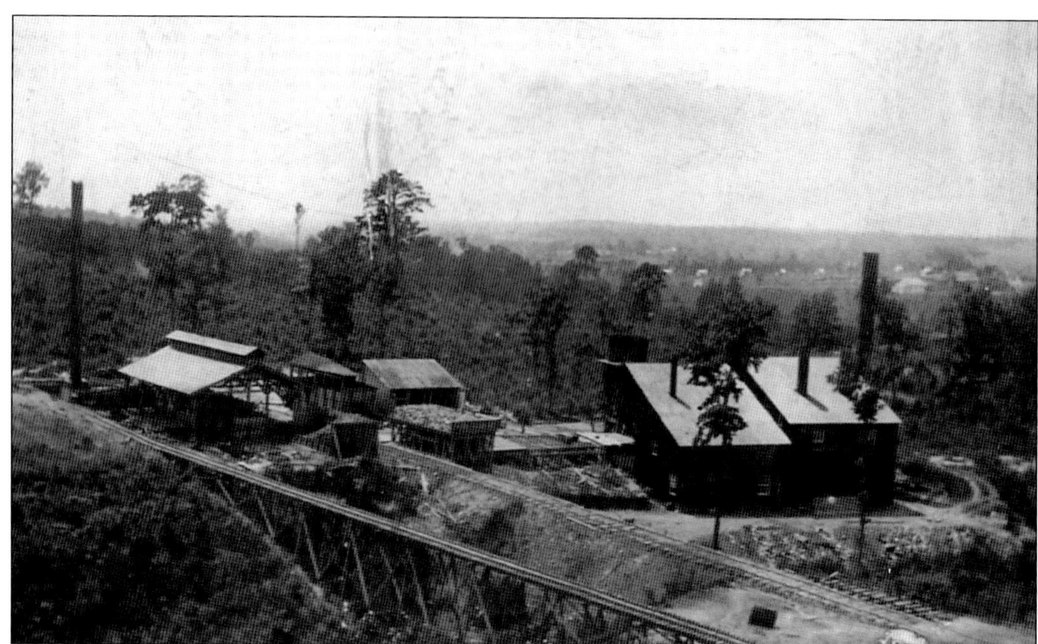

North Carolina Smelting Works. These never-before-published images show the North Carolina Smelting Works in Thomasville, between present-day Carmalt and Fisher Ferry Streets. Henry Rapp came from Baltimore, Maryland, with his family to manage the facility. In 1893, a narrow-gauge railroad known as the Pole Cat Road was laid from Thomasville to Silver Valley so that ores could be hauled by a small engine. It was stated in the local newspapers that the smelting plant had cost $200,000. This was by far the most money invested in a business at the time and resulted in a very important industry that thrived between 1890 and 1895. However, the "pay dirt" became more dirt than pay, and the operation was abandoned by the turn of the 20th century. Amazon Cotton Mill was later built on this site. (Both, courtesy Jane Cox Leonard).

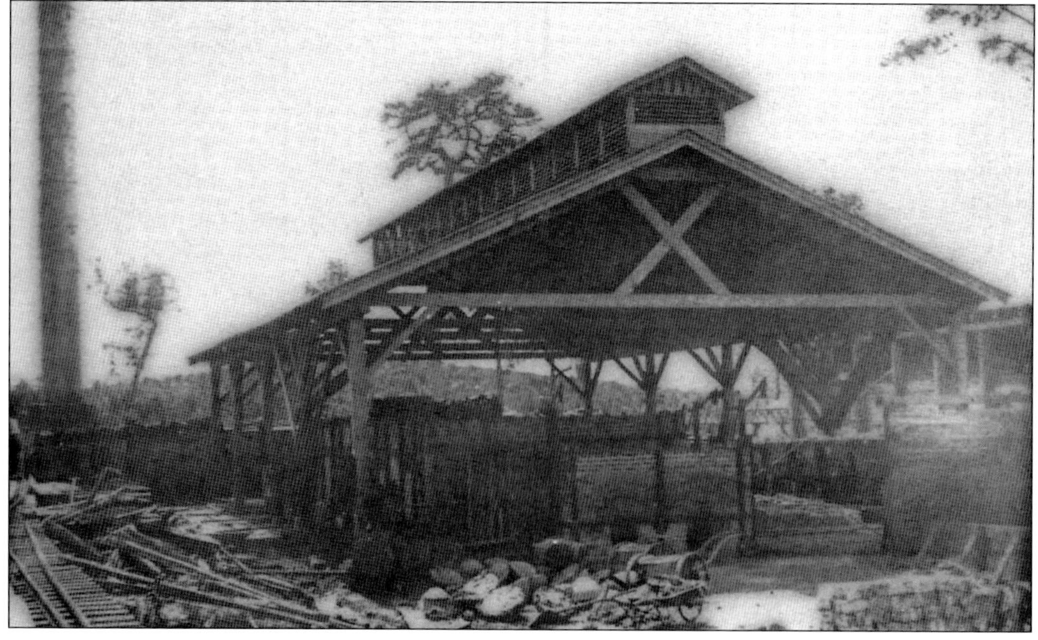

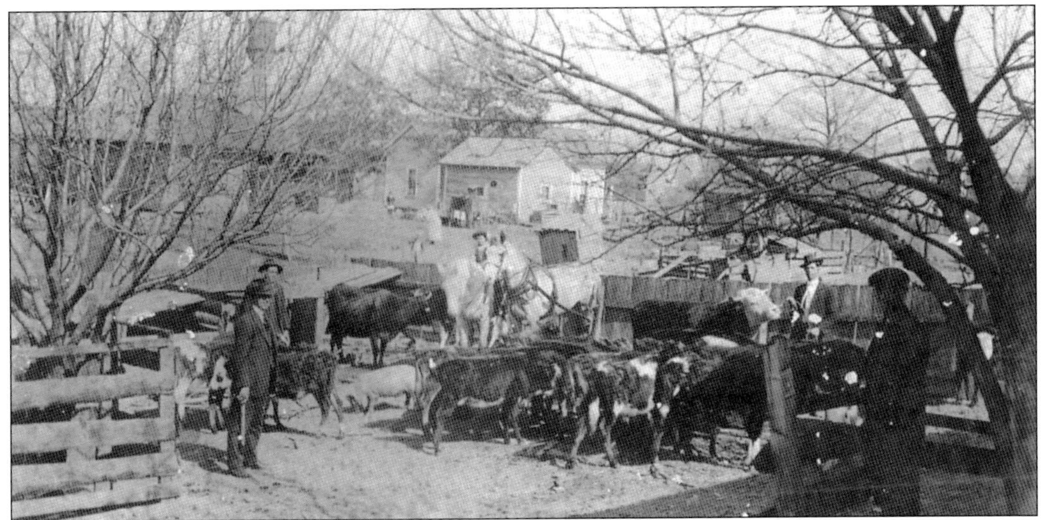

J.H. Everhart Brothers Livestock, 1920. The man with the stick is unidentified, but on horseback to his right is Willard Everhart. Joe Everhart is on the right holding the reins of a steer. The barn lot was on Worrell Street. In the left background is the home of the Damerons and the Standard Chair water tank.

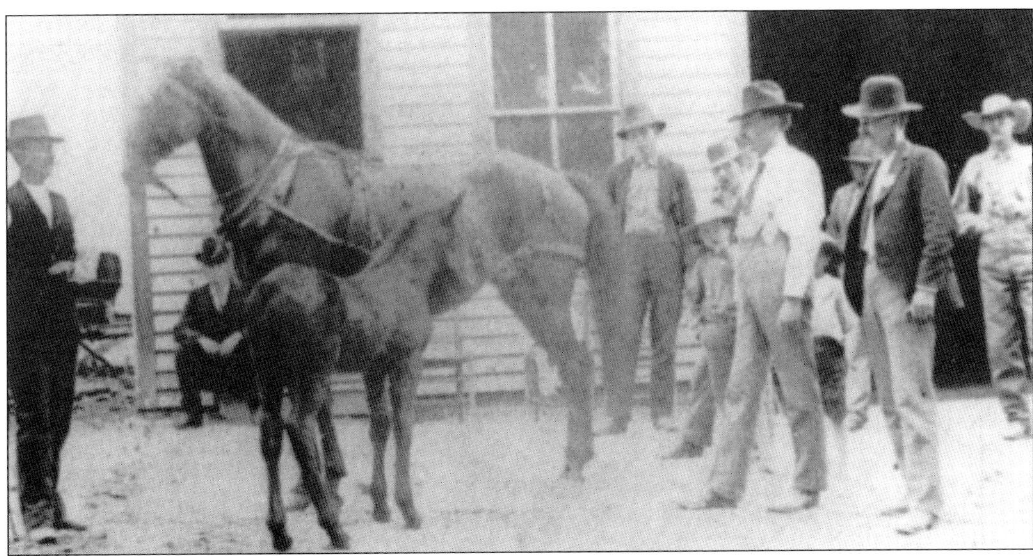

Wagner's Livery Stables, 1906. For many years, there were watering troughs on the main streets of town, and enterprising merchants also had them at the back of their stores along with hitching posts. Braxton B. Wagner's livery stables opened in 1898 on Guilford Street after being converted from the Wetmore Shoe Factory.

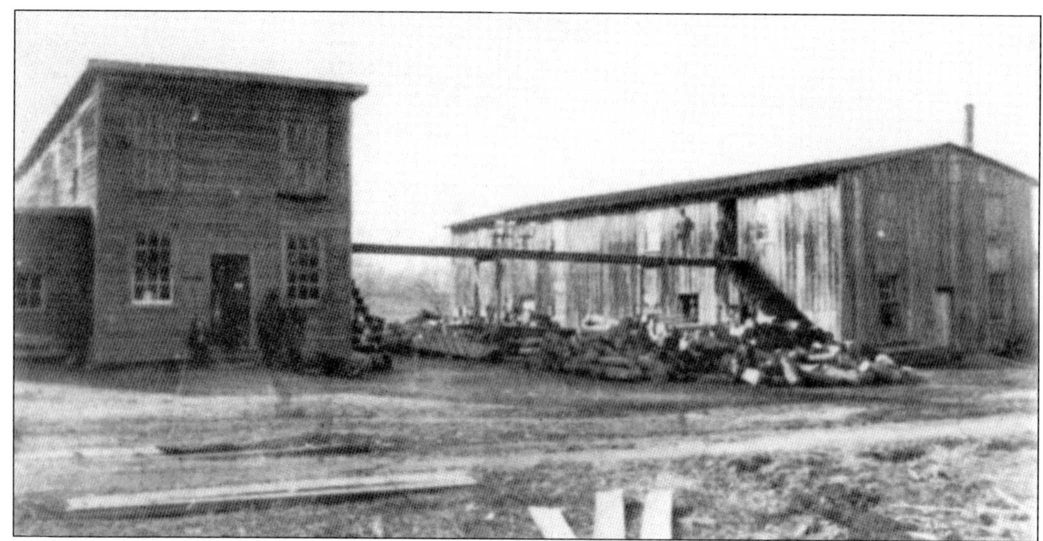

D.S. Westmoreland Chair Factory. Thomasville's—and quite possibly North Carolina's—first chair factory was opened by David Stephen Westmoreland in 1879. Westmoreland, a city councilman, sold his plain straight-back chairs for $12 a dozen. The factory burned down in 1897. Westmoreland's brother John F. was a North Carolina state senator and published Thomasville's first newspaper, the *Times*.

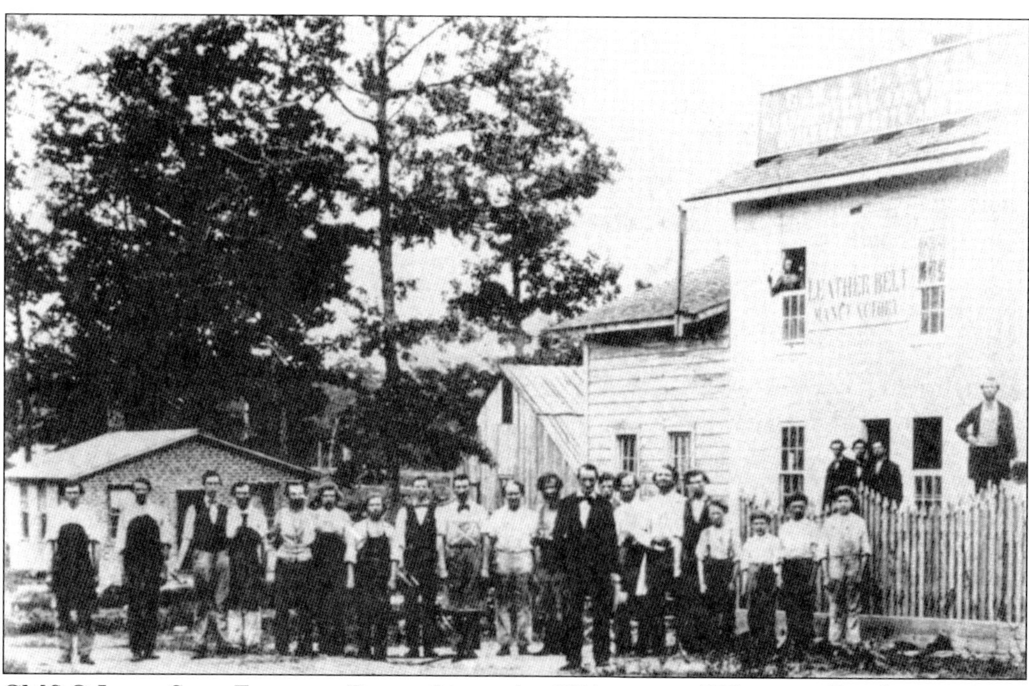

CM&G Lines Shoe Factory. George Lines, the 1874 mayor of Thomasville, along with his brother Charles Mix Lines, built a factory for making leather belts and brogan shoes for farmers. The shoe line grew and became so successful that CM&G Lines was given the title of "Largest Shoe Factory in the South." The brothers also operated CM&G Lines Hardware and Grocery on Salem Street.

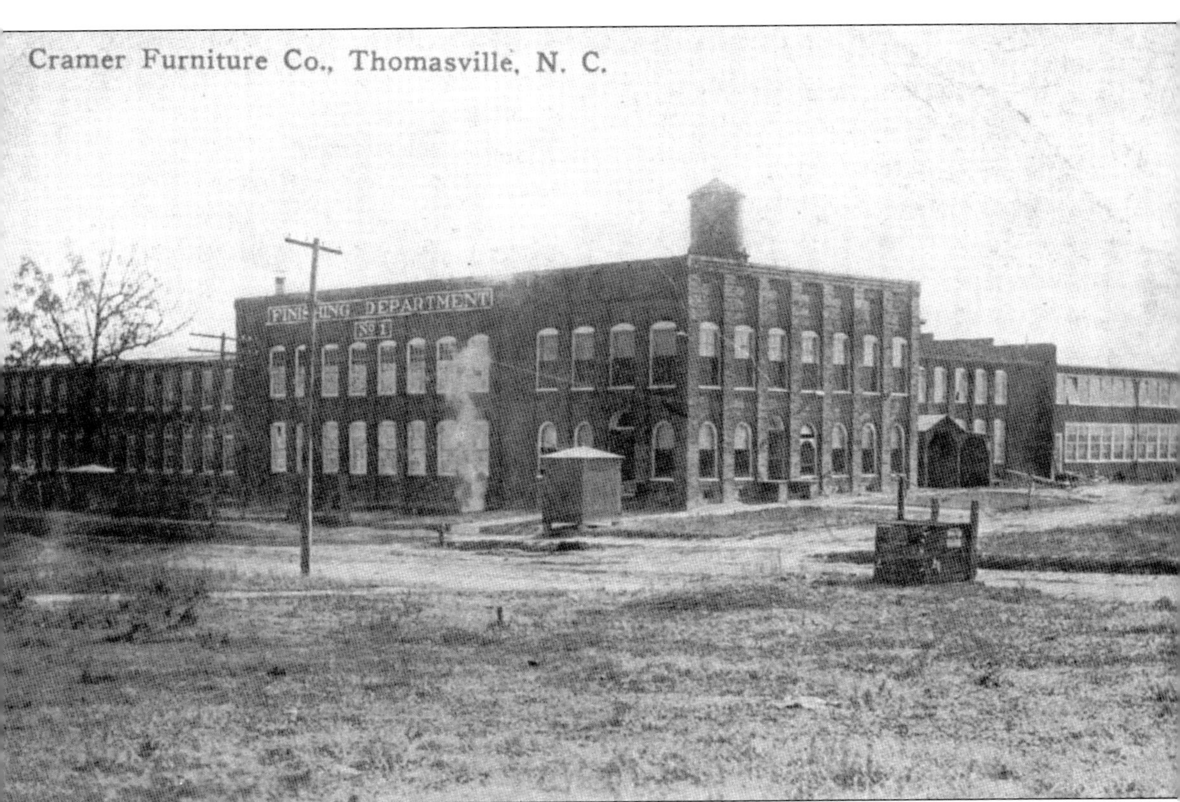

Cramer Furniture Company. A year after its founding in 1900, Cramer Furniture was the second-largest furniture manufacturer in the South; by 1913, it was the largest. It was safely piloted in its infancy by S.W. Cramer, its founder, who also served as president until he retired in 1913 and S.W. Cramer Jr. became president. Cramer Furniture Company was sold to Thomasville Chair Company in 1914.

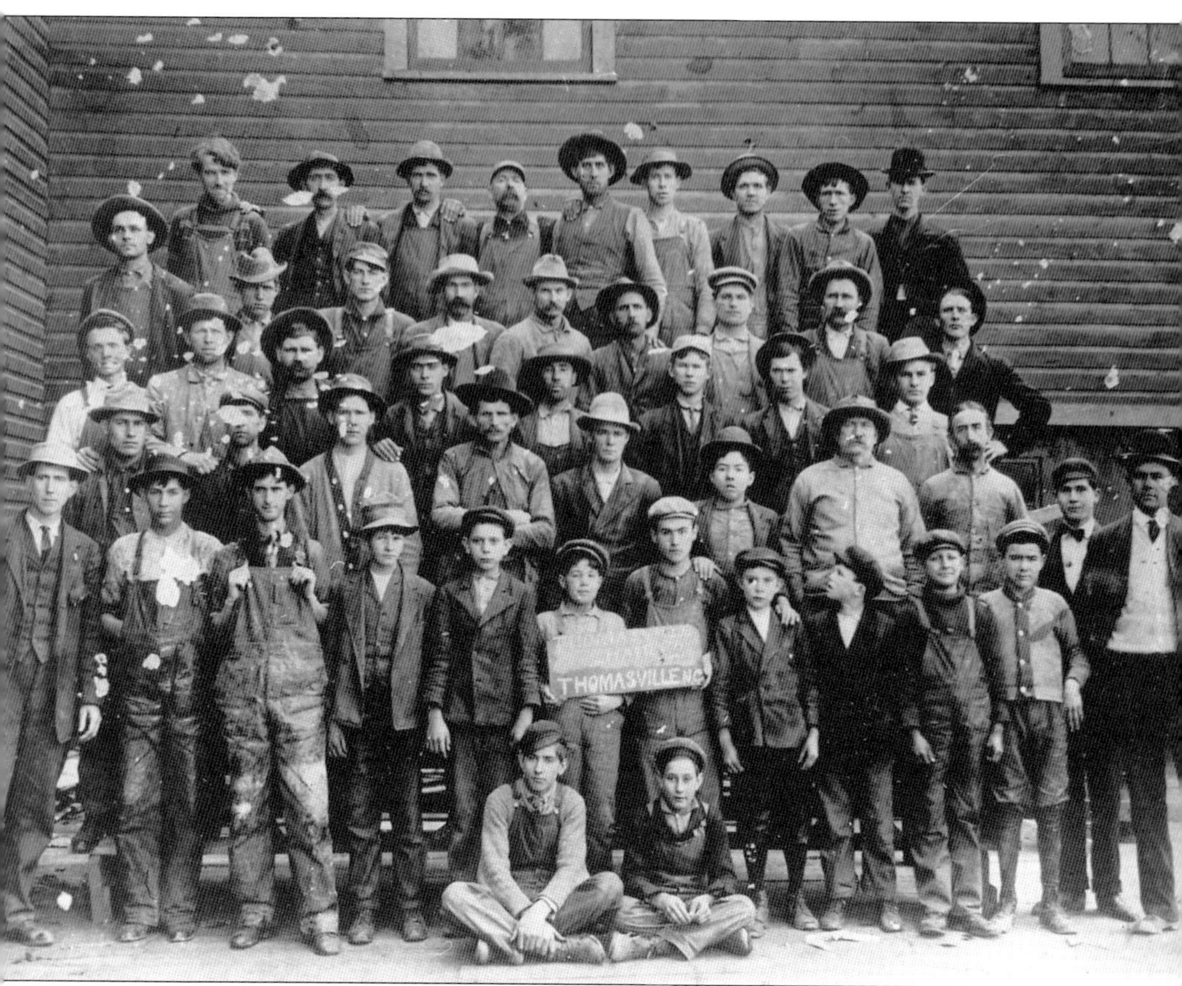

THOMASVILLE CHAIR COMPANY EMPLOYEES, 1910. Plant A employees were responsible for finishing the furniture, since Plant B did not have a finishing room. Seated in front at right, beneath the sign, is Jake Sechrest. He went to work at Plant A in 1909, making 40¢ per day and working 10 hours per weekday and 8 hours on Saturdays.

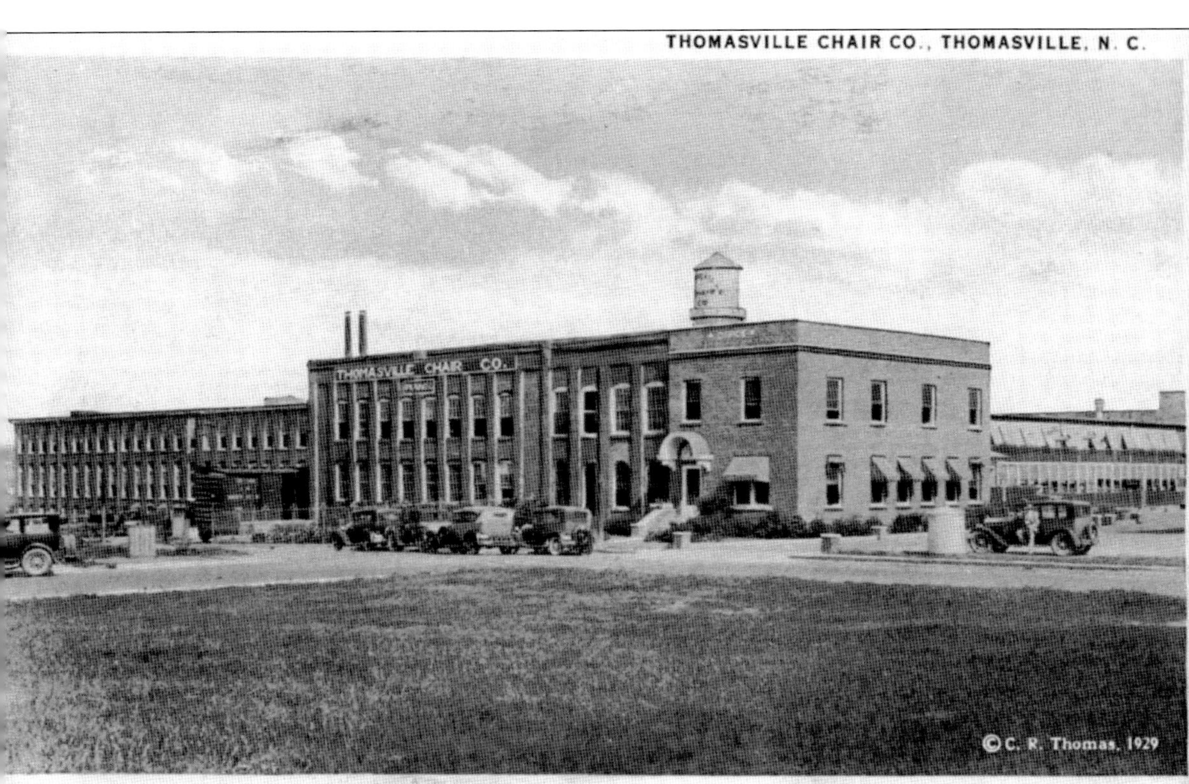

THOMASVILLE CHAIR COMPANY, 1929. Formed in 1904, Thomasville Chair Company grew into Thomasville Furniture Industries, one of the world's largest producers of fine household furnishings. Pictured is Plant C (for Cramer Furniture, the plant's originator) on East Main Street. Note the railroad car in front of the building; this car was used to transport the fine furniture nationwide.

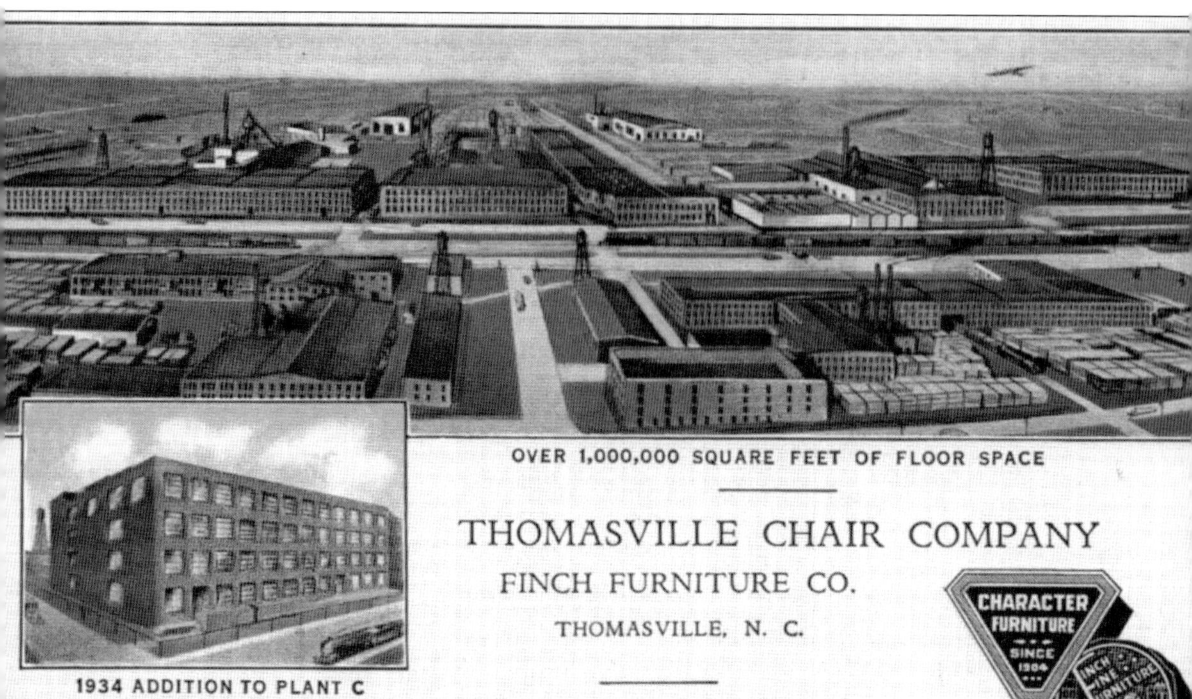

THOMASVILLE CHAIR COMPANY POSTCARD, 1930s. Thomasville Chair Company (originally Finch Furniture and most recently Thomasville Furniture Industries) started selling chairs for $8 to $21 per dozen. The company followed the custom of giving the customer a bonus, throwing in a 13th chair at no additional cost. Thomasville experienced an industrial surge thanks to Thomasville Furniture Industries, and led the country in furniture manufacturing.

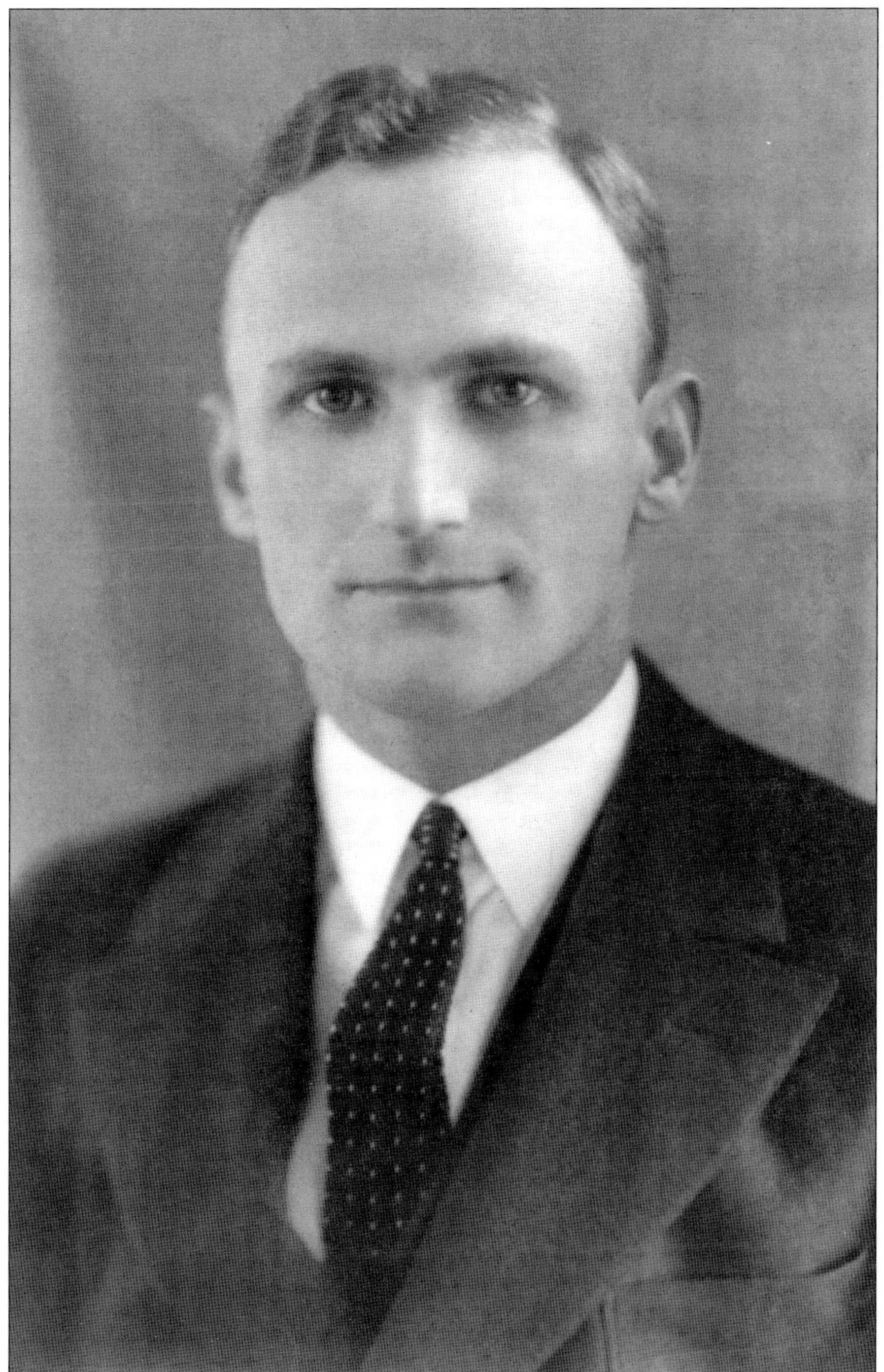

T. Austin Finch Sr., 1909. Tom Austin Finch was a man of great wisdom and vision. He served as president of Thomasville Chair Company from 1929 until his death in 1943 and was the key figure in the growth and development of the company. Finch was so successful that his friend Pres. Franklin D. Roosevelt called him during the Great Depression to ask for advice on how to get Americans back to work. (Courtesy Andrew Clement.)

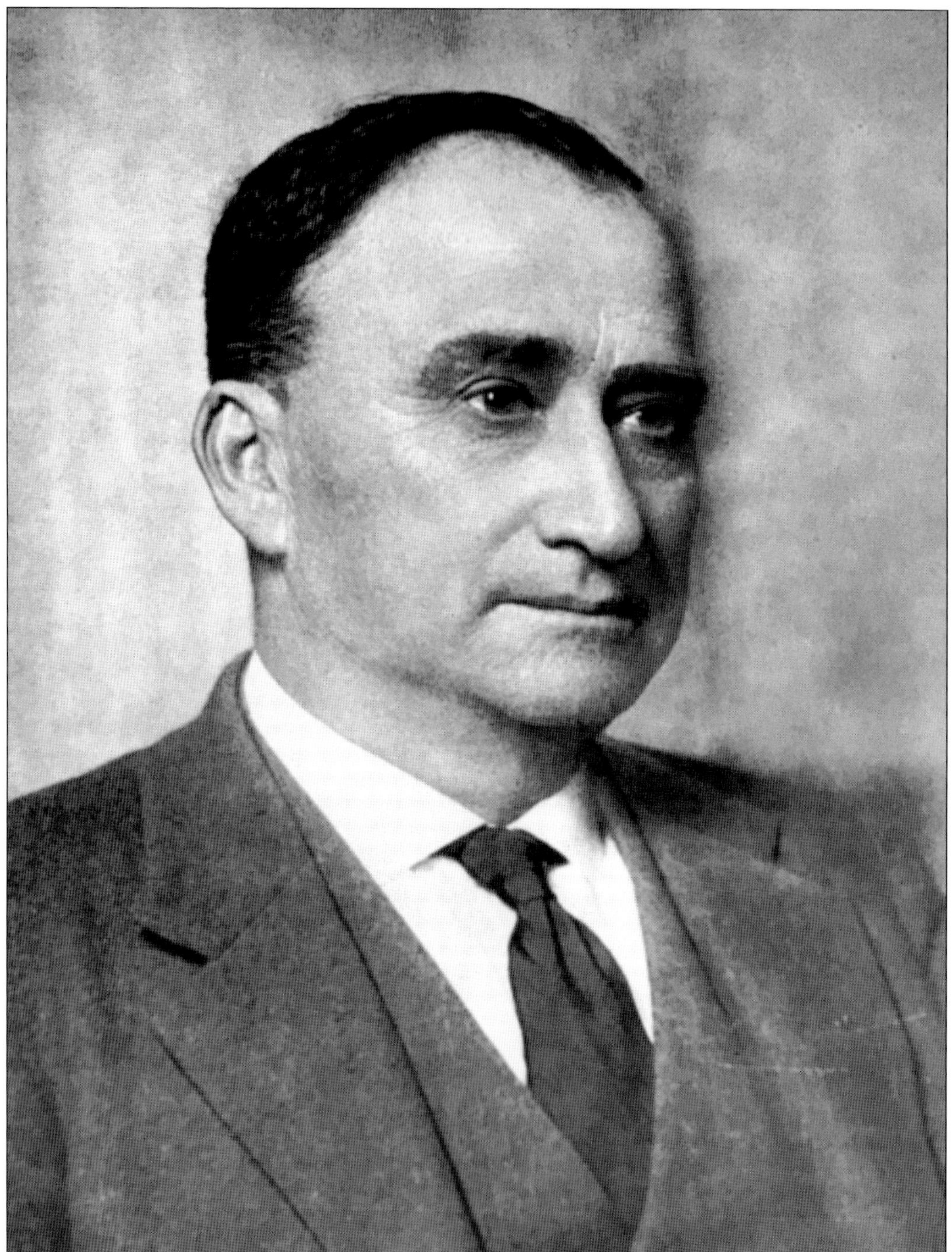

T.J. Finch, 1929. Thomas Jefferson Finch was one of the early business leaders in Thomasville and father to T. Austin, George, and Doak. T.J. graduated from Trinity College (now Duke University) and opened a general store with C.L. Harris in 1897. He was also one of the three men who organized the Bank of Thomasville. T.J. Finch was a farmer, sheriff, and highly successful businessman. (Courtesy Andrew Clement.)

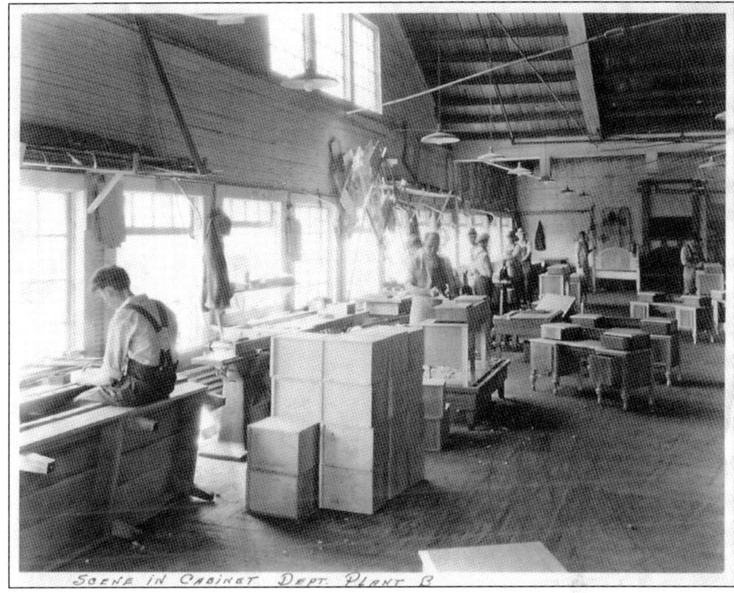

PLANT B, 1920s. This is a rare glimpse into the cabinet department of Thomasville Chair Company's Plant B. In the early days, the transportation department of Thomasville Chair Company was a wagon and a white mule. To get chairs and other furniture from Plant B to Plant A, workers would load the wagon, and it would be hauled over to the other plant. (Courtesy Andrew Clement.)

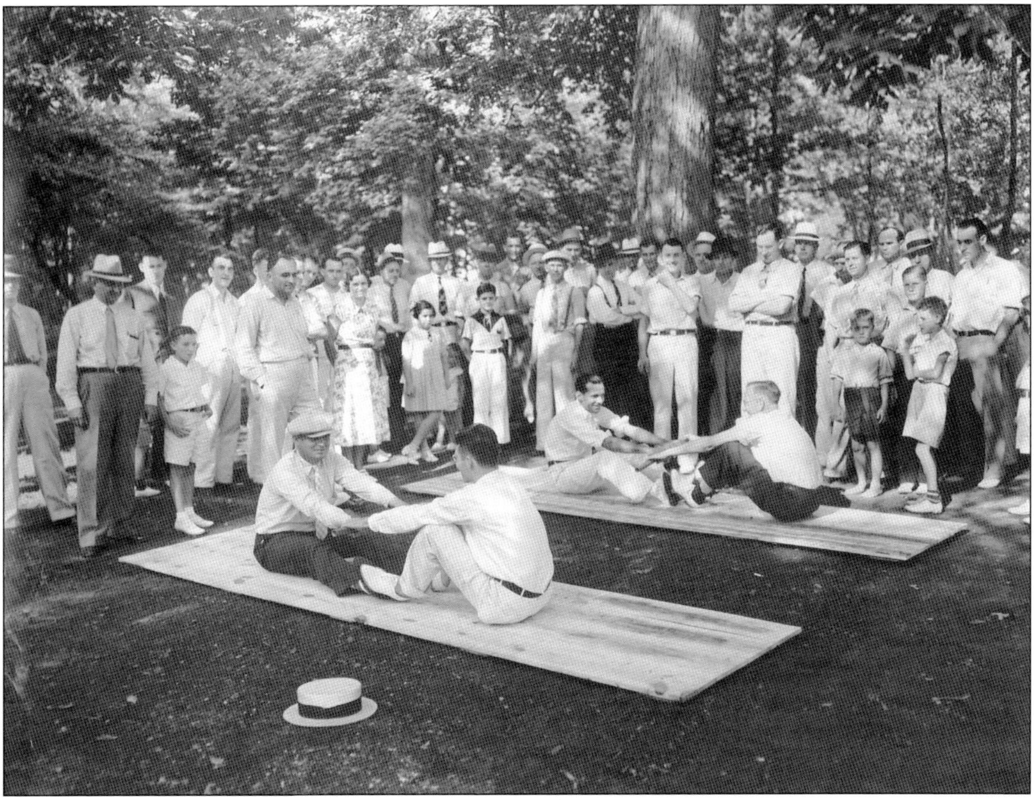

RECREATION DAY, 1930s. Wheatmore Farm (now Adaumont Farm) was home to the Finch family and the original Wheatmore School, which is where the Finch boys were educated. In the first half of the 20th century, Thomasville Chair Company employees were invited to annual recreational days, where they could compete in relays and games with their families and coworkers. (Courtesy Andrew Clement.)

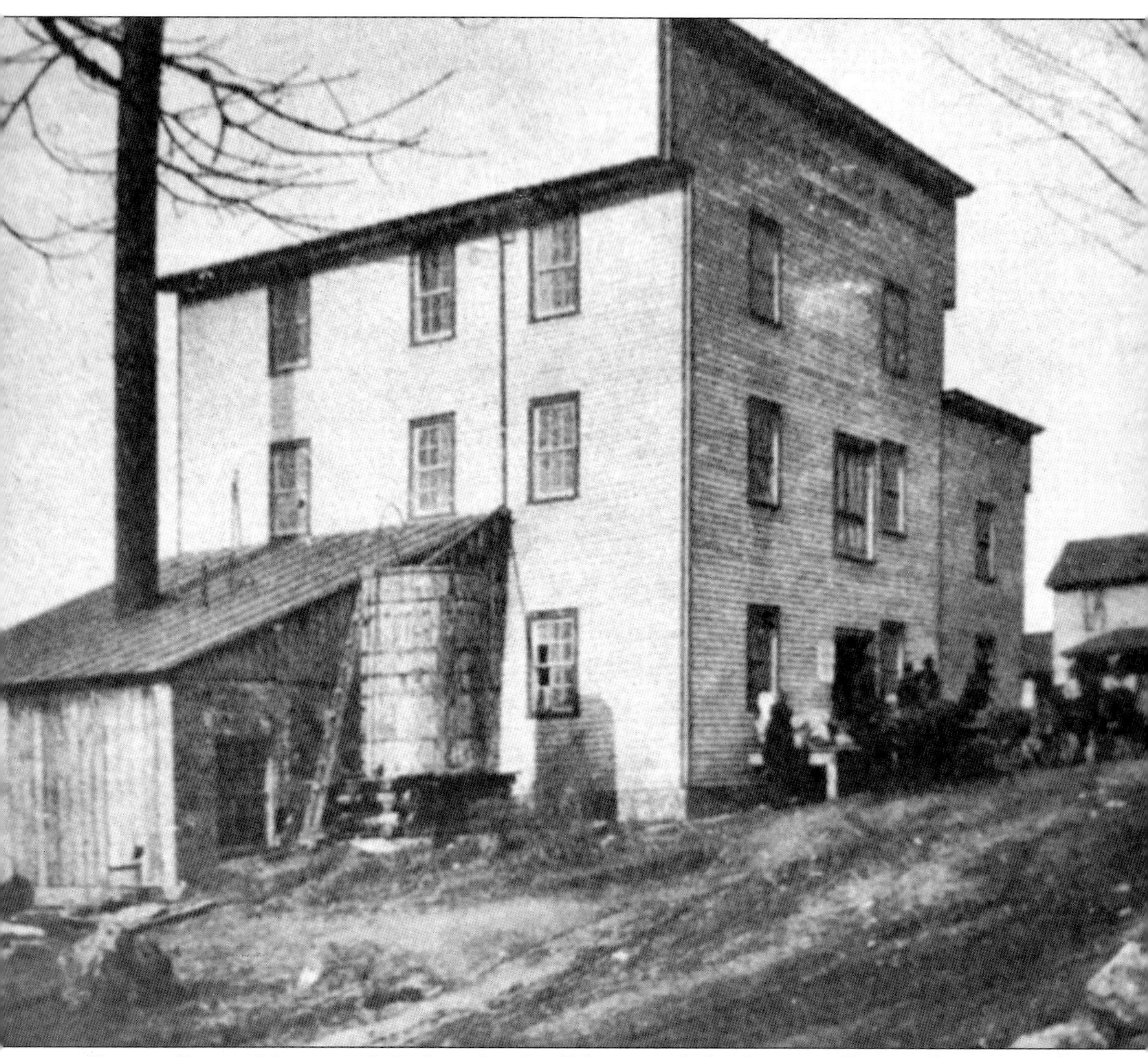

EUREKA ROLLER MILLS, C. 1897. Completed in February 1892 by George Miller, Eureka Roller Mills was sold later that year to Capt. J.E. Sumner (grandfather of J. Walter Lambeth Jr.), who operated the mill until 1896. The mill changed hands several times: D.T. Lambeth & Sons (1896–1899), Lambeth Roller Mills (1899–1905), Thomasville Roller Mills (1905–1914), and finally Hinkle Milling Company (1914–1989).

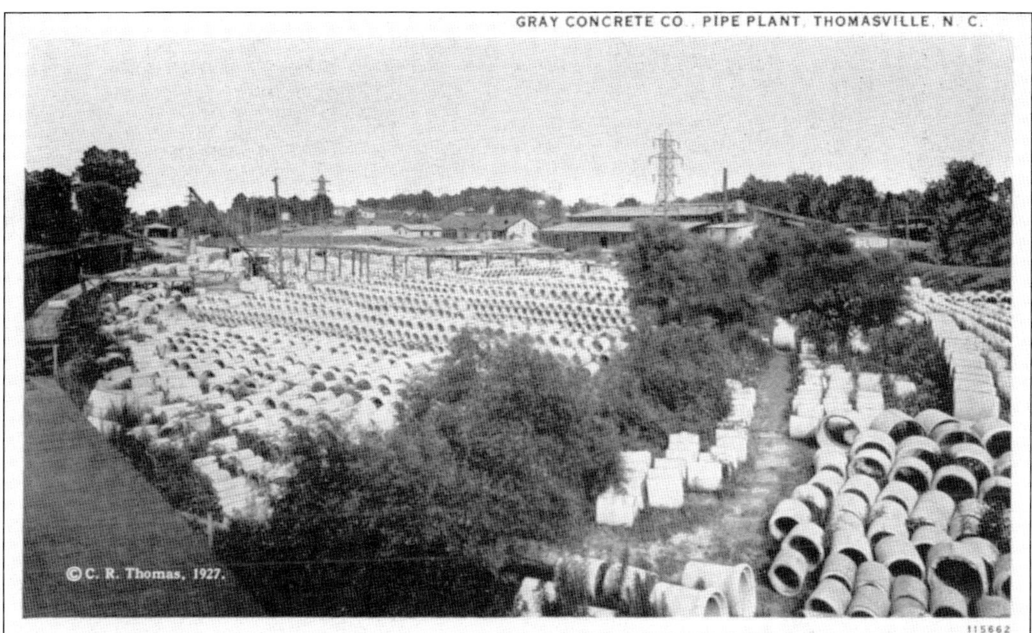

Gray Concrete Company, 1927. Fred B. Gray organized Gray Concrete Company in 1908 and started producing concrete farm drain tiles, septic tanks, and concrete blocks. Production evolved into concrete pipes and storm drainage for highway work. The company was responsible for erecting Colonial Drive School, City Memorial Hospital, and a few other buildings, as well as paving Spring Street and Colonial Drive.

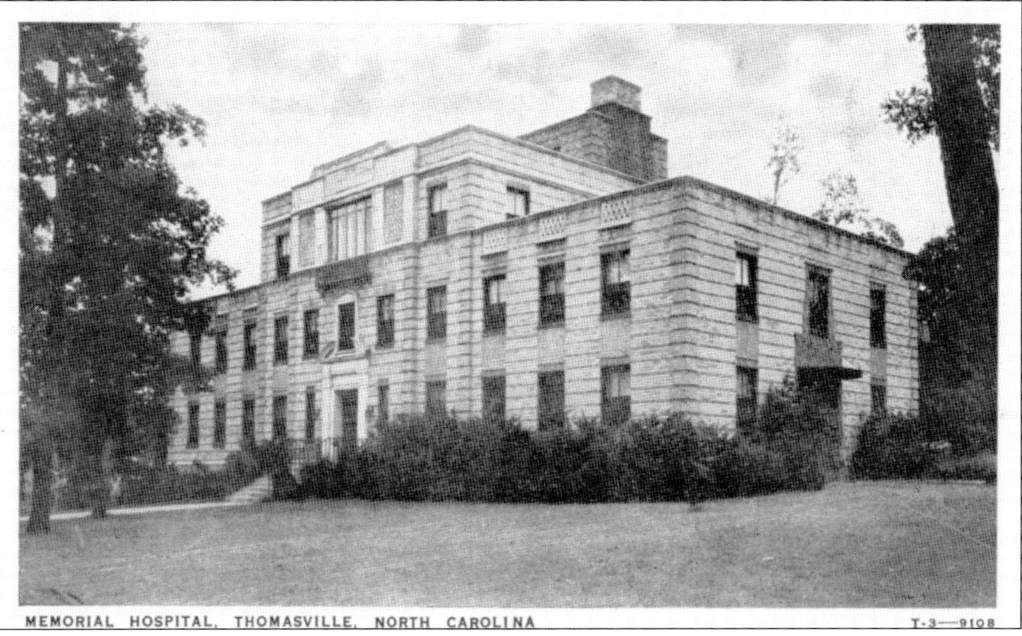

City Memorial Hospital, 1930. Thomasville's first hospital opened on Pine Street in 1930 with 31 beds at a cost of $105,000. Brothers George and Doak Finch contributed $40,000 from a sum netted in a lawsuit against Southern Railway over the death of their brother Brown Finch, who died instantly when a Southern passenger train crashed into his car at a Thomasville crossing.

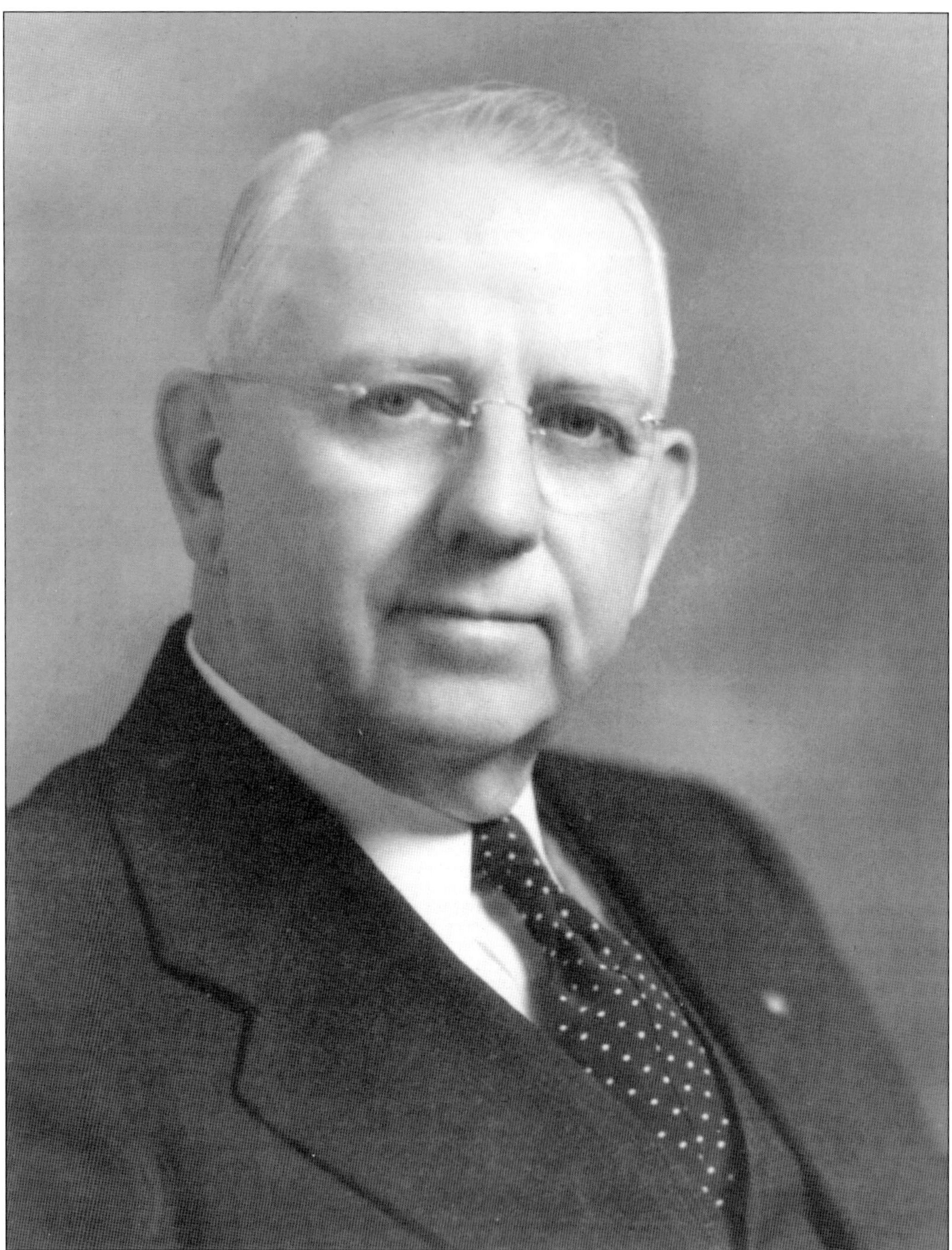

Dr. C.H. Phillips. Dr. Charles Hoover Phillips of Fuller's Mill was a general physician who moved to Thomasville in 1920. He attended to many patients in his home before making the move to 101 Spruce Street. Dr. Phillips had a large practice and was a key leader in the formation of City Memorial Hospital. He was known for his philanthropy and providing no-cost care for patients who were unable to pay for his services. He is a great-great-grandfather of the author.

Three

Houses

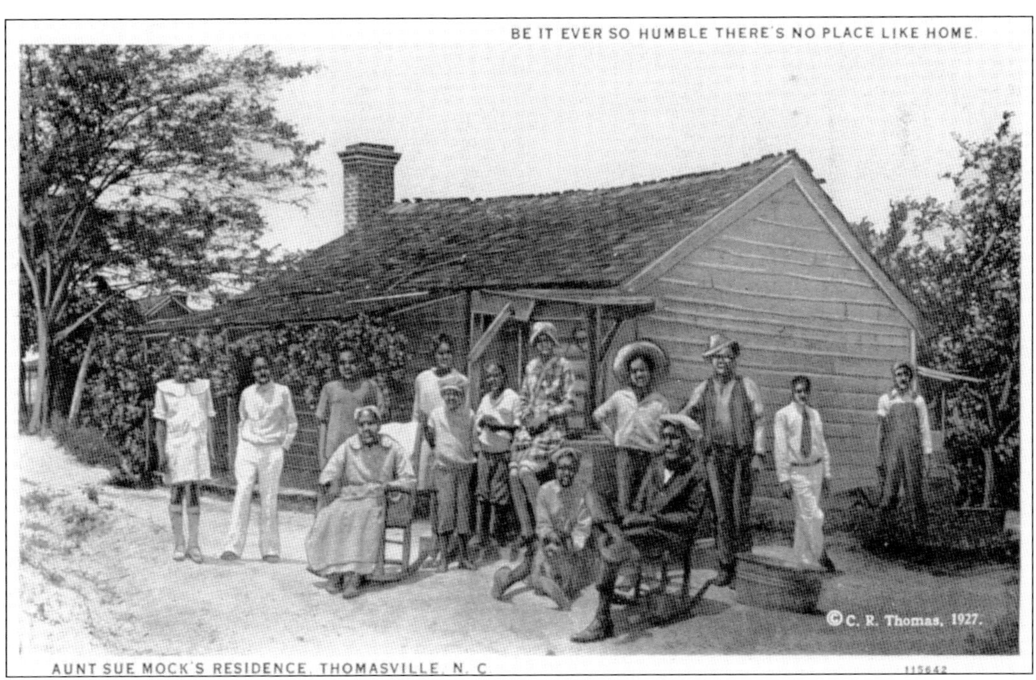

Aunt Sue Mock's Residence, 1927. "Aunt" Sue Mock was a practicing midwife in Thomasville until her death in 1933 at age 87. She was regarded as the chief midwife in both the Black and white communities. She is pictured sitting in a rocking chair in front of her home with her family.

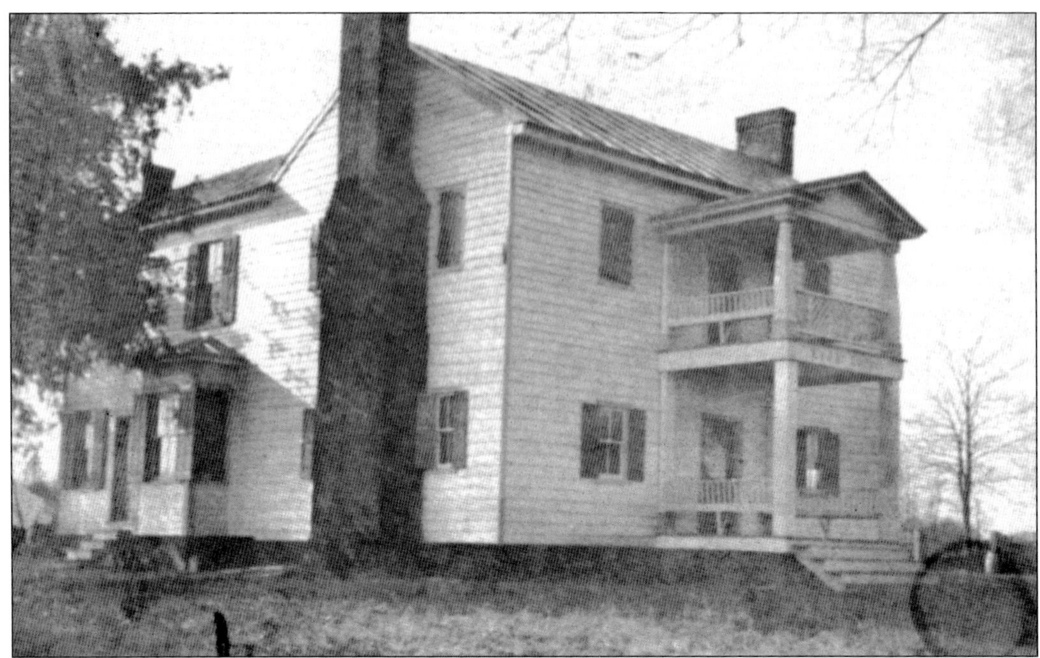

John W. Thomas Residence, 1903. This photograph shows how Thomas's onetime home at Fair Grove looked around the time the farm was bought by Maj. Frank Fleer. Major Fleer, a chewing-gum manufacturer, gave it the name Cedar Lodge and helped it grow into Cedar Lodge Farm & Dairy. Fleer is responsible for the creation of Double Bubble and Chiclets.

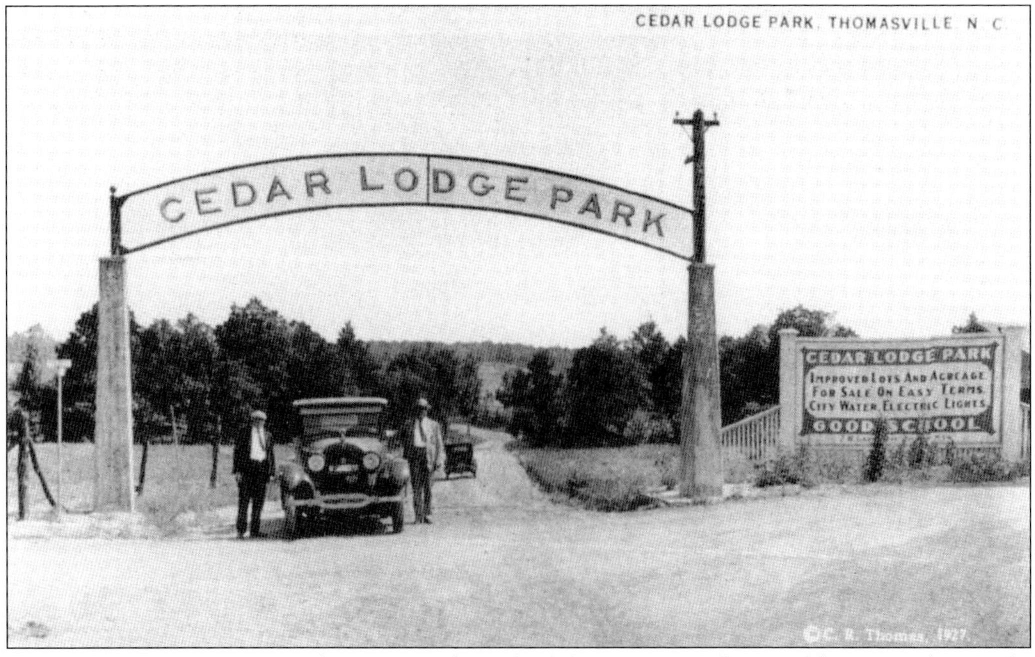

Cedar Lodge Park, 1927. This new residential subdivision was advertised by a sign that reads, "Improved Lots And Acreage / For Sale On Easy Terms / City Water Electric Lights / Good School." The sign includes contact information for J. Walter Lambeth who is pictured (right) with his Cadillac and C.R. Thomas. This metal arch is now part of a gate to Mills Home.

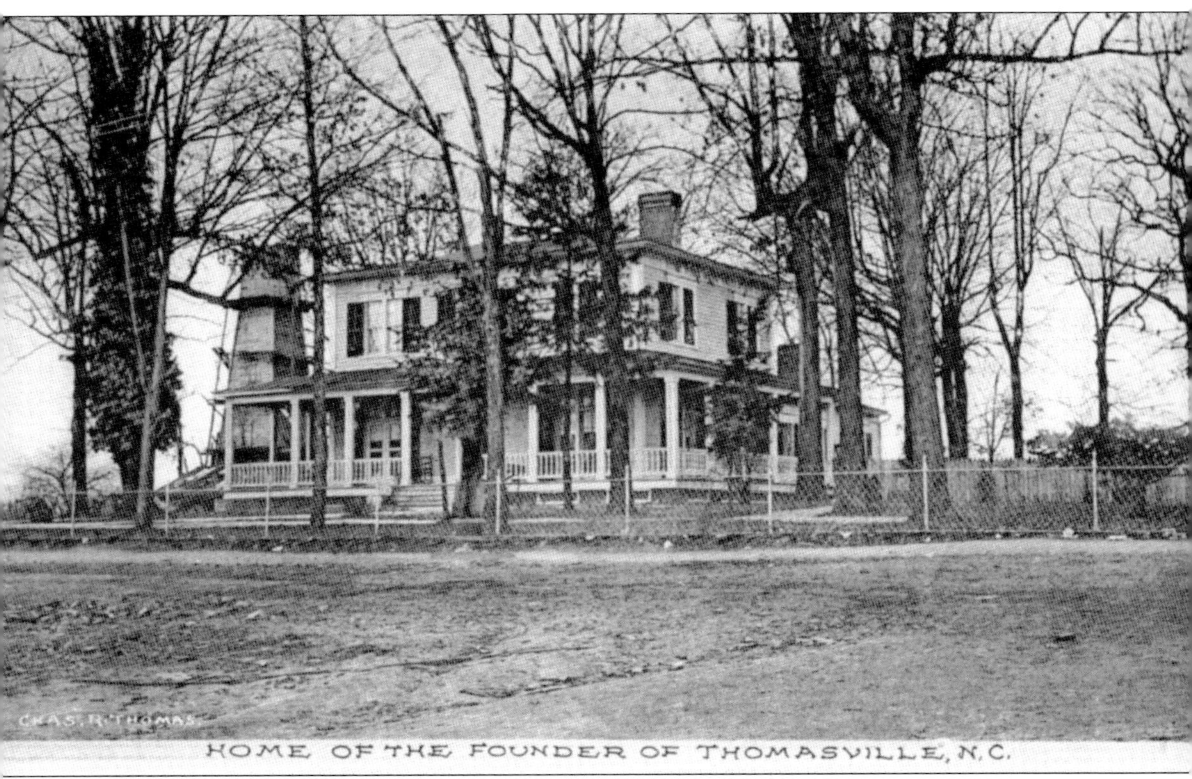

JOHN W. THOMAS RESIDENCE. A 1921 *Chairtown News* article described this house as a "grand mansion." It was built in 1857 by contractors Foster and Winslow and was surrounded by oaks, cedars, cherry trees, and an iron fence. It sat north of the railroad tracks behind the current Lambeth block and was razed in the mid-1930s.

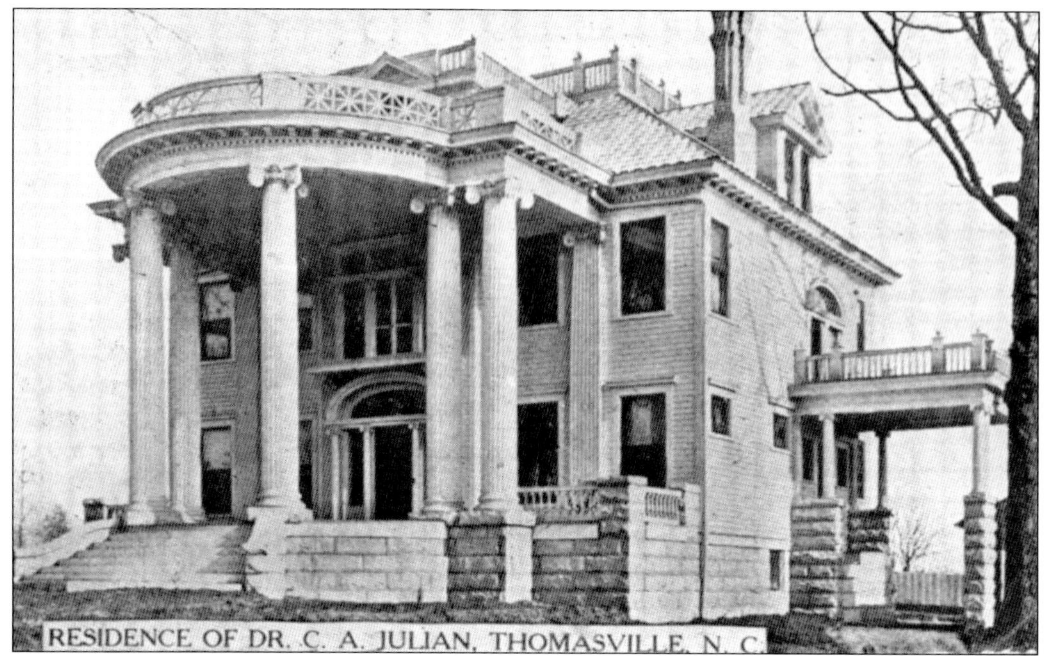

Dr. C.A. Julian Residence, 1916. In the early 1900s, Gerald Johnson said: "I have . . . seen the columns of the Madeline in Paris, and the circle of the monoliths in the National Gallery of Art in Washington, but they impressed no less than the columns on Dr. Julian's house, fifty years ago." Perhaps the finest neoclassical house of its day, the large and squarish two-story main block was covered with a modified pyramidal roof finished with a balustrade. Gracing the front porch was a colossal two-story Ionic-columned semicircular porch built on a masonry foundation; a porte cochere was attached to one side. The house sat on the corner of Cramer and East Main Streets and burned down in the early 1940s.

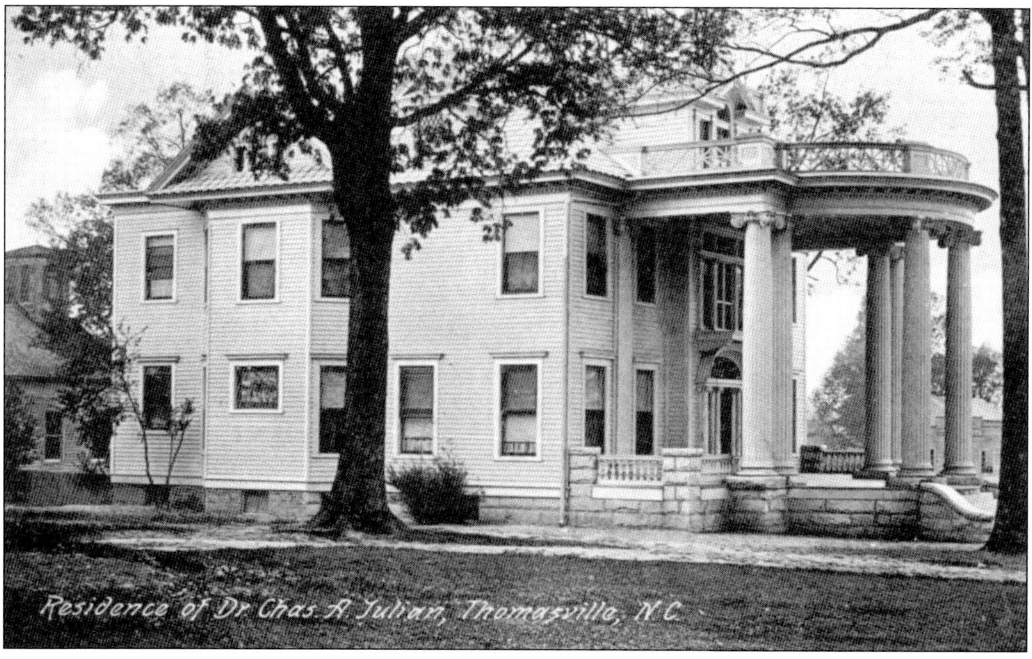

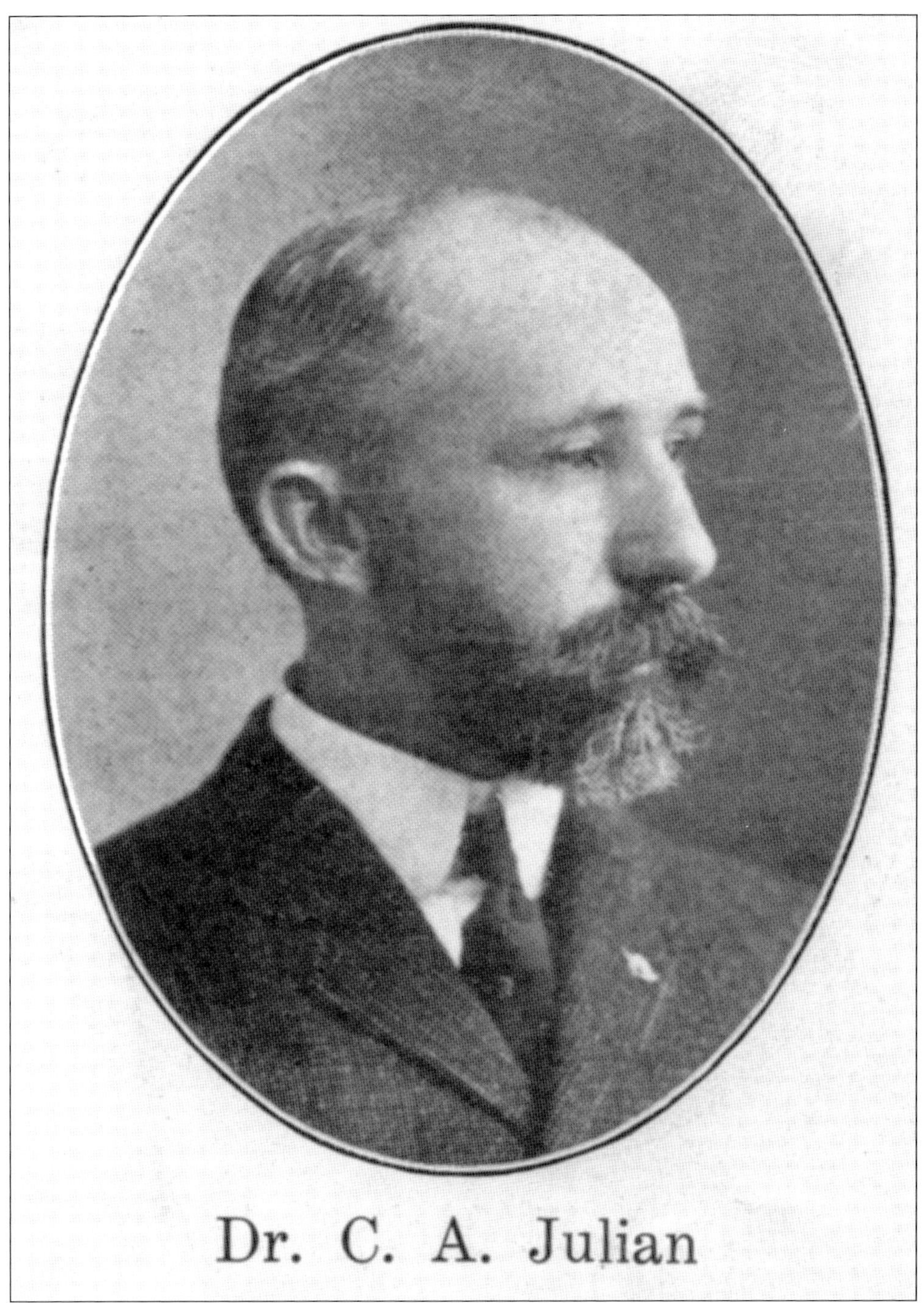

Dr. C.A. Julian, 1914. Dr. Charles A. Julian, who served as a city councilman from 1894 to 1896 and 1899 to 1900, married Carrie Cramer, granddaughter of John W. Thomas. Dr. Julian was a brilliant physician credited with the discovery of hookworm. A World War I Army veteran, he served as the North Carolina tuberculosis board secretary, a North Carolina nurses' board examiner, the North Carolina Medical Society vice president, and the L. Richardson Memorial Hospital president.

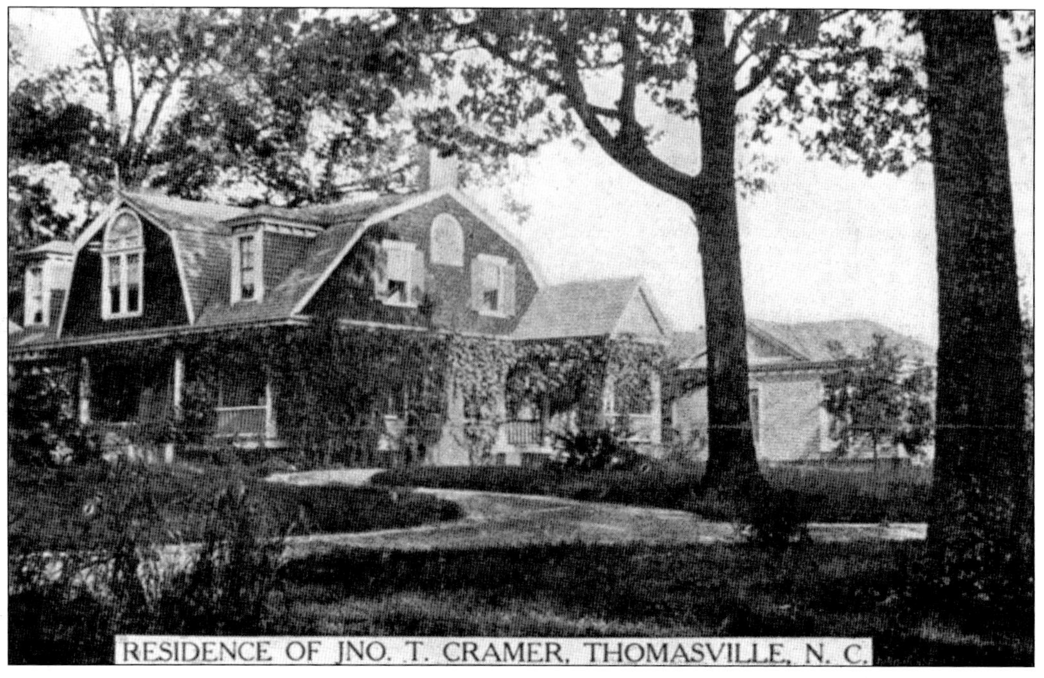

J.T. Cramer Residence. The John Thomas Cramer home was at the corner of Cramer and East Main Streets, one block east of Randolph Street. Originally the Lewis Thomas Hotel, this residence served as the hospital depot during the Civil War, and one room was later used as the ticket office for the North Carolina Railroad. Cramer served as a Union soldier and participated in 33 battles. He was Dr. C.A. Julian's father-in-law.

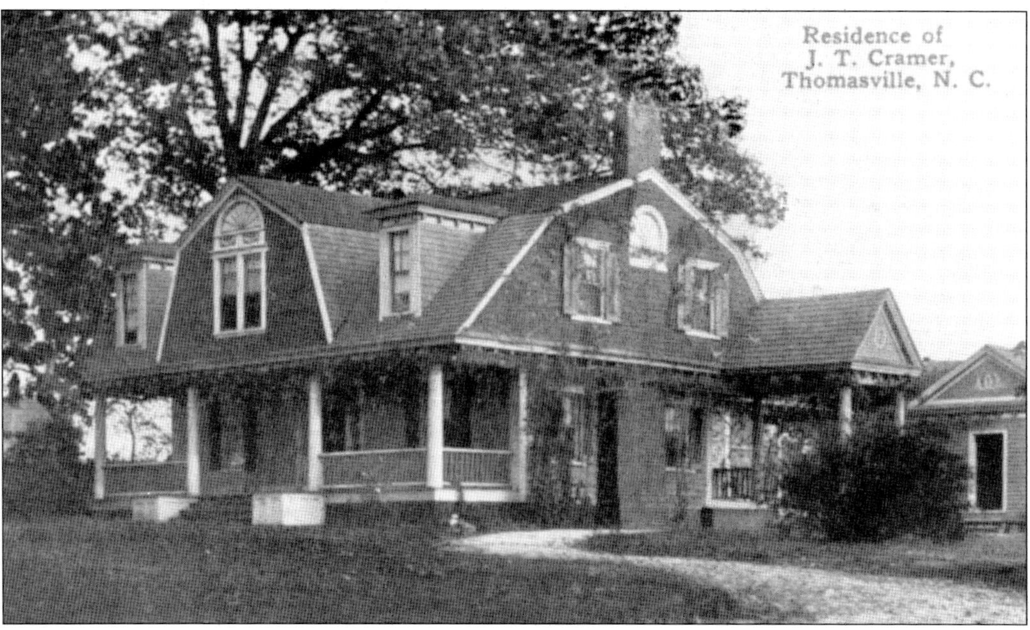

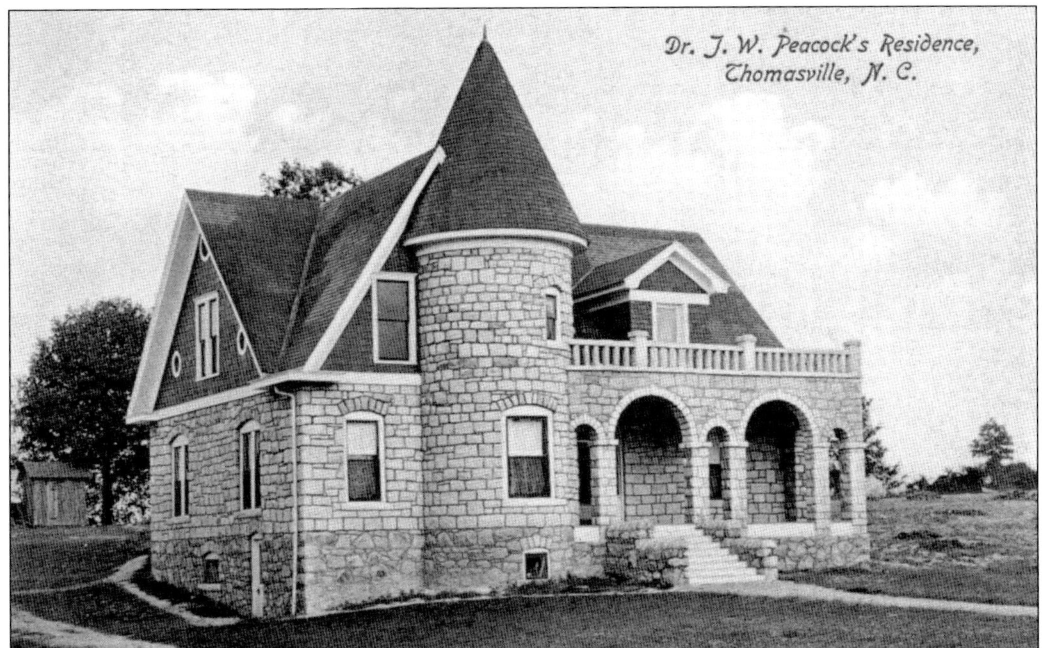

Dr. J.W. Peacock Residence. This beautiful stone structure still stands as a private residence on Salem Street. Conflicting reports say it was built in either 1907 or 1911 for Dr. J.W. Peacock. In 1924, Thomas Jefferson Finch bought the house from the Peacock family and later sold it to R.L. Pope, who worked at First National Bank and served on the city council.

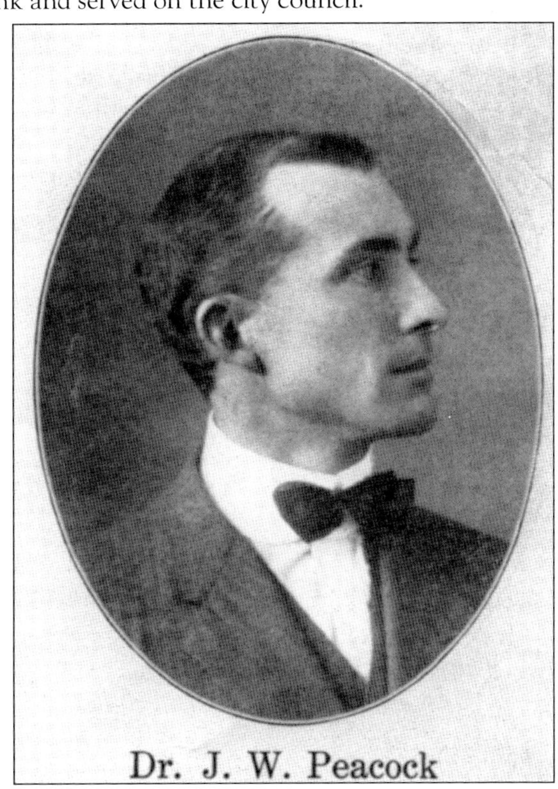

Dr. J.W. Peacock, 1914. Dr. James Walter Peacock was undoubtedly the most admired of Thomasville's four physicians at the time this photograph was taken. He cared extensively for the sick during the 1918 influenza pandemic. A Prohibition feud with police chief John Edgar Taylor led Peacock to shoot and kill Taylor in 1921. After a trial, confinement in prison, and an escape, Peacock wound up living in California. He died in a mining accident in 1928.

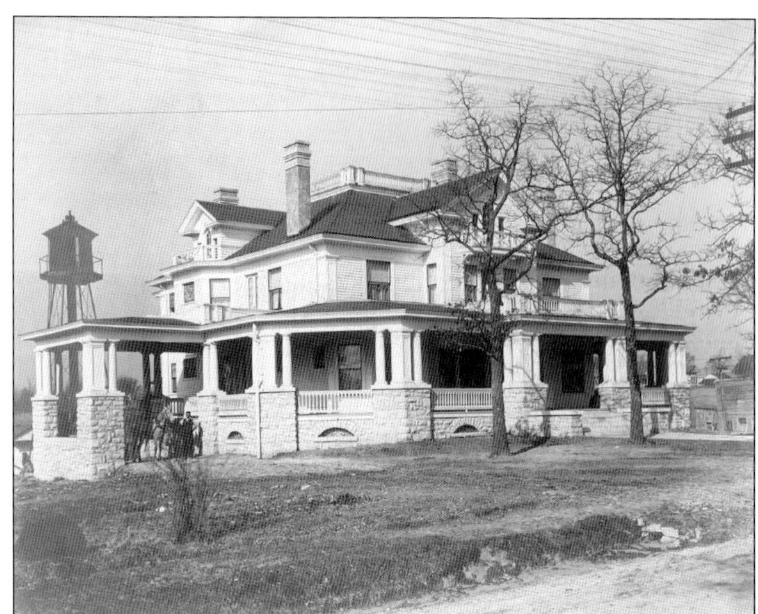

F.S. Lambeth Residence "Arlam," 1914. Col. Frank S. Lambeth, one of the organizers of Standard Chair Company, built this house with his wife, Ella Arnold. The magnificent structure, built sometime between 1900 and 1910, is one of the most prominent houses that still stands on present-day Randolph Street. It aptly represents the wealth that once flowed through the "Chair City."

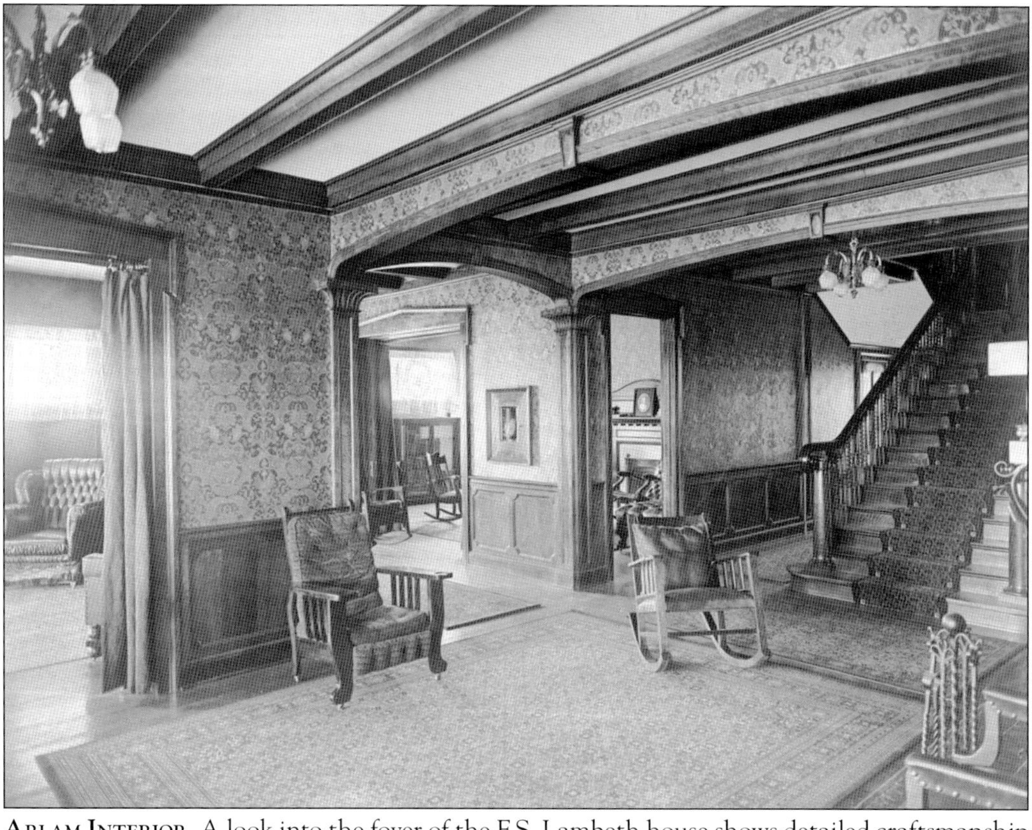

Arlam Interior. A look into the foyer of the F.S. Lambeth house shows detailed craftsmanship and wealth. The wooden chairs at center were likely produced by Standard Chair Company in the early 1900s. It is rumored that a man died at the house, and his ghost still haunts the interior; his death gave rise to questions that were never answered.

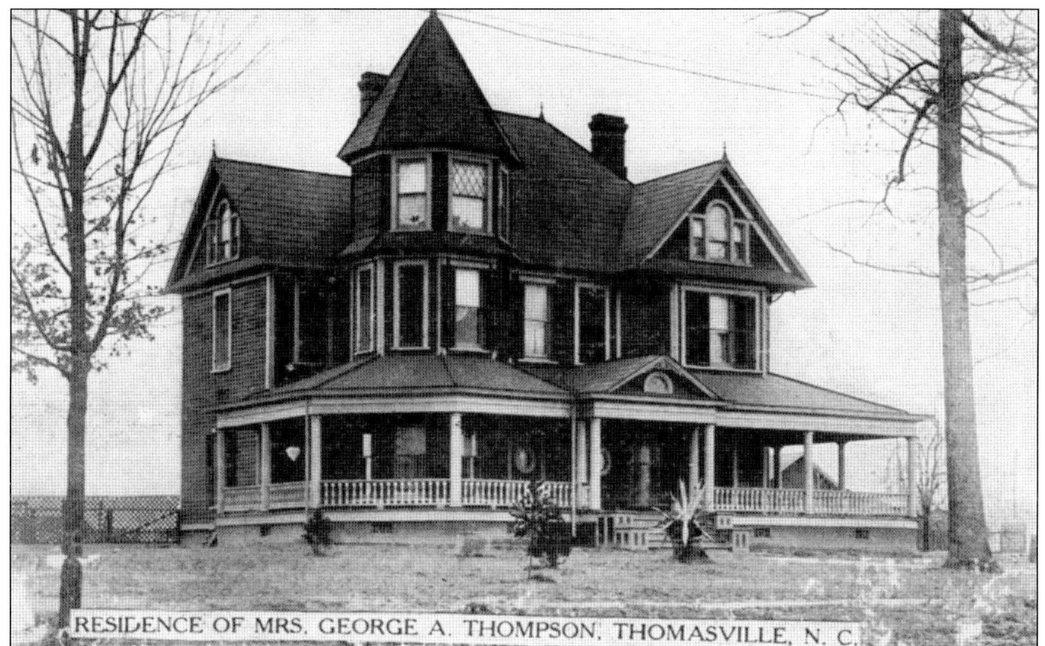

Mrs. George A. Thompson Residence. According to Mrs. G.A. Thompson, "In 1838 John W. Thomas, my grandfather, the founder of the town, bought a tract of 1500 acres from a Mr. Goldsberry, paying for this land a four-horse load of bacon. . . . Later [he] built a home [in present downtown], which was called in those days 'The Mansion,' and moved his large family there."

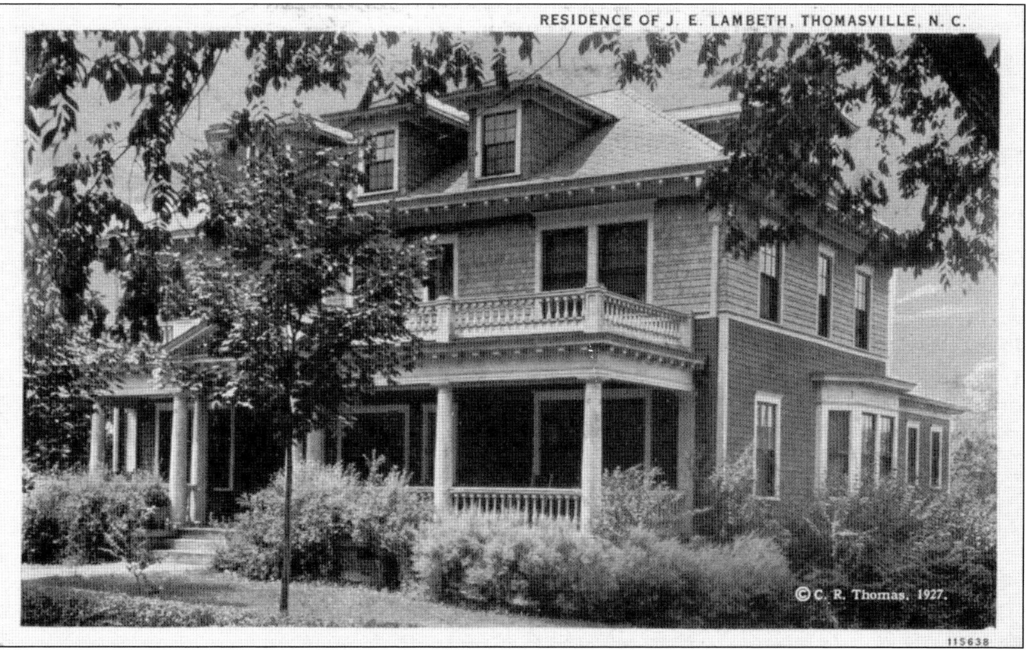

J.E. Lambeth Residence, 1927. James Erwin Lambeth Sr. was the son of F.S. Lambeth and served as mayor of Thomasville from 1929 to 1935. J.E. Lambeth served as president and vice president of Standard Chair Company, the first large furniture factory in Thomasville, which was built in 1898 and continued operations until the 1940s. This house, built in 1910 on Randolph Street, no longer stands.

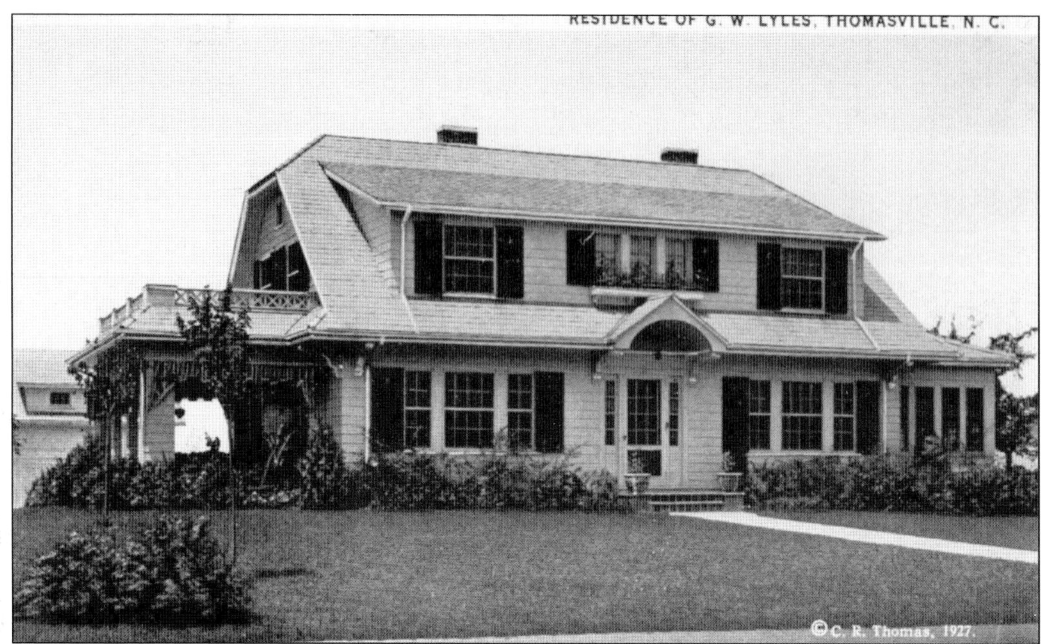

G.W. Lyles Residence, 1929. The Dutch Colonial residence that once belonged to the Lyles family is another house that still stands on Salem Street. It was built for the Lyles family in 1924 by a Mr. Wellingham. G.W. Lyles owned an automobile agency in Thomasville, and later in High Point. The home remained in the Lyles family until 1992.

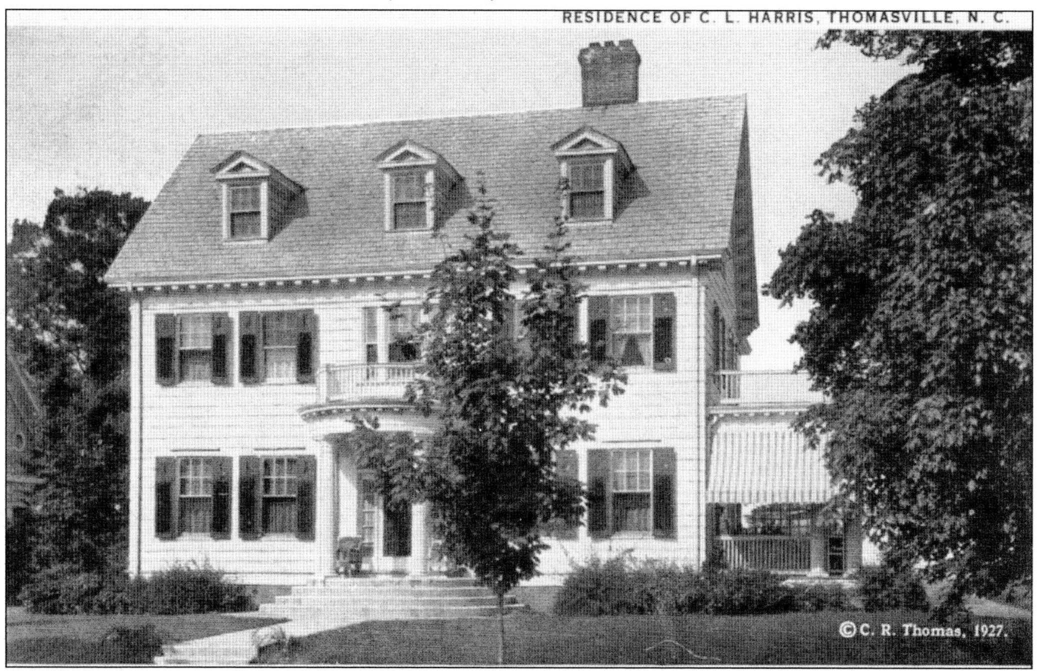

C.L. Harris Residence, 1929. The Cepha Lee Harris home still stands at 207 Salem Street. Arthur Morris built the house but only lived in it for a short period. Harris purchased it from Morris, and it remained in the Harris family until the late 1960s. Harris relocated to Thomasville in 1896, founded Davidson Wholesale, and cofounded Thomasville Store Company.

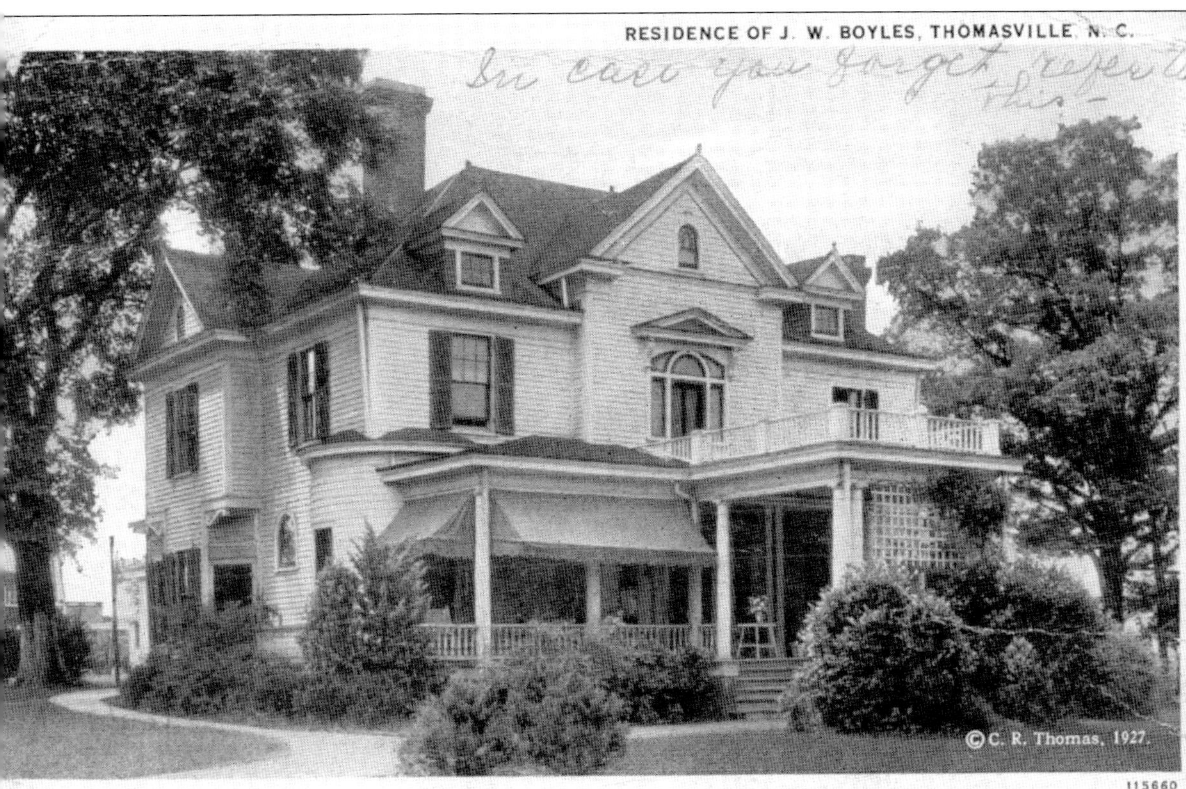

J.W. BOYLES RESIDENCE, 1927. J.W. Boyles was a business and civic leader in the community. His home once stood at the location of the current post office on the corner of Fisher Ferry and West Main Streets. The house was originally built in 1907 for banker J.L. Armfield by M.L. Ritchie, Thomasville's foremost building contractor at the time. The house was torn down in 1964.

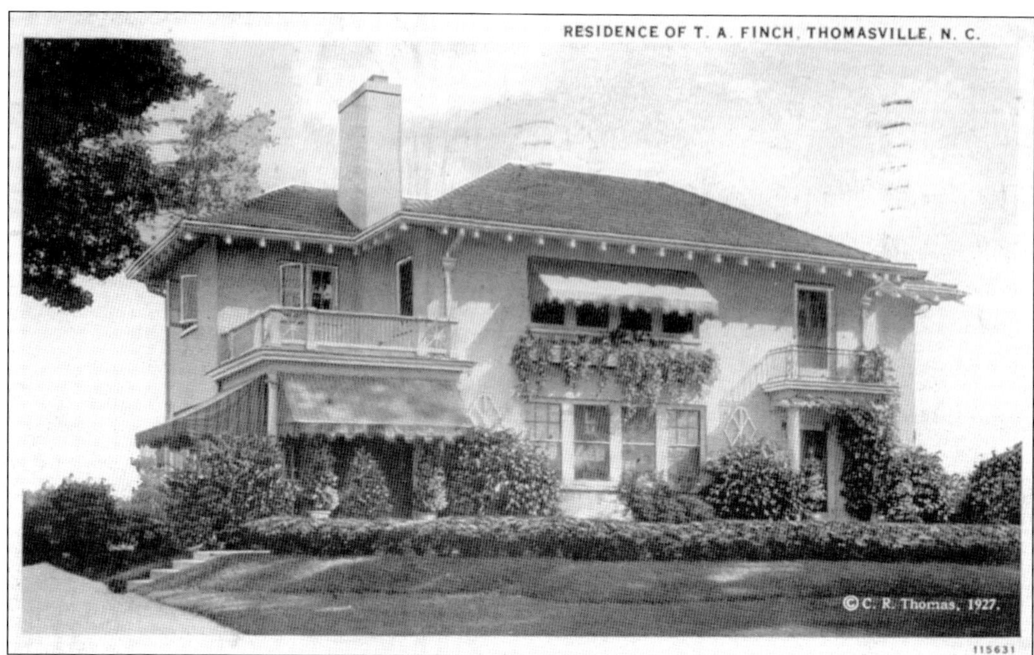

T.A. FINCH RESIDENCE, 1929. The T. Austin Finch House conveys a refined, subtle sense of permanence and wealth. The expansiveness of the austere yet sophisticated edifice is unequaled in Thomasville's 1920s and 1930s residential architecture. The green Ludowici-Celadon tile hip roof, deep eaves, shaped rafter ends, and large multipane windows and French doors exhibit the influence of the Renaissance Revival style. The spacious two-story residence was erected in two phases: the original dwelling was completed in 1921, and a 1938 west addition doubled its size.

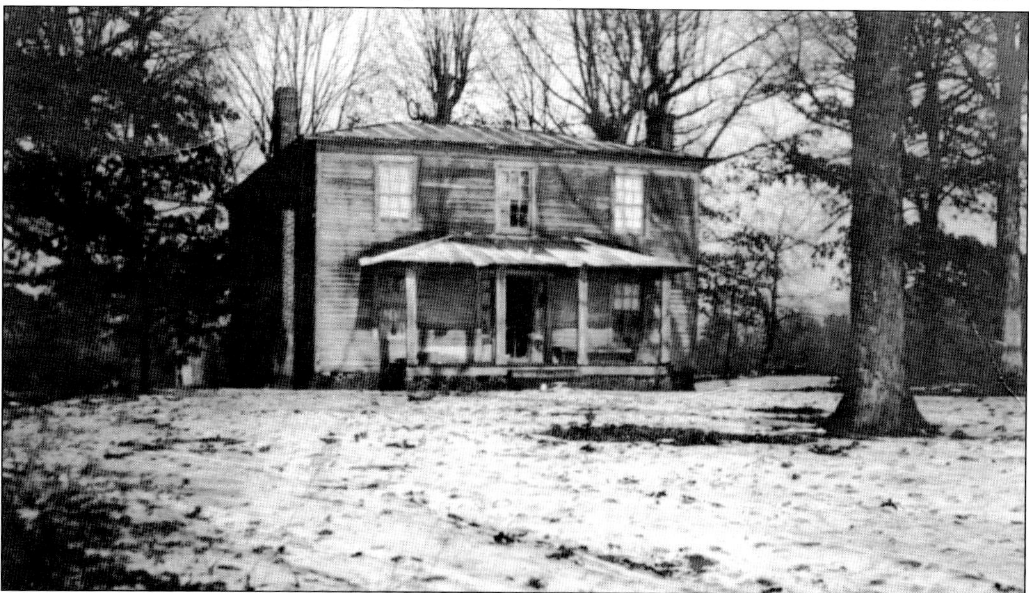

TOMLINSON FARM, 1857. Now a private residence on Trinity Street Extension, the Tomlinson Farm is an excellent and intact example of a mid- to late-19th-century farm complex in Thomasville. The property consisted of over half a dozen structures mostly dedicated to tobacco farming. This house was home to Everett Swaim Sr., who is pictured on the front cover, and his wife, Annie Tomlinson.

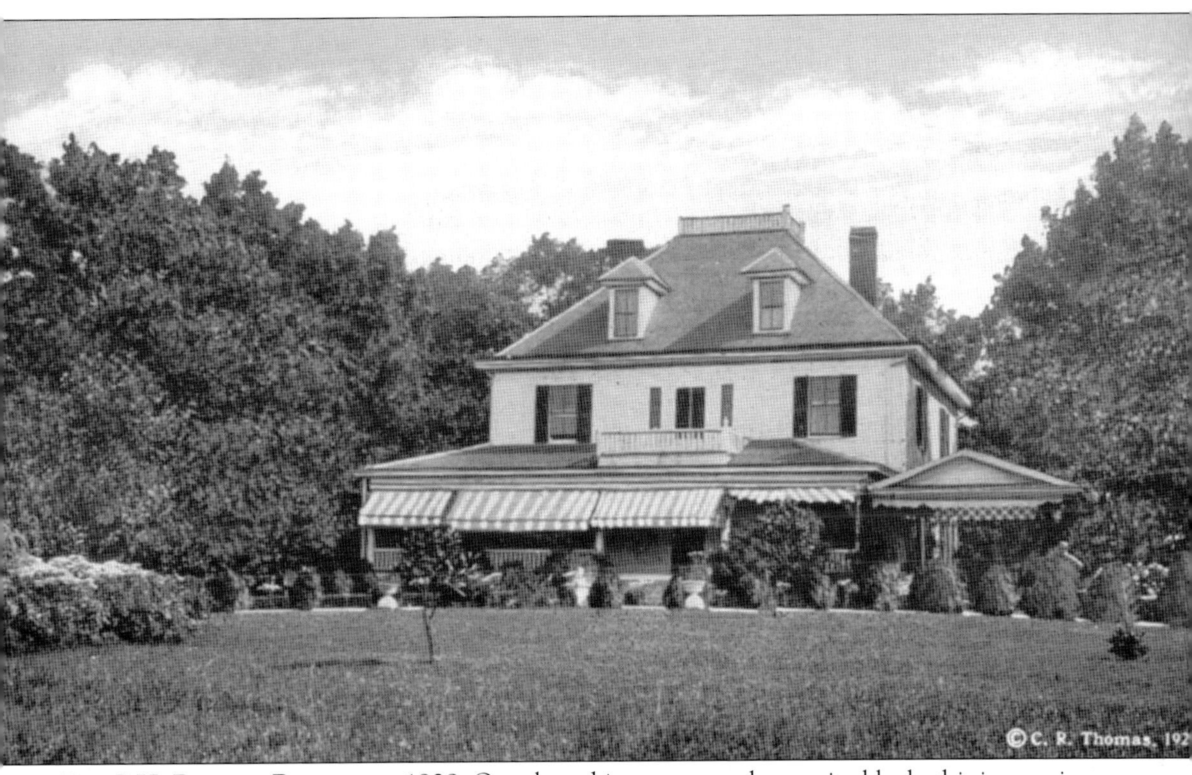

Dr. C.H. Phillips Residence, 1929. On a lot taking up more than a city block, this impressive structure that once sat at 101 Spruce Street was home to Dr. Charles Phillips and his wife, Bessie. It later became the residence of optometrist Dr. Nathaniel Walker and his wife, Pauline, a daughter of Dr. Phillips who worked tirelessly for the beautification of Thomasville. The house had a rose garden with underground irrigation designed by the Olmstead Brothers landscape architectural company and a crow's nest on top with a spectacular view of Pilot Mountain. It was demolished in 1998.

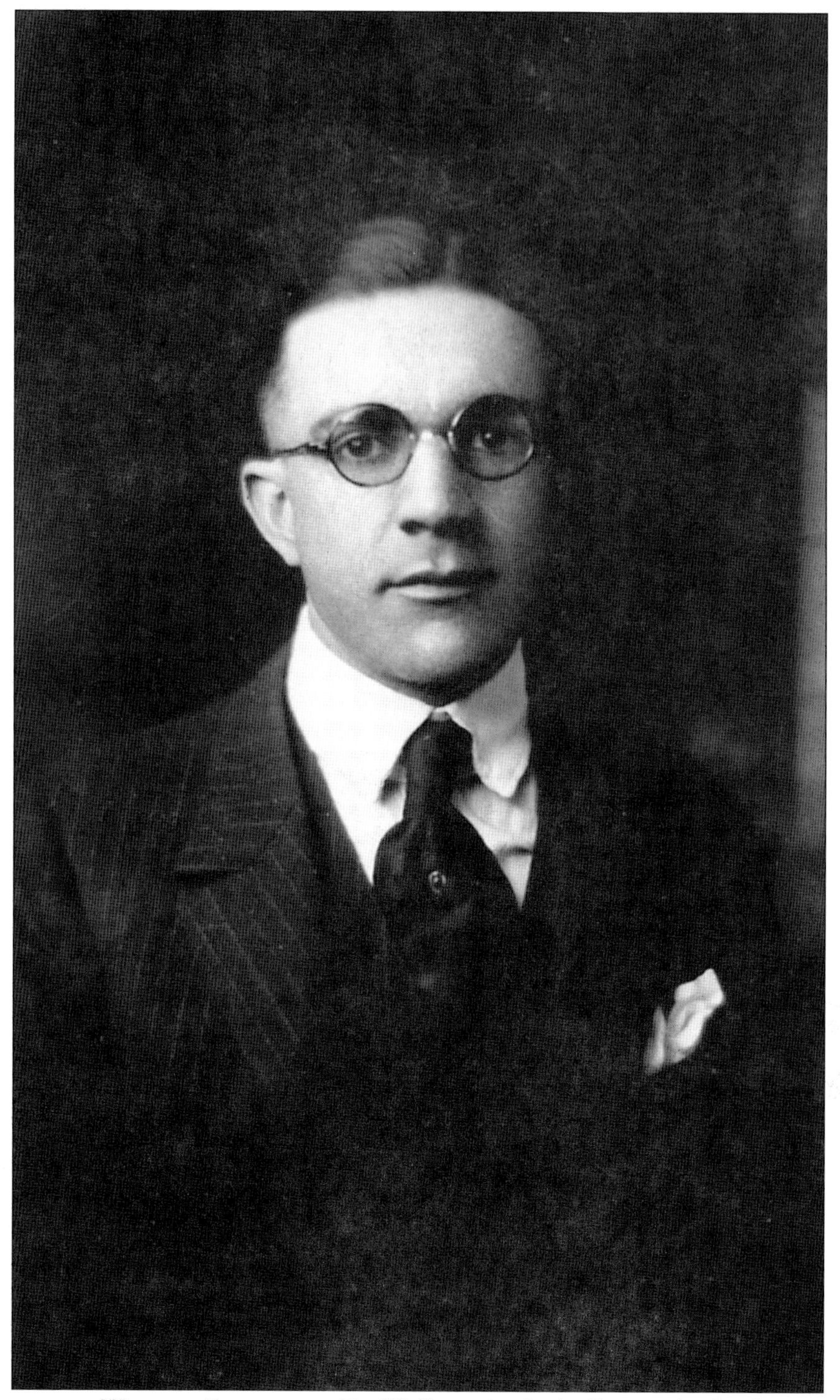

Dr. Nathaniel Walker. Optometrist Dr. Walker, who had offices in both Thomasville and High Point, was a professional man dedicated to his practice. He was married to Pauline Fuller Phillips, daughter of Dr. Charles Phillips. The Walkers called 101 Spruce Street home for many years and had six children. Dr. Walker was a man of deep faith and was beloved by the community.

Four

CHURCHES

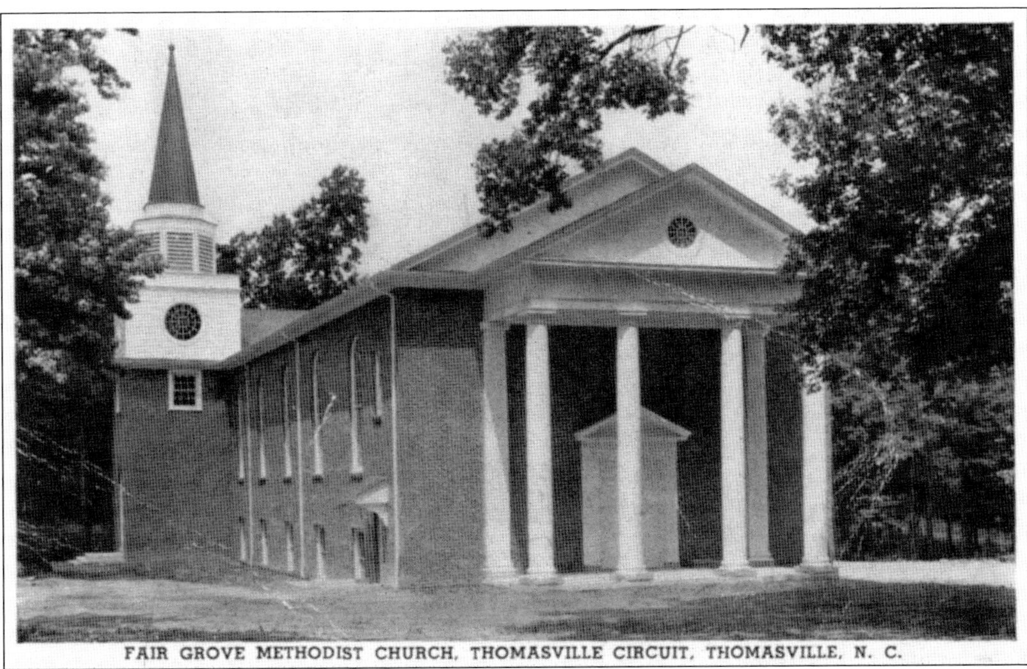

FAIR GROVE CHURCH. Fair Grove Methodist Church is the oldest Methodist church still in existence in Davidson County. In 1828, John Myers deeded four acres for the church grounds, and John Thomas served as one of the nine trustees. This church had more influence than any other on the religious life of Thomasville. (Courtesy Caroline Swaim Hill.)

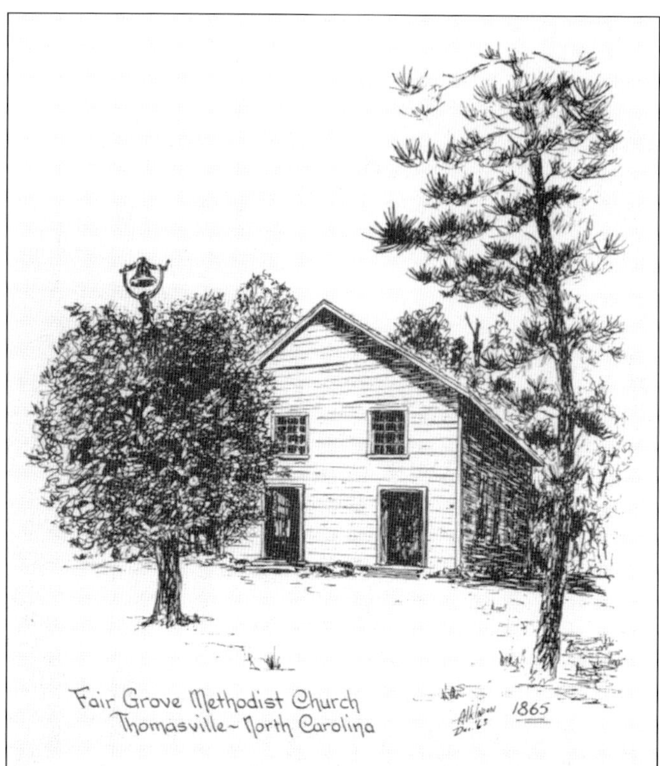

Fair Grove Church, 1865. The first Fair Grove School was housed in the old Fair Grove Church, a small log structure that burned down in 1865. The same year, a wood structure was erected with two doors at the entrance to replace the original building. The new structure had a large wood stove in the middle of the main room and shelves for lunches. There were always two buckets of water inside; these were carried over from the well where the current Fair Grove Church parsonage stands.

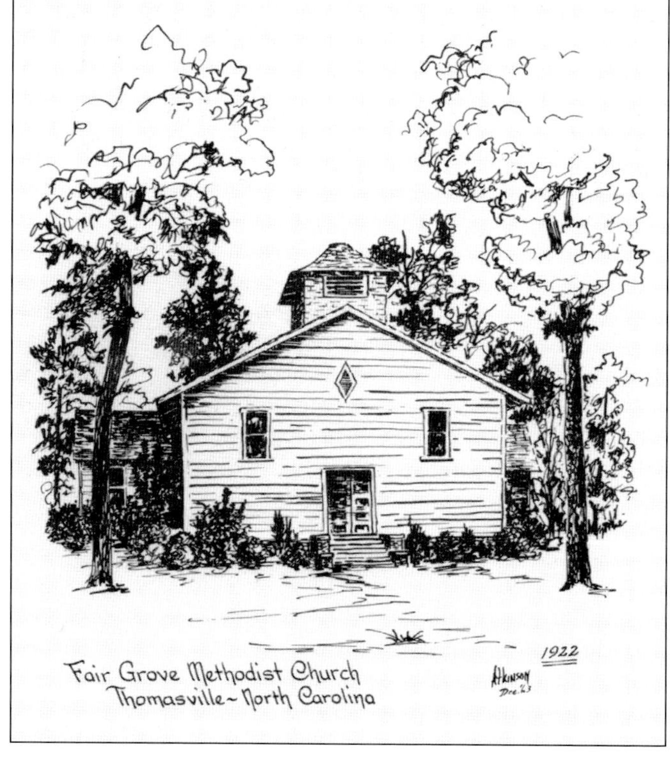

Fair Grove Church, 1922. A total of four frame churches were constructed in this spot before the present-day brick church. The Fair Grove Church cemetery is the resting place for many of the men and women who were important in early Thomasville. A small group of approximately 15 headstones beneath ancient cedar trees in front of the church are the earliest locally made grave markers.

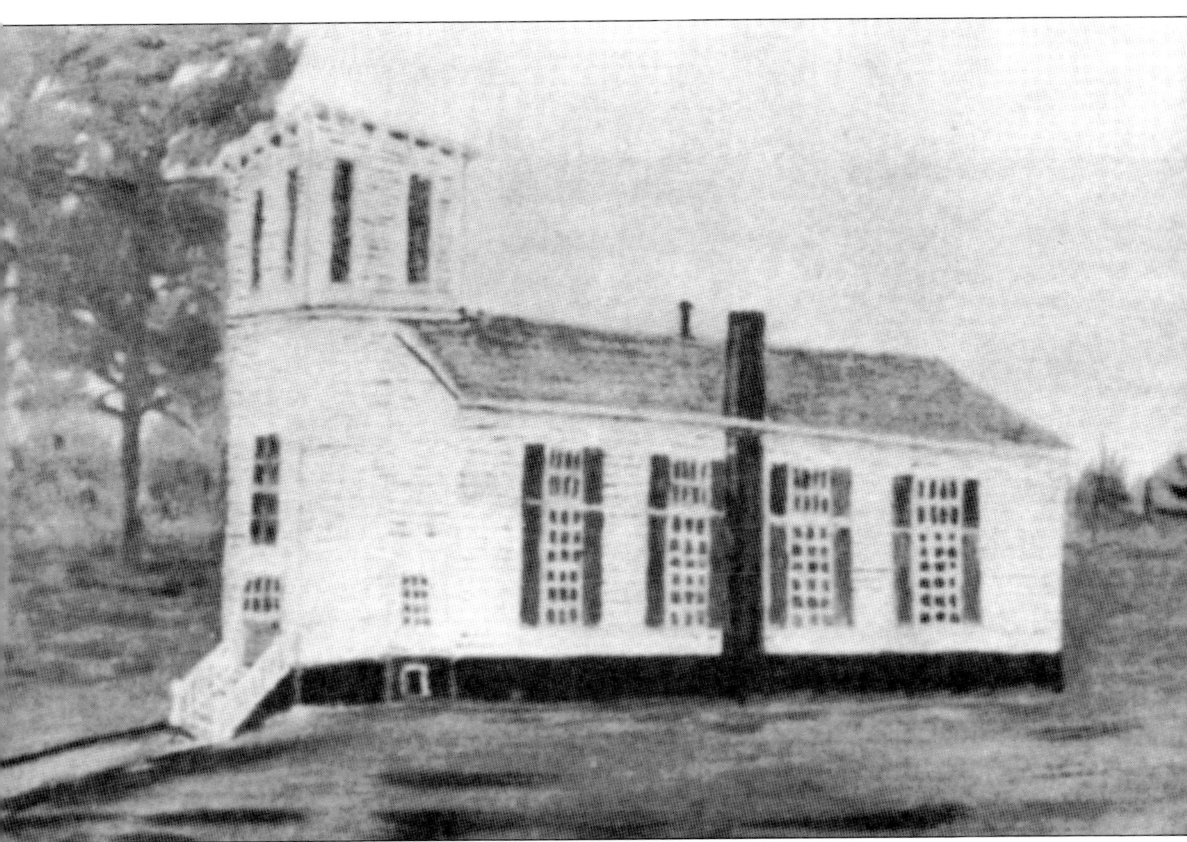

Thomasville Methodist Church, 1863. This painting by R.L. Pope depicts Thomasville Methodist Church north of the railroad on East Main Street. The church began with a Sunday school conducted in an arbor by John Carmalt in 1855. When cold weather came, it was held in the Lewis Hotel lobby, Lines Shoe Factory, and the seminary building until the first frame building was completed in 1863.

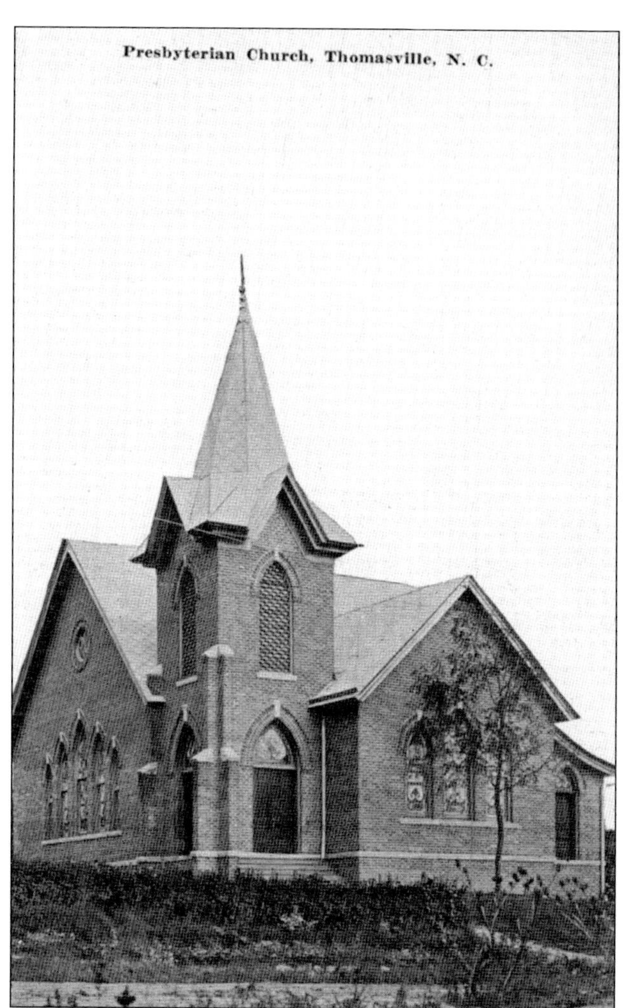

PRESBYTERIAN CHURCH, 1914. There were few of the Presbyterian faith in Thomasville before 1860. Rev. Willis L. Miller lived on Salem Street and occasionally preached as an evangelist for Orange Presbytery. Reverend Miller organized a company of soldiers, the Thomasville Rifles, which he led as both captain and chaplain. In 1911, the first Presbyterian church was built on Randolph Street.

CALVARY CHURCH, 1948. Rev. J.C. Leonard of Lexington organized Calvary Church in 1892 just west of town. Leonard was given a sum of $200 toward the construction of a church building. In April 1948, a handsome brick building replaced the old frame building. Moffit's Grove schoolhouse was on an adjoining lot. (Courtesy Chalmous Sechrist.)

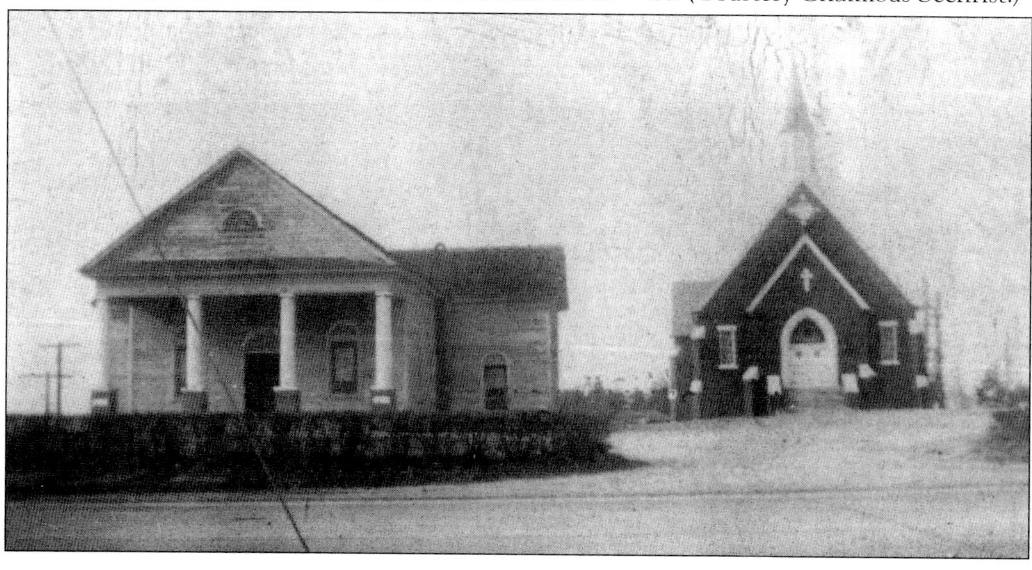

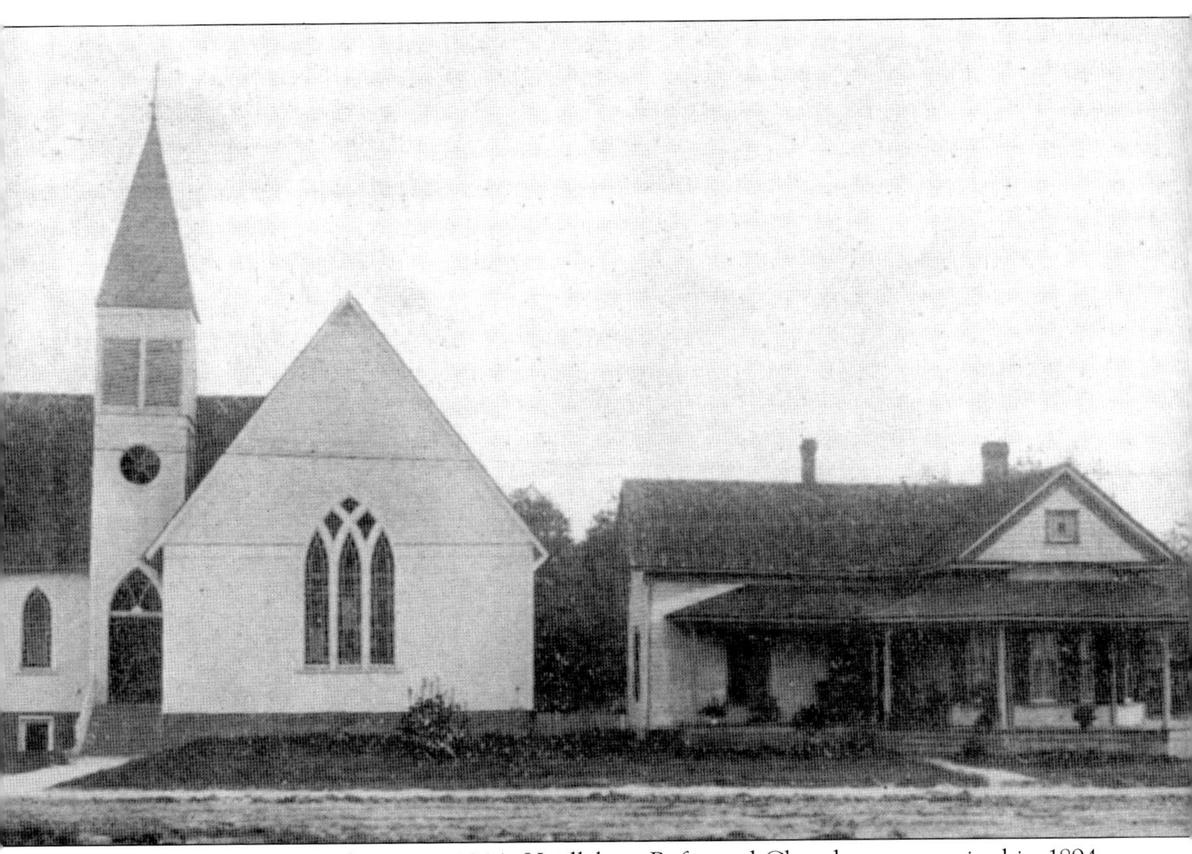

Heidleberg Reformed Church, 1914. Heidleberg Reformed Church was organized in 1894. Reverend Leonard organized the church with 16 charter members. The church slowly grew and moved to its third location (not pictured) on Salem Street in the 1920s; the Whitaker place was purchased with an adjoining lot. The old Whitaker residence still serves as the church parsonage, and the brick church stands among the prominent houses lining Salem Street.

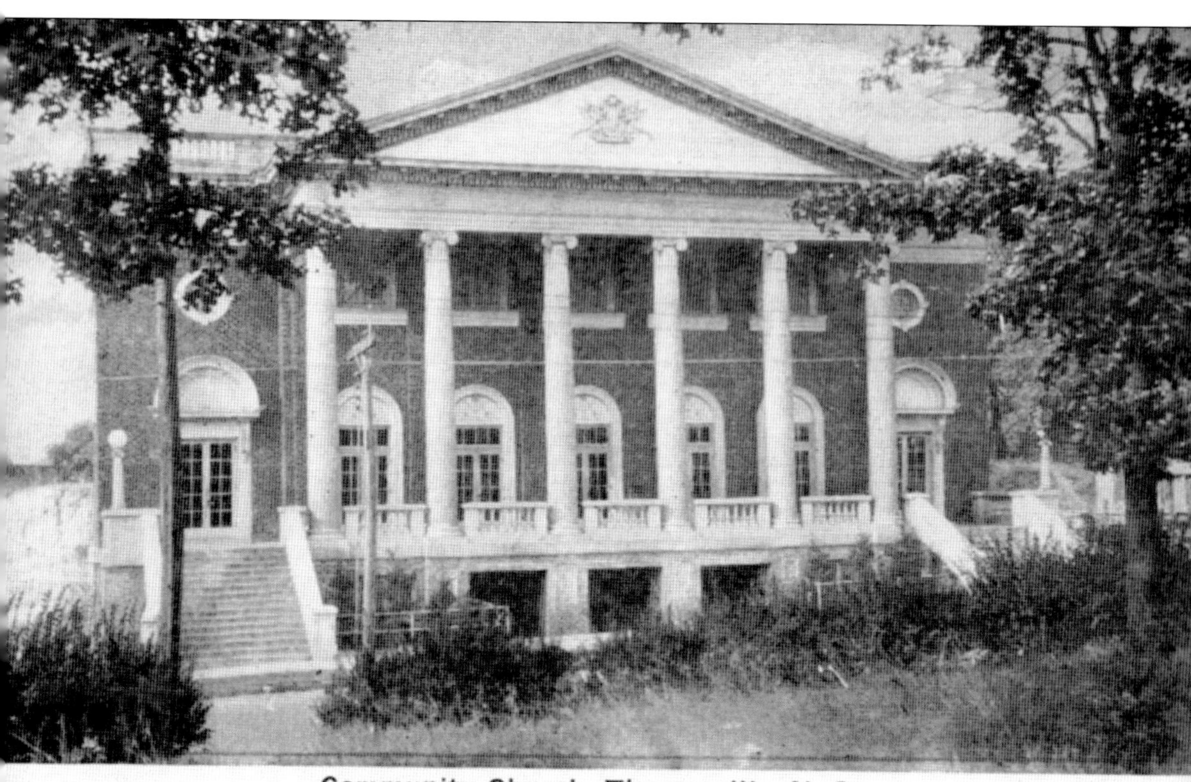
Community Church, Thomasville, N. C.

COMMUNITY METHODIST PROTESTANT CHURCH. Charles Finch erected Community Methodist Protestant Church in 1923 as a memorial to his wife. Finch's vision was for the building "to meet not only the demands of spiritual development but the natural demands of children for social and physical exercise." After the merging of Community Methodist and Main Street Methodist to form Memorial Methodist Church, the building was recycled and became the city-owned Civic Center.

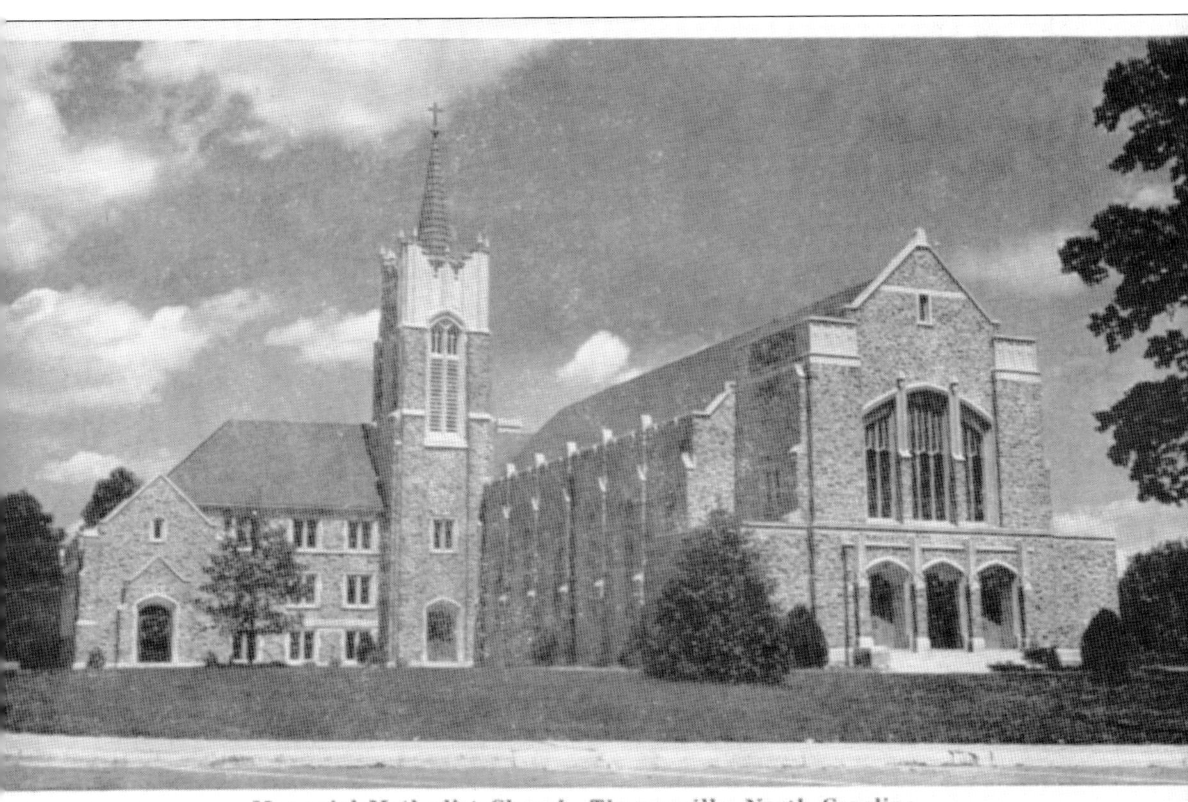

Memorial Methodist Church, Thomasville, North Carolina

MEMORIAL METHODIST CHURCH, 1951. Memorial Methodist Church opened in 1951. Since then, the building has never been in danger of losing its distinction of being the most prominent and beautiful church in Thomasville. The fieldstone structure was erected at a cost of more than $650,000. (Courtesy Jane Cox Leonard.)

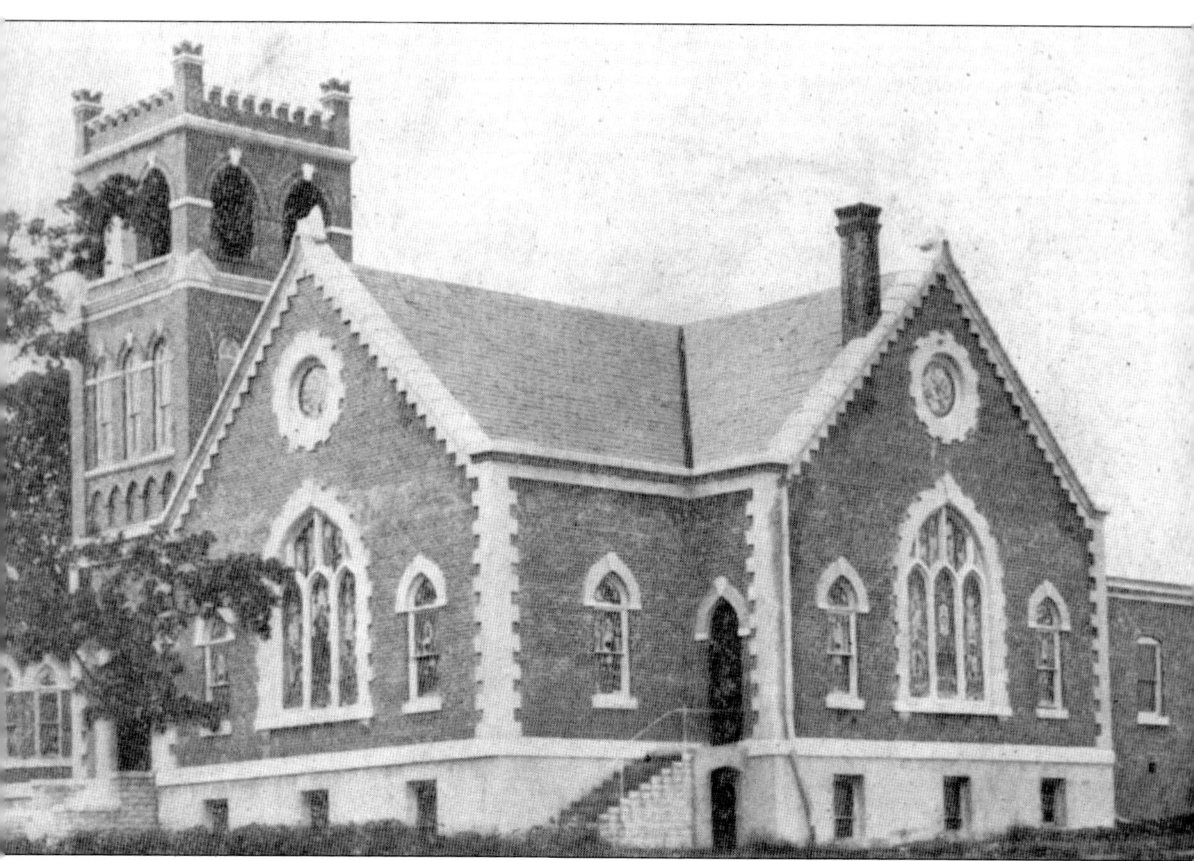

MAIN STREET METHODIST CHURCH, 1914. According to Wint Capel in his book *In Words & Pictures: Thomasville in the Nineteen Twenties*, "An example of a social event during the early 1920s was the annual Chrysanthemum Show at Main Street Methodist Church. It was managed by Mrs. Henry Rapp, wife of the former superintendent of the North Carolina Smelting Works. Show entries winning honors were auctioned off, with proceeds going to the church, after which an oyster supper was served."

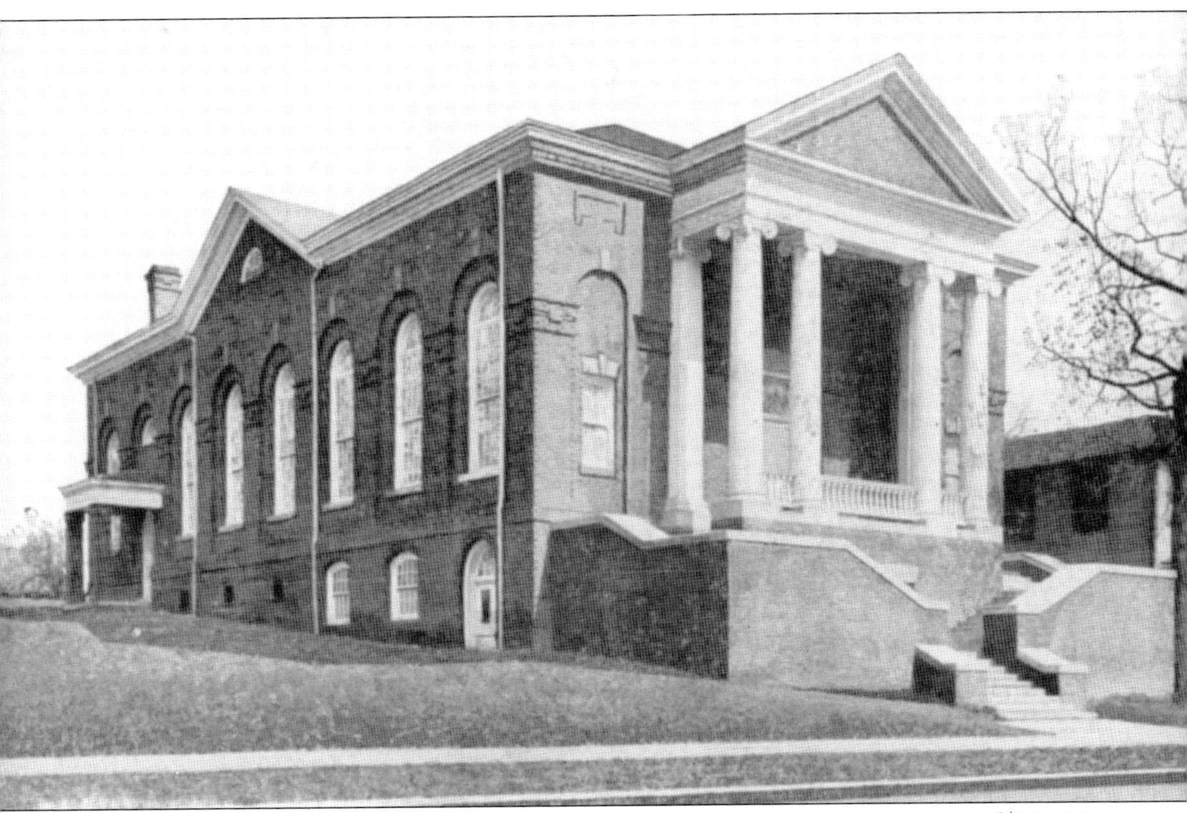

First Baptist Church, 1913. Erected in 1913, First Baptist Church was built for a cost of $12,000. It contained one large room on the ground floor for the men's bible class and two stories of Sunday school rooms at the back in addition to a large auditorium. Fifty years after the initial church was erected, the congregation removed it and replaced it with the building that currently stands.

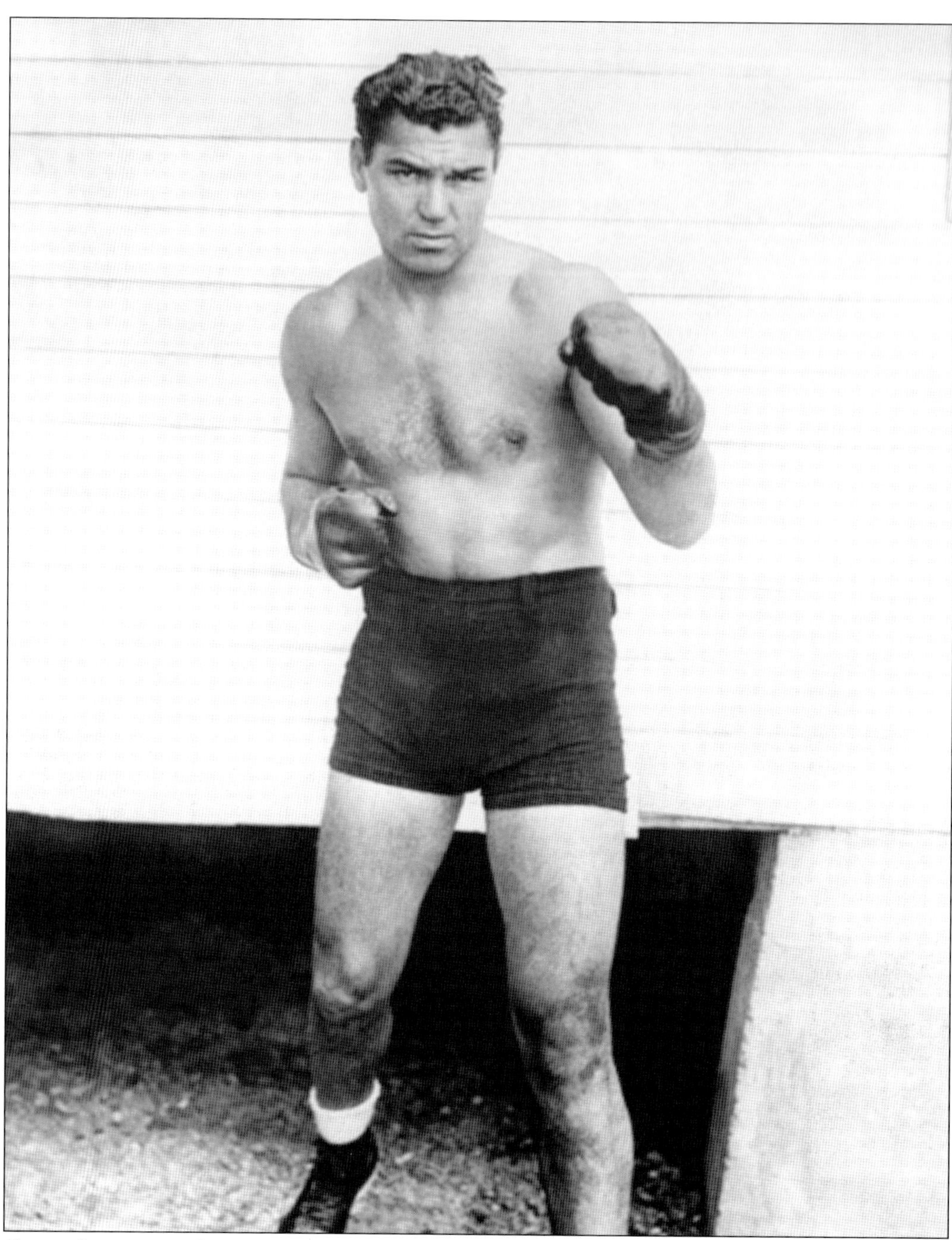

GRACE LUTHERAN CHURCH AND JACK DEMPSEY. Rev. Charlie Patterson of Thomasville's Grace Lutheran Church had a short-lived close relationship with boxer Jack Dempsey. The Manassa Mauler was training in Asheville to defend his heavyweight title against Luis Fripo in 1923. Reverend Patterson attended the workout and agreed to step in for a tardy sparring partner. The preacher, who boxed some while in the Army, later bragged that he never hit the canvas during five rounds with the champ, but he lost one tooth and parts of two others.

Five

SCHOOLS

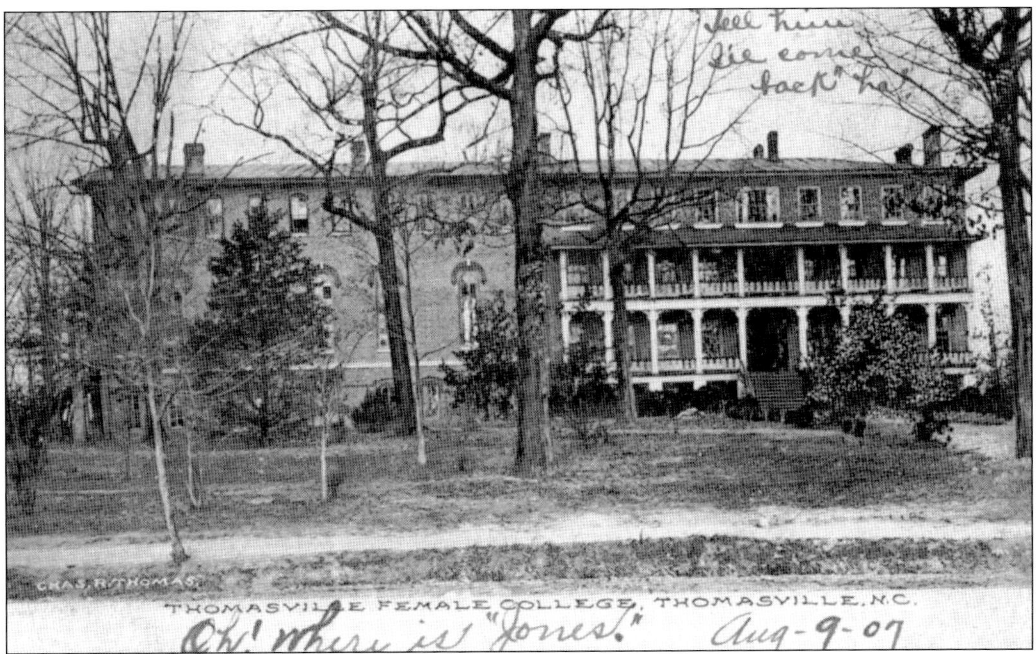

THOMASVILLE FEMALE COLLEGE. The Glen Anna Female Seminary was erected in 1857 as a finishing school for girls from across the state. After the Civil War, it become known as Thomasville Female College and drew students from Raleigh, Durham, Chapel Hill, and Statesville. It flourished until the late 1880s, later becoming Ragan Knitting Mills.

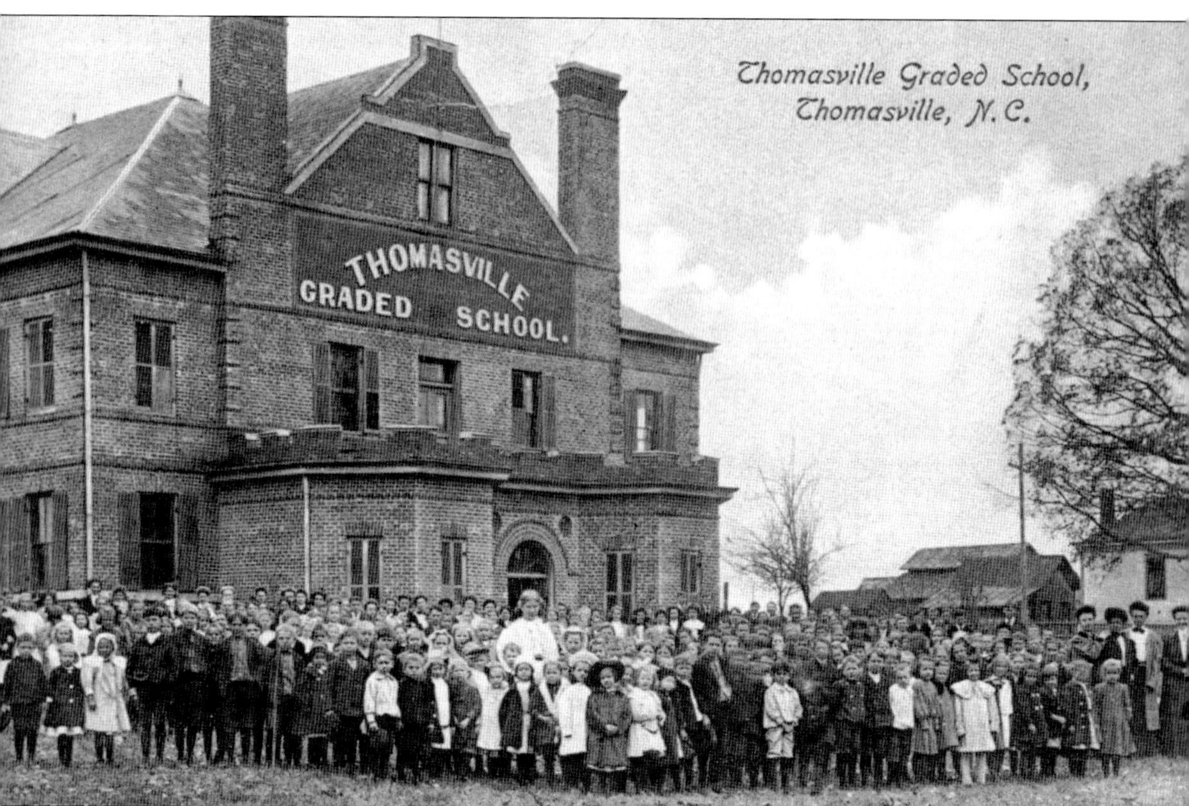

THOMASVILLE GRADED SCHOOL. Thomasville Graded School was built in 1902 as Thomasville's first public school. The campus consisted of eight classrooms, a large auditorium, two small offices, a playground, a water pump, and two frame houses on either side that served as lavatories. It burned on Good Friday 1922, and Main Street School replaced it. The Central Recreation Center now sits on this site.

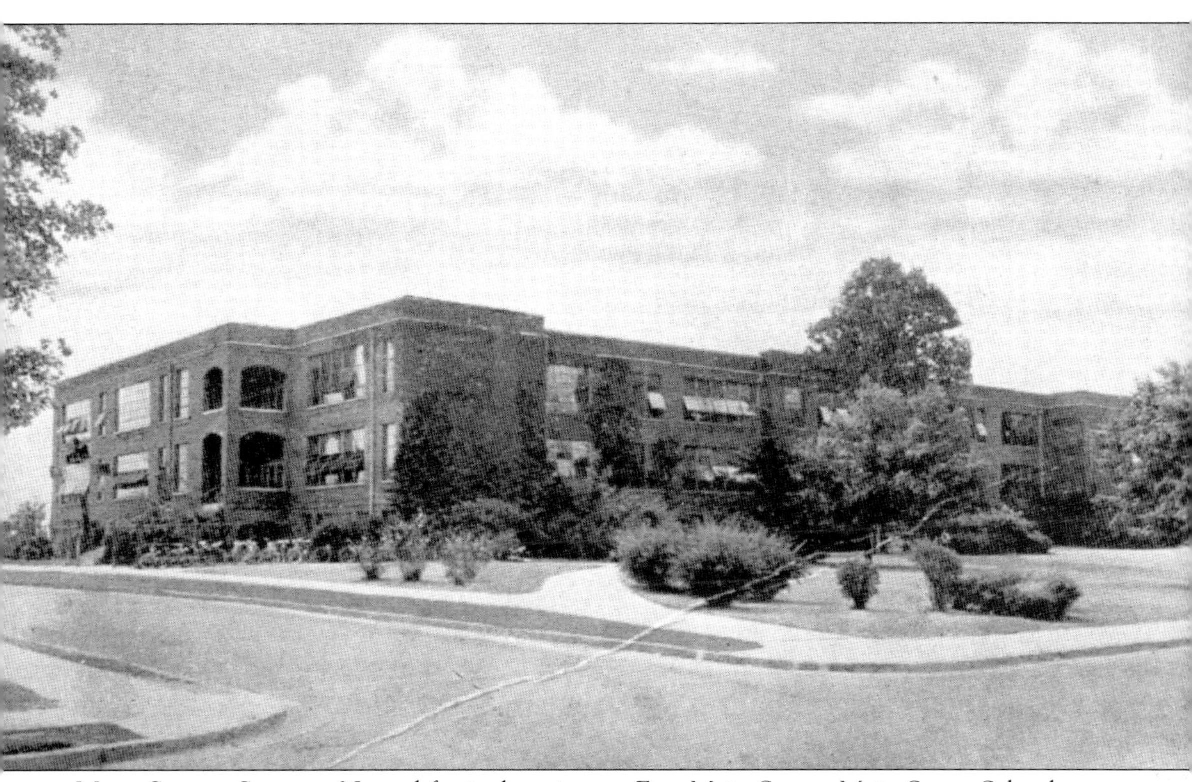

Main Street School. Named for its location on East Main Street, Main Street School was completed in 1923 and was adequate for all the children of Thomasville. The building featured improvements in heating, lighting, and sanitation for the time it was constructed. It later became Thomasville Senior High School after the lower grades moved to other locations.

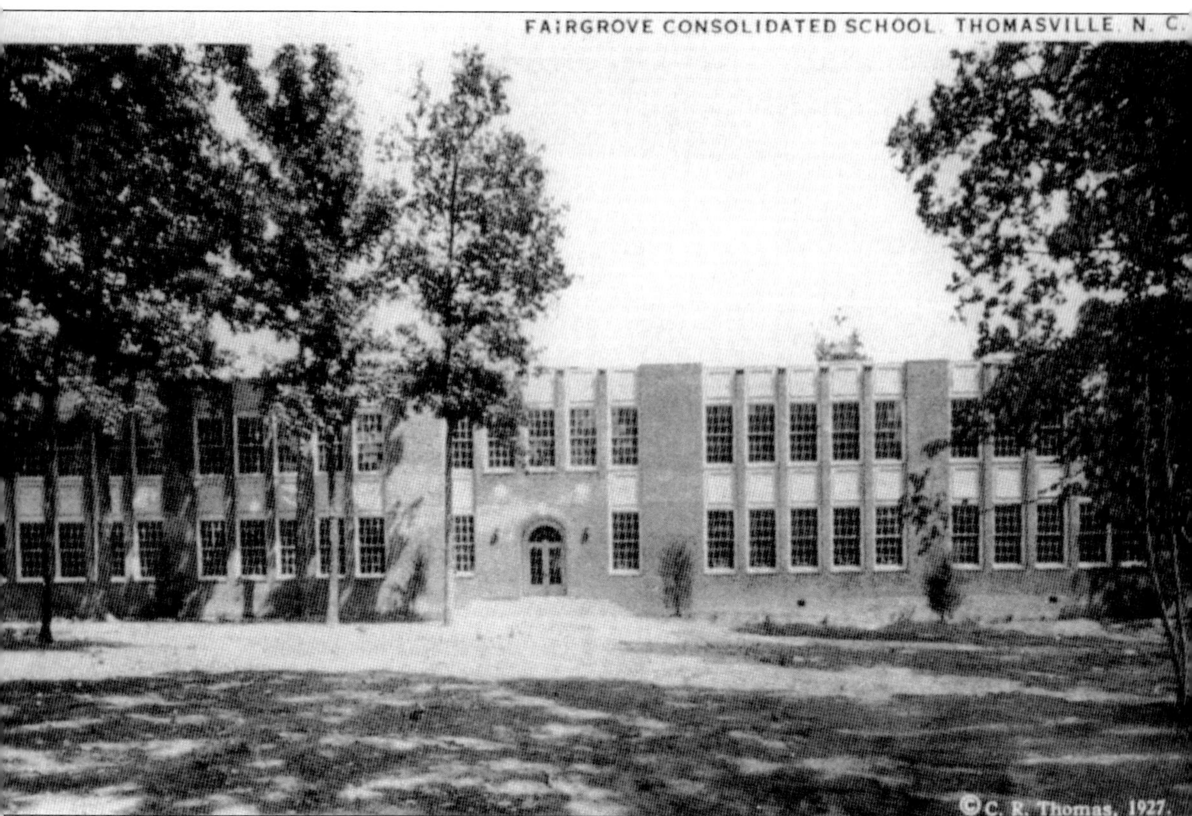

FAIRGROVE CONSOLIDATED SCHOOL, 1927. On November 2, 1925, the Davidson County Board of Education allocated $18,000 to a special building fund for construction of a consolidated school to be erected in Fair Grove. The schools included in the consolidation were Hall's Chapel, Byerly School, Kendall School, and Davidson Academy. November 1926 saw the completion of the school with its indoor plumbing.

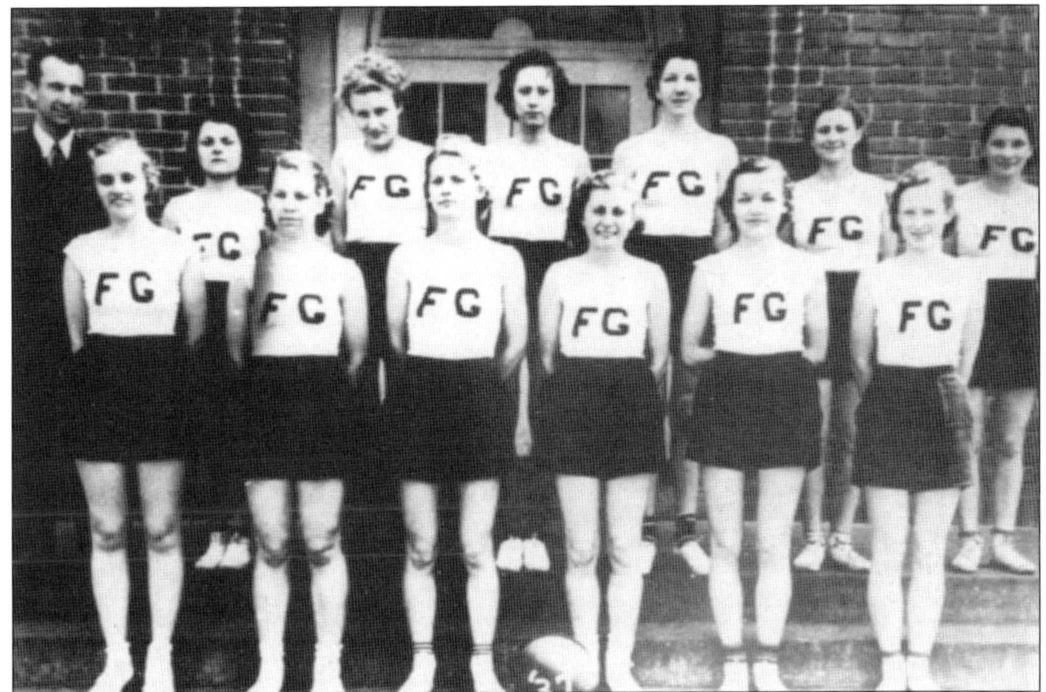

Fair Grove Girls' Basketball Team, 1937. Pictured here are, from left to right, (first row) Bertha E. Crouse, Mozzelle Bodenheimer, Clara Brown Trotter, Mabel Hepler, Thelma Fritts, and Odessa Templeton; (second row) coach David Diamont, Virginia Clodfelter, Ruby Myers, Margaret Lee, ? Mauldin, Eula Mae Beck, and Ruth Hepler.

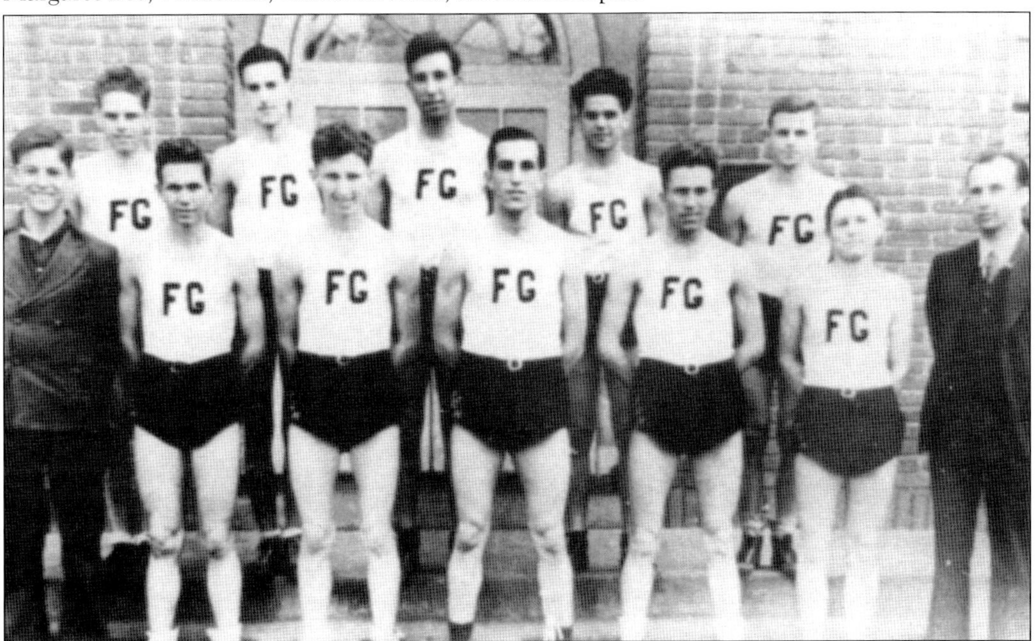

Fair Grove Boys' Basketball Team, 1937. From left to right are (first row) Joe Don Fouts, Colin Cranford, Hillard Nance, Johnnie Everhart, Harvey Black Jr., George Welborn, and coach David Diamont; (second row) Howard Bean, Wilbur Jarrett, Edwin Pierve, J.R. Hamilton, and Austin Swaim.

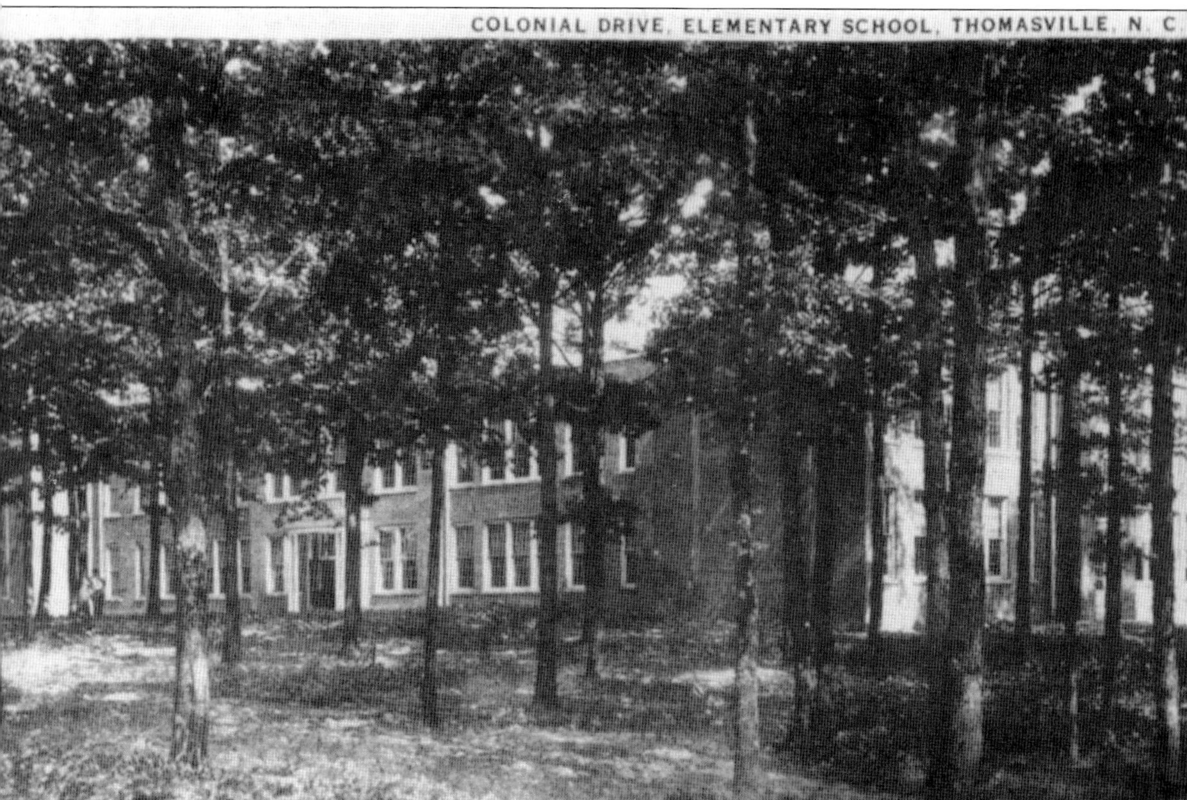

Colonial Drive Elementary, 1929. Built in 1928, this was Thomasville's second public school building and eased the overcrowding at Main Street School. Elsie Doxey served as Thomasville's first female principal and remained in the position for 10 years at Colonial Drive Elementary. This building is now a center of Davidson County government services.

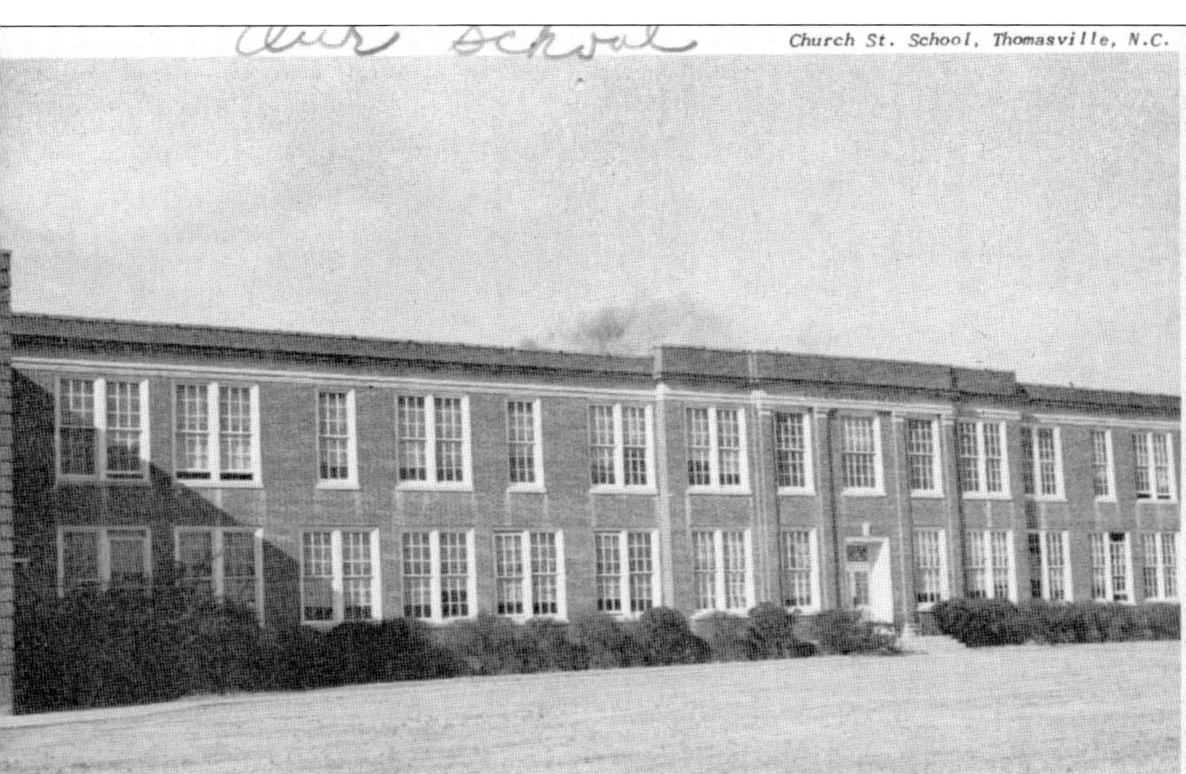

CHURCH STREET SCHOOL. In 1868, John W. Thomas deeded the lot on Church Street for use as an AME church. He also specified that the church be used for a school. In 1937, a large frame structure was built to meet the growing needs of the community. From 1937 until 1968, before desegregation, the school held 12 grades; after 1968, it served only up to eighth grade until 1974 and then up to sixth grade until 1982, when Thomasville Middle School opened.

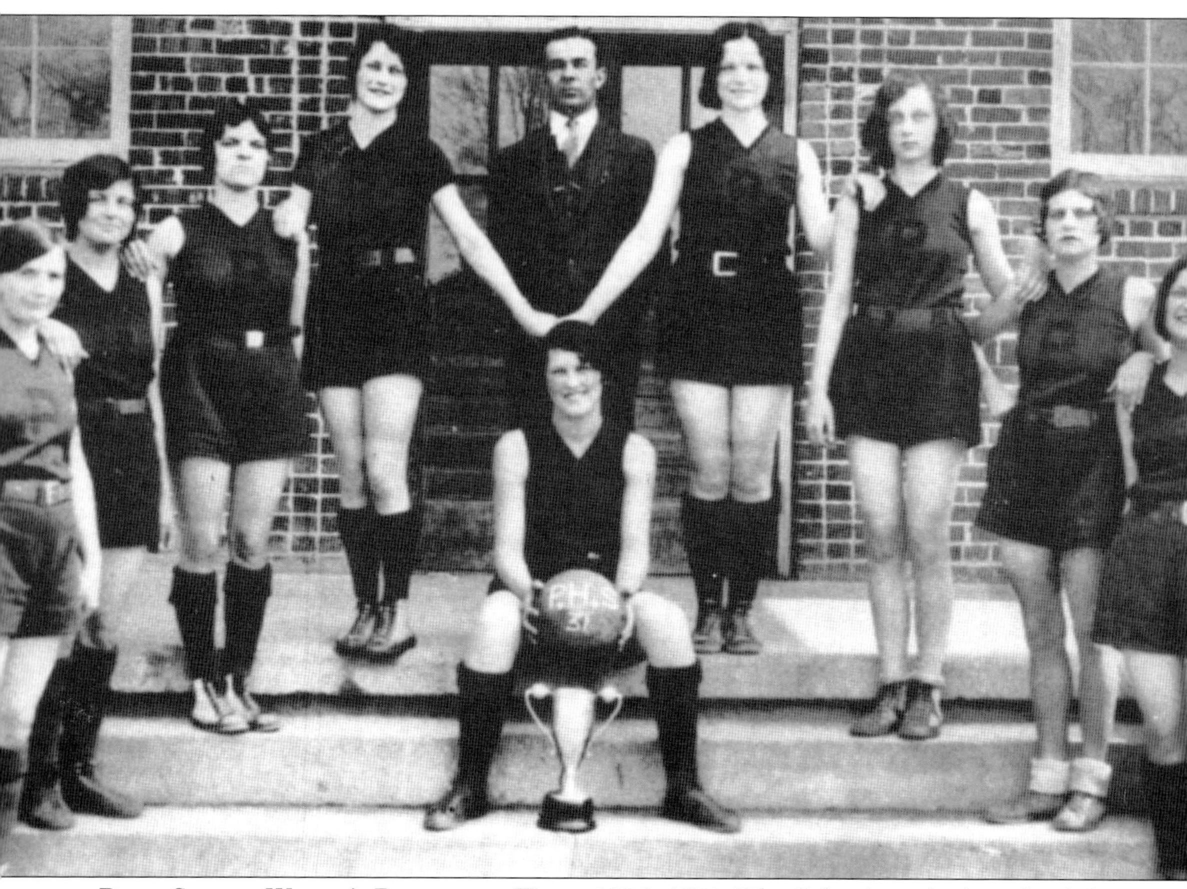

Pilot School Women's Basketball Team, 1930–1931. Pilot School was built on land that once belonged to descendants of Pres. John Quincy Adams. Using donated lumber, community men volunteered and pulled long shifts to complete the building while women prepared food at the building site. Brick, which was made by hand on site, framed the front section of the school, which opened its doors in 1923.

Six

Mills Home

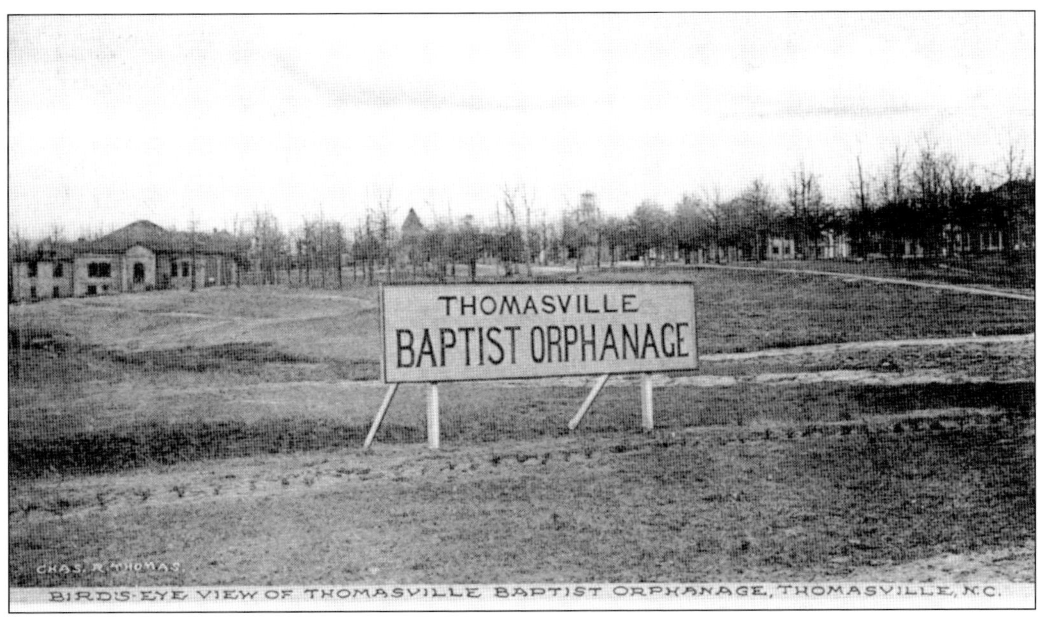

Thomasville Baptist Orphanage. The first campus of Baptist Children's Homes of North Carolina was founded as Mills Home in 1885. Children were received between the ages of 5 and 12 and were released according to preparation rather than age. The first child was received on November 11, 1885.

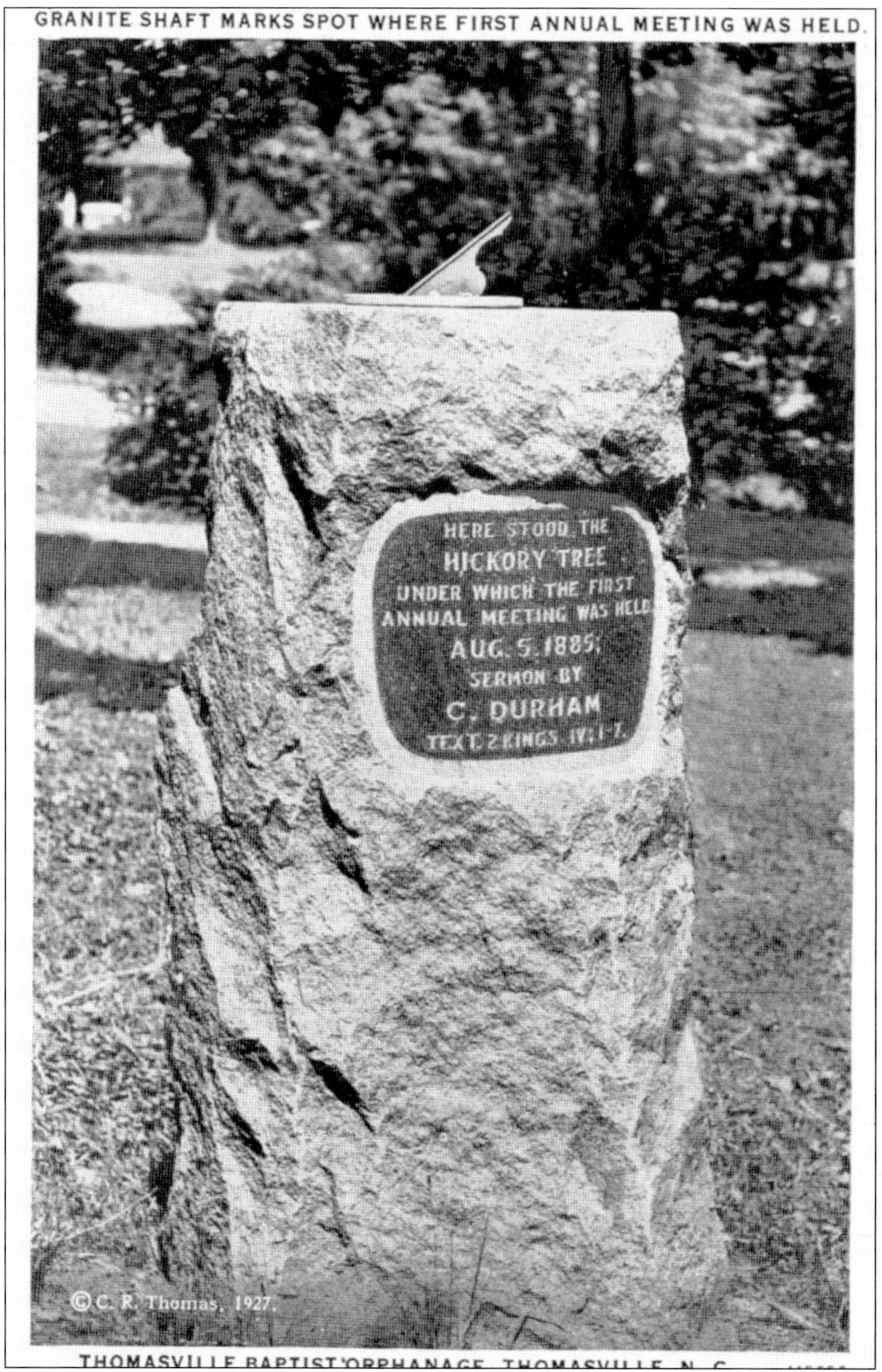

First Annual Meeting Marker, 1927. The first annual meeting of the Thomasville Baptist Orphanage was held on August 5, 1885. The first hymn sung was "Come Thou Fount," and C. Durham preached the sermon from 2 Kings 4:1-7 while standing under a hickory tree just below the general manager's house.

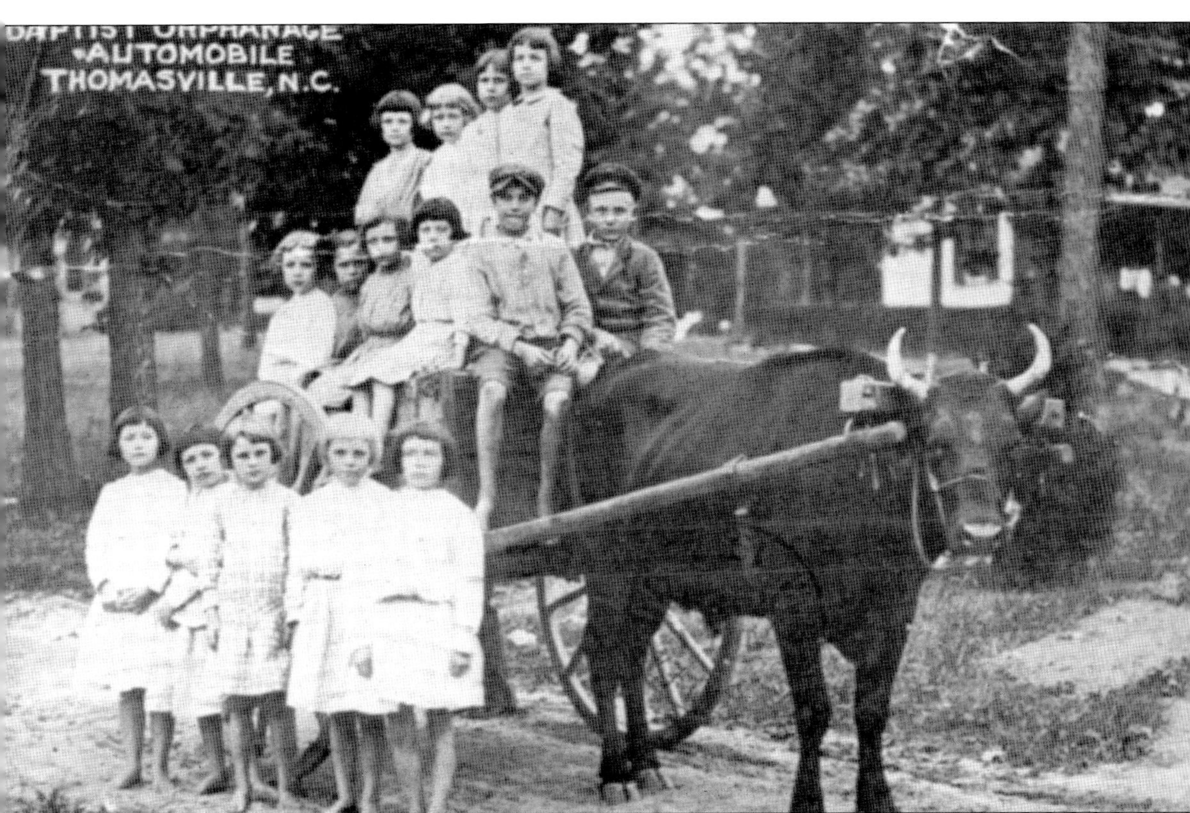

OLD BUCK. Old Buck had his work cut out for him as he transported luggage and freight between the orphanage and the railroad depot. He faithfully pulled the cart for many years before being fattened, slaughtered, and eaten by the same youngsters in this photograph. A meal of beef was a rare treat in those days.

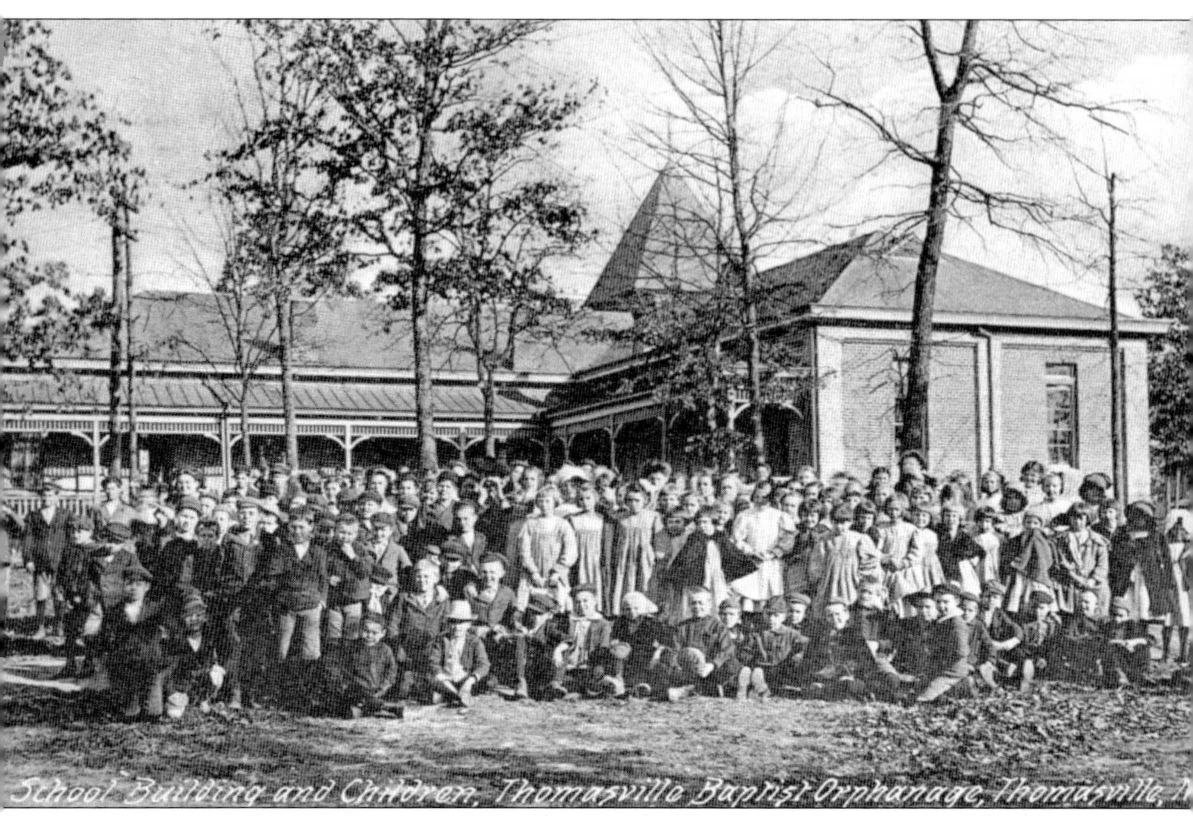

ORPHANAGE SCHOOL BUILDING. The Thomasville Baptist Orphanage school building was completed in 1897. Schoolwork was on a graded system and consisted of nine grades. Children went to school for half the day and worked for the other half. There were two sets of teachers—one for the morning and one for the afternoon.

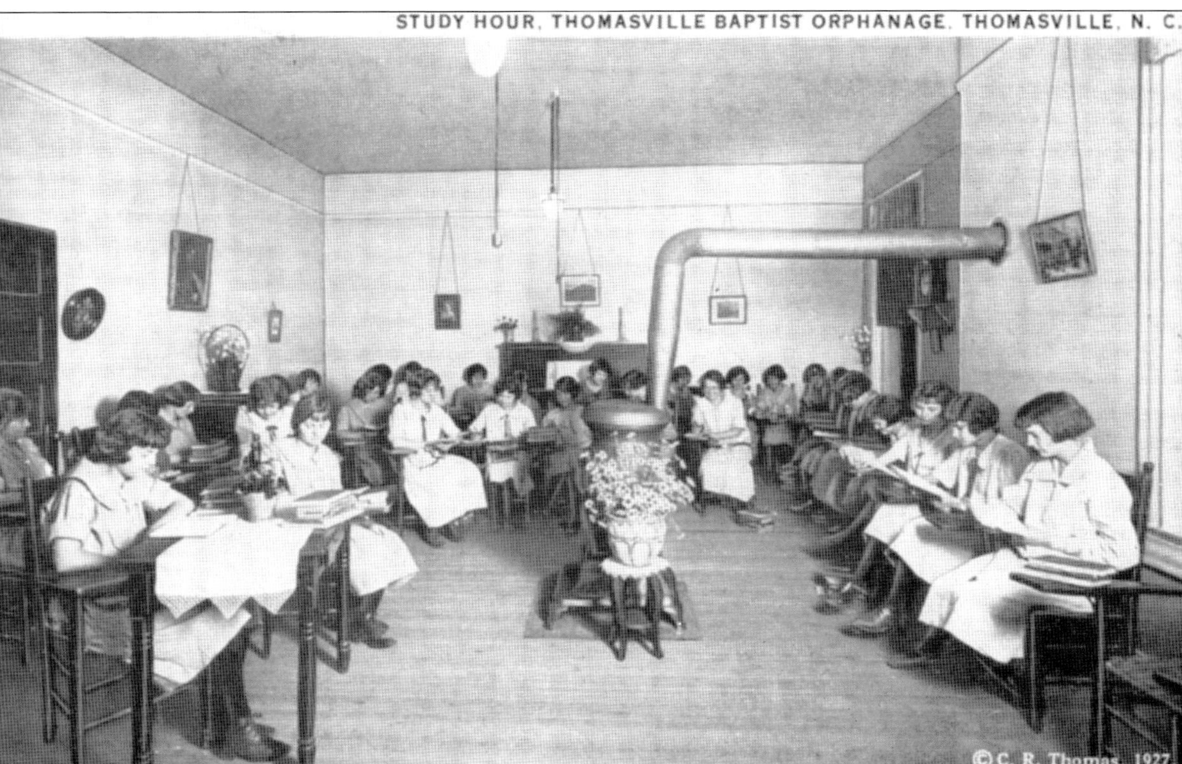

STUDY HOUR, 1927. Long before Thomasville was providing its children with adequate educational opportunities, full schooling was given to the orphans. Classes taught at the Thomasville Baptist Orphanage included reading, arithmetic, language, drawing, history, physiology, nature study, geography, writing, spelling, and singing. Boys were trained in various trades, and girls were trained in homemaking arts.

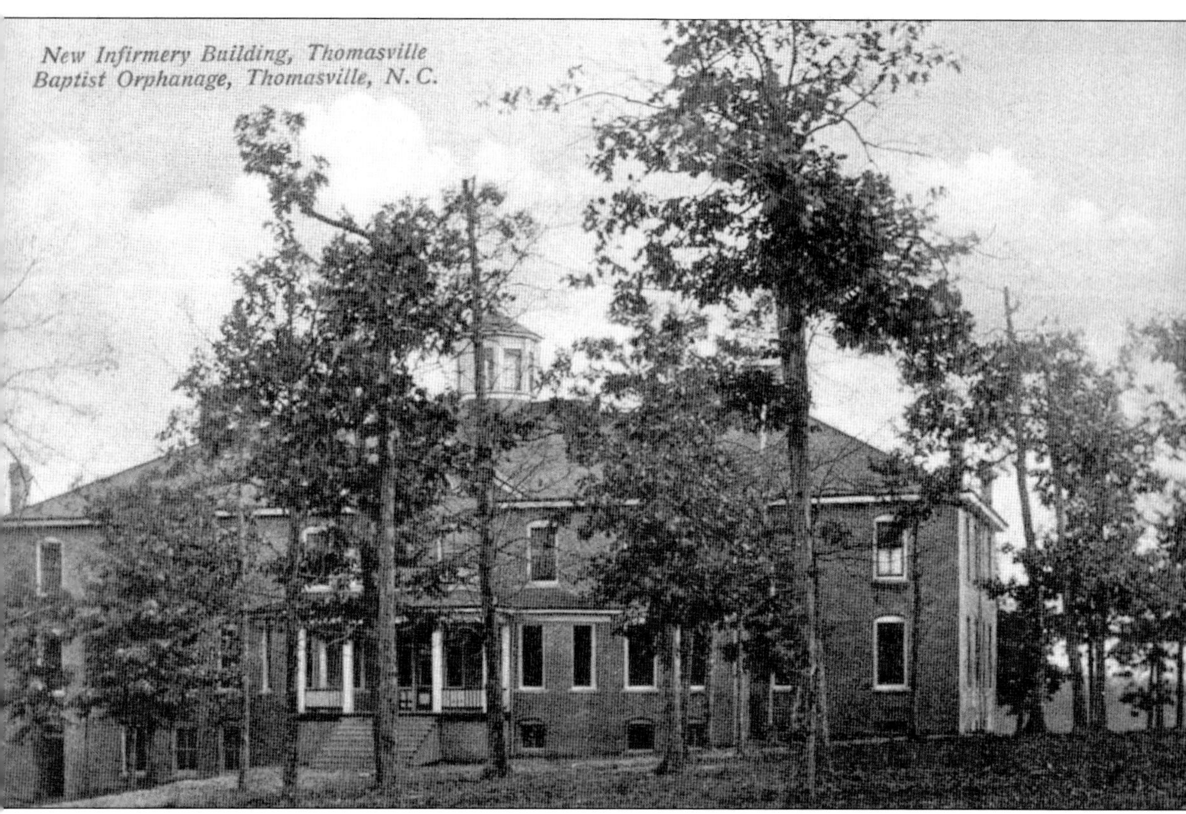

INFIRMARY BUILDING. The largest and finest building on the Thomasville Baptist Orphanage grounds was the infirmary or "woman's building." It cost $12,000 and proved to be a wonderful blessing during a slight scourge of scarlet fever and smallpox not long after the orphanage opened. It served as a year-round haven for children with milder forms of sickness.

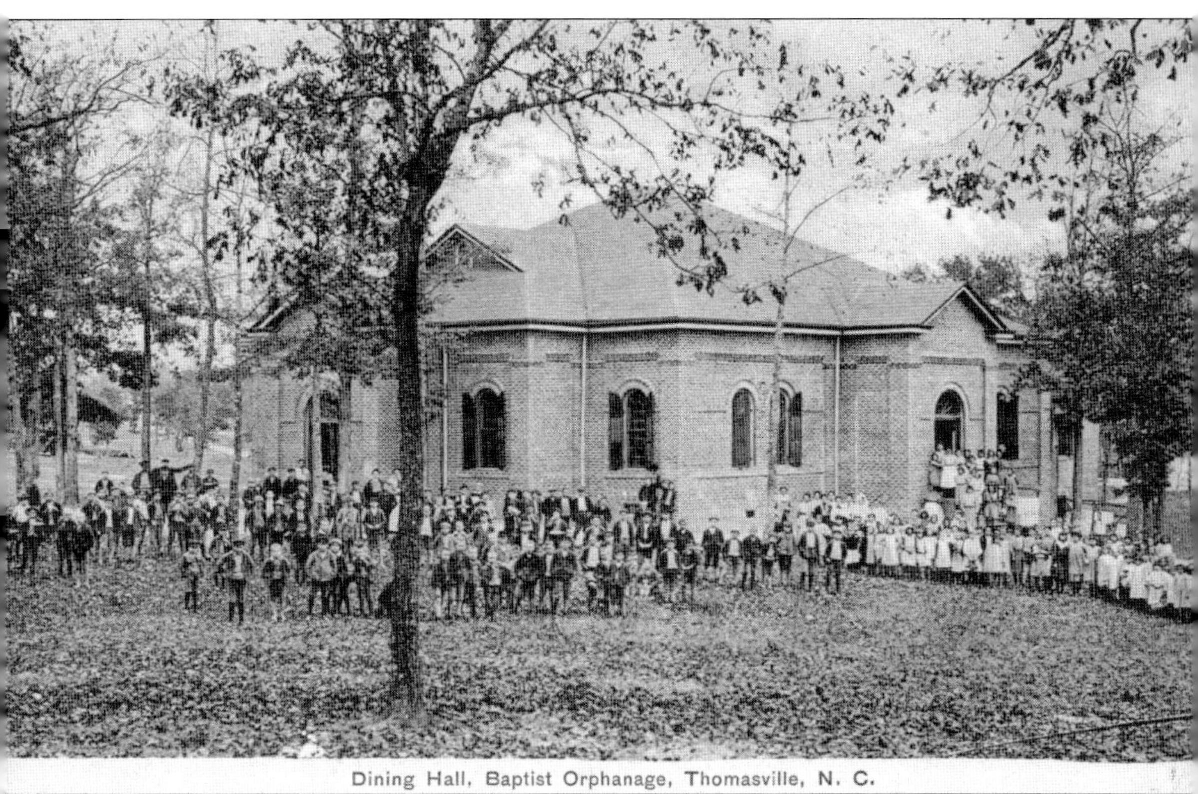

DINING HALL. Meals at the orphanage were served at the dining hall, which first opened its doors in 1904. Barely visible to the right of the folks on the staircase is a bell that blends in with the branches of the young oak. Affixed atop a pole, the bell was rung to signal across the grounds that it was time to eat.

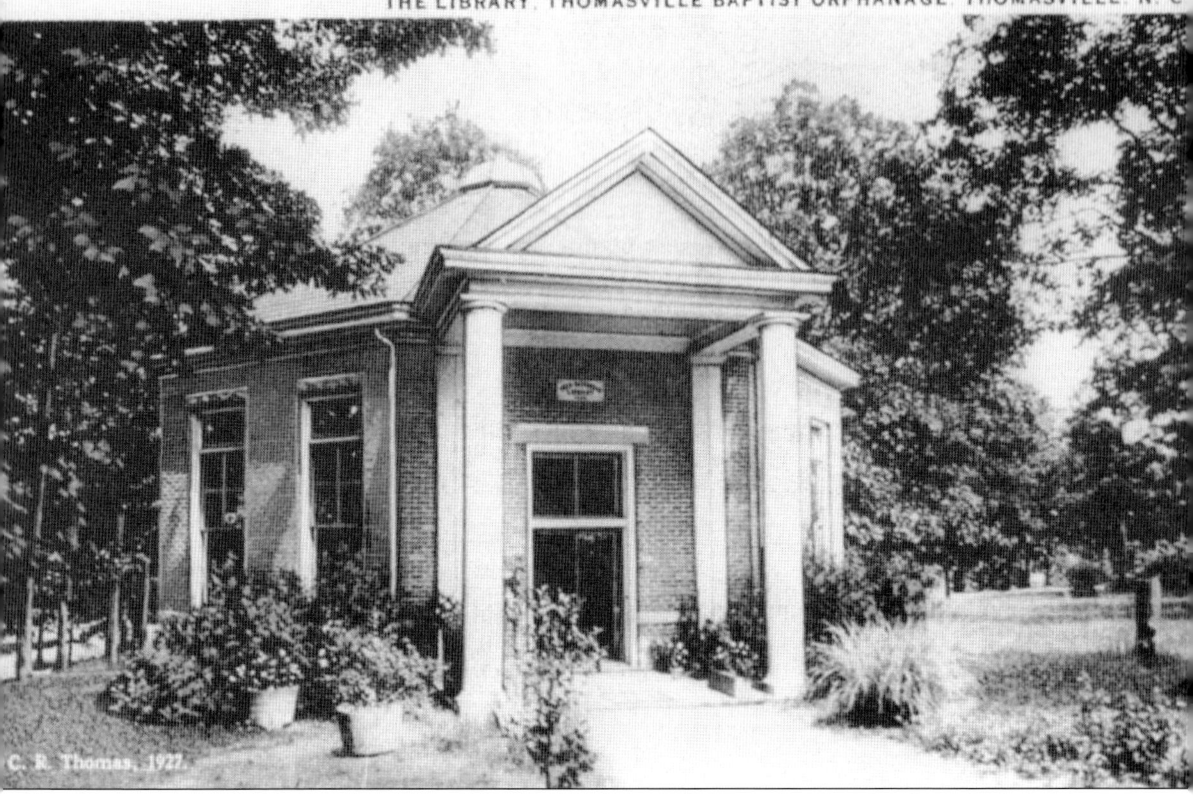

ORPHANAGE LIBRARY, 1927. The doors of the Thomasville Baptist Orphanage library were closed to "any novel that is not of pure and elevating character." It was built in 1908 and added beauty to the grounds. There was a fireproof vault for the safekeeping of orphanage records. The present-day orphanage library stands in its place.

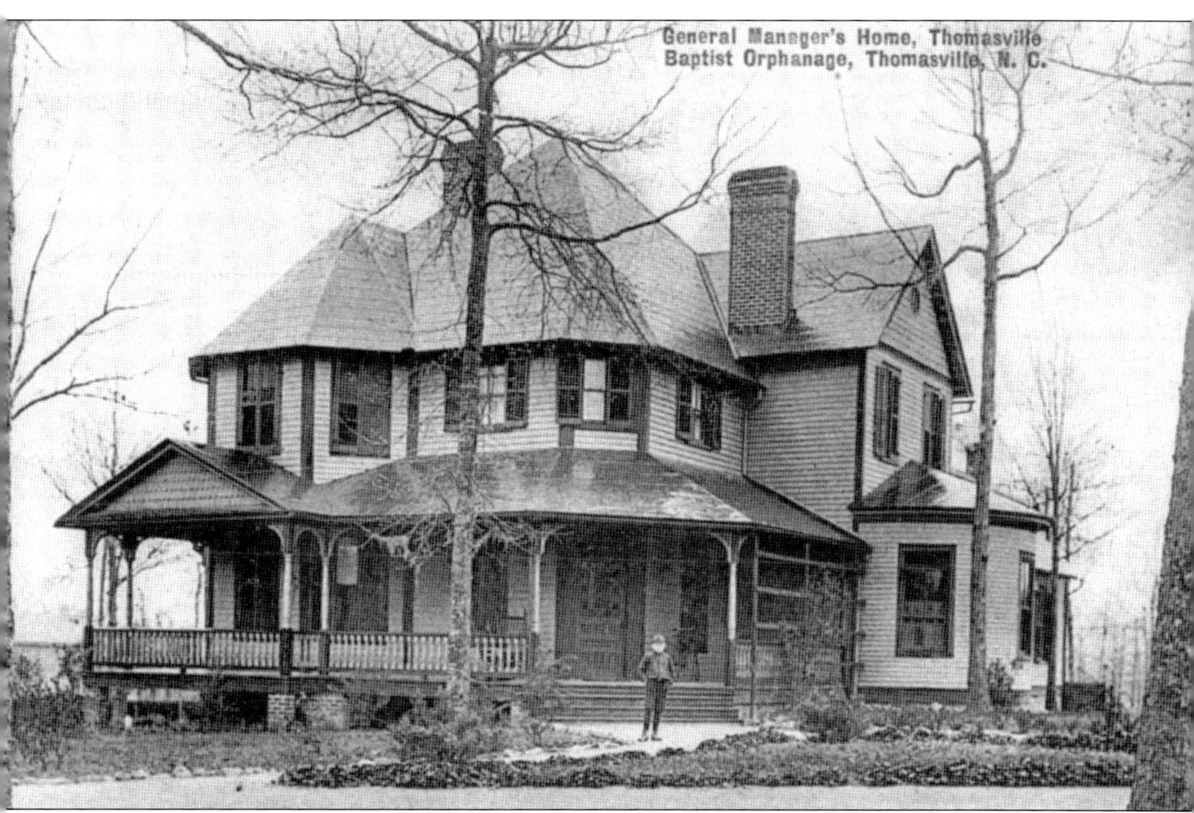

General Manager's Home. Completed in 1898, the general manager's home was on the site of Paradise Hill, a Black camp meeting ground. Carpenter L.E. Peace and worker Ransom Oakes were assisted by three mules—Sandy, Samson, and Delilah—in clearing the site.

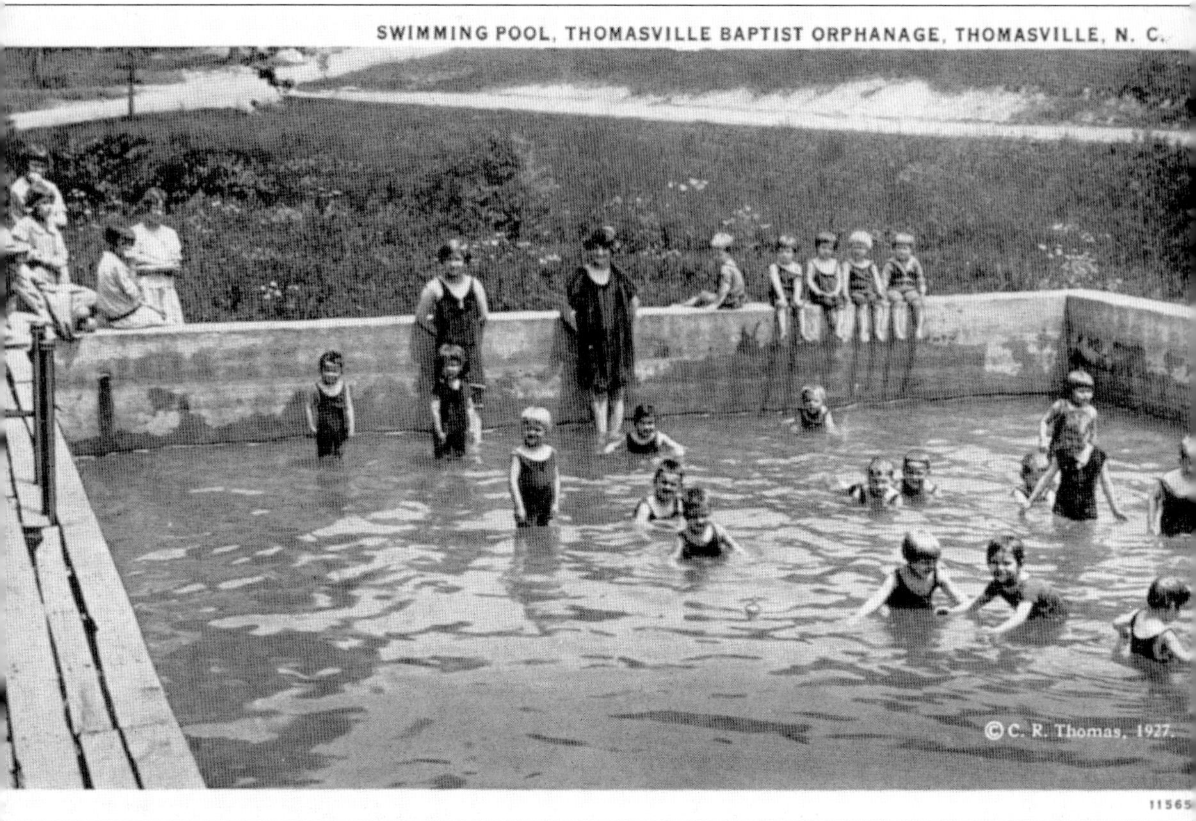

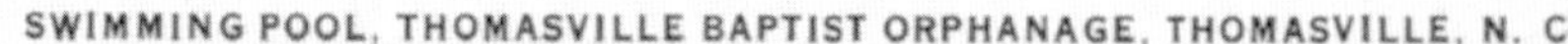

SWIMMING POOL, 1927. The Thomasville government was thankful to draw on the orphanage's deep well to undergird the town's fledgling water system. The well was drilled 876 feet deep through granite until a stream was struck, furnishing an unlimited supply of water. In the hot summer months, the orphans were thankful to draw from it too, but in the form of a swimming pool.

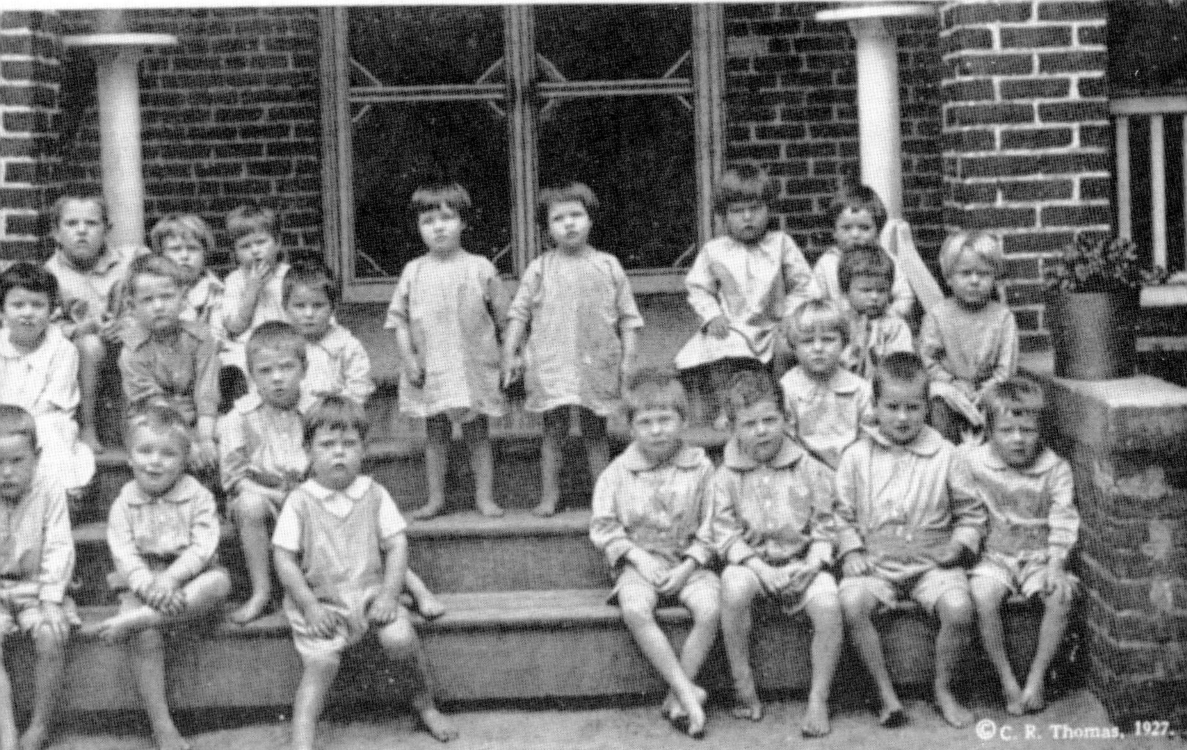

LITTLE FOLKS, 1927. The Mitchell House for girls and the Watson House for boys were erected at the time of the founding of Mills Home. Each house was designed to accommodate 24 children, a teacher, and a matron. Both houses had a separate building with a kitchen, dining room, pantry, and cook's sitting room.

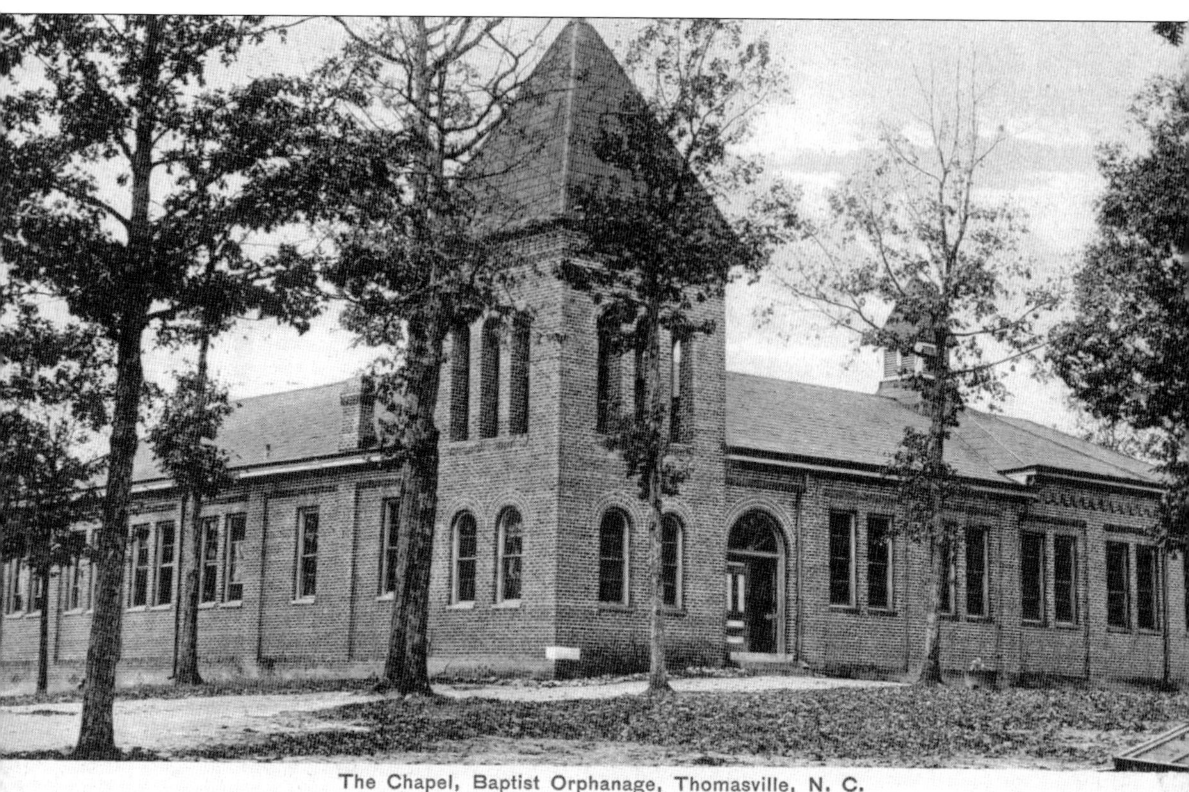
The Chapel, Baptist Orphanage, Thomasville, N. C.

THE CHAPEL. As soon as houses were erected to shelter orphan boys and girls, John Mills asked for a place of worship for them, and in 1886, the brick Lea Chapel was built a short distance north of the Mitchell Cottage. Visiting ministers preached here, and Mills taught daily bible classes.

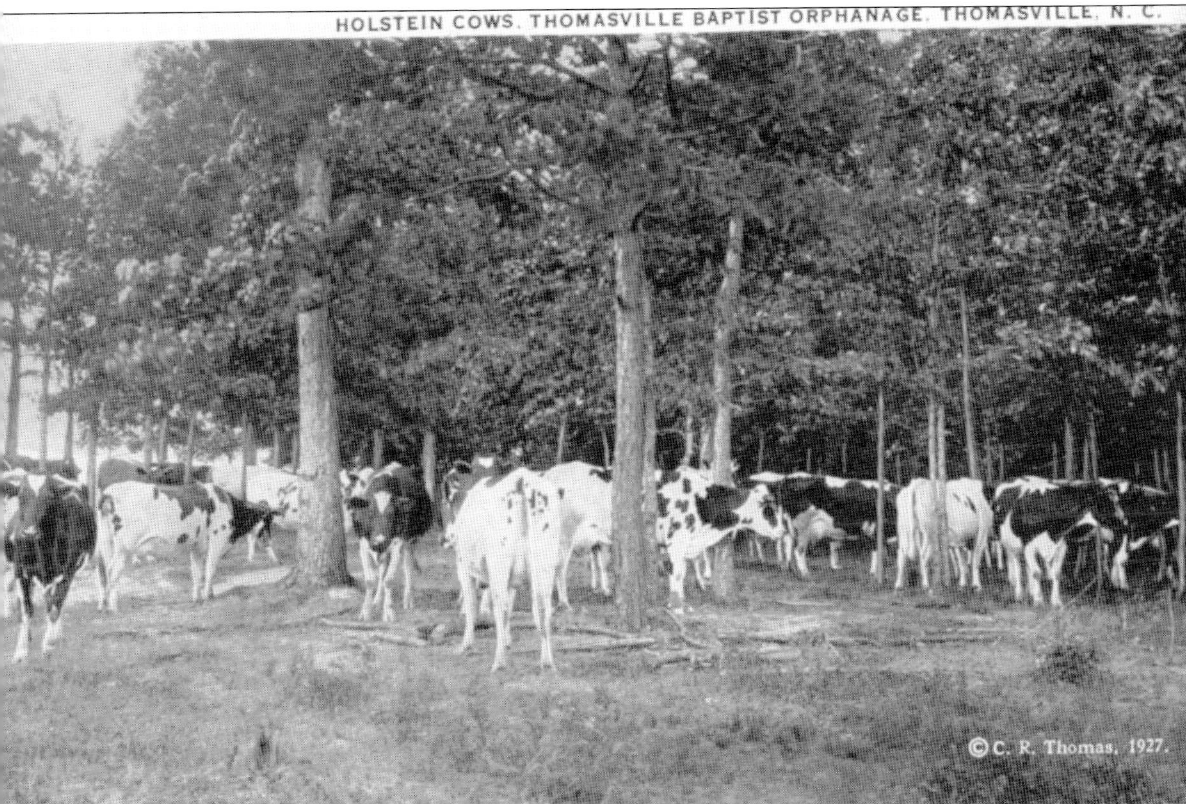

HOLSTEIN HERD, 1927. The orphanage farm was a leader in improved methods, machinery, pastures, and purebred Holstein cows. Farm manager C.C. McKoin bought a few registered Holsteins in 1926, and a gradual conversion to exclusively registered animals ensued. A herd was developed that stood out for its breeding and high production.

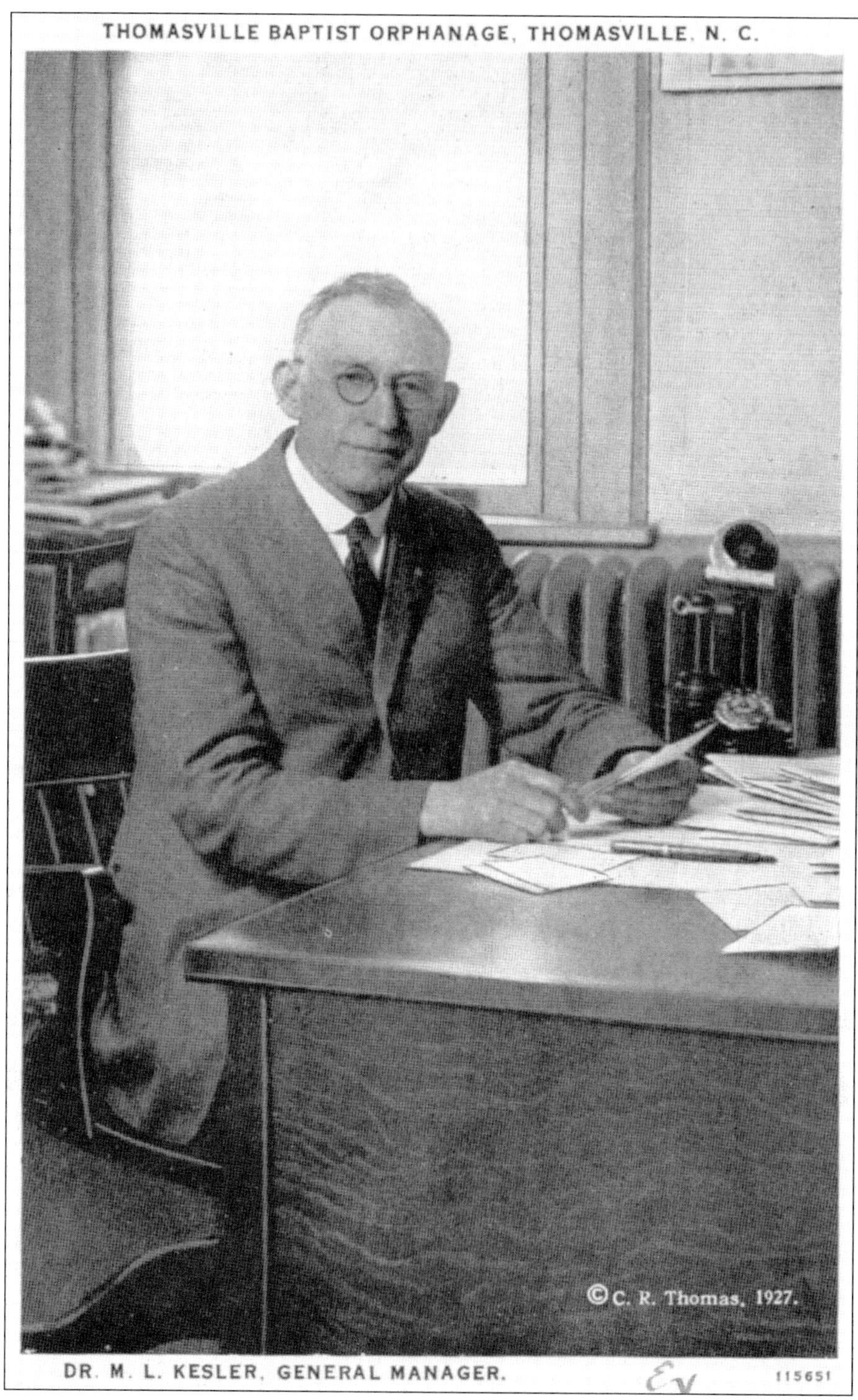

DR. M.L. KESLER, 1927. Dr. Martin Luther Kesler succeeded J.B. Boone as general manager in 1905. Based on the foundations laid by his predecessor, Kesler set about improving the appearance of the houses and grounds. Every child and worker was encouraged to plant, cultivate, rake, and prune to help make the orphanage a beautiful, clean, wholesome, and healthful place.

Seven

Thomasville Shooting Club

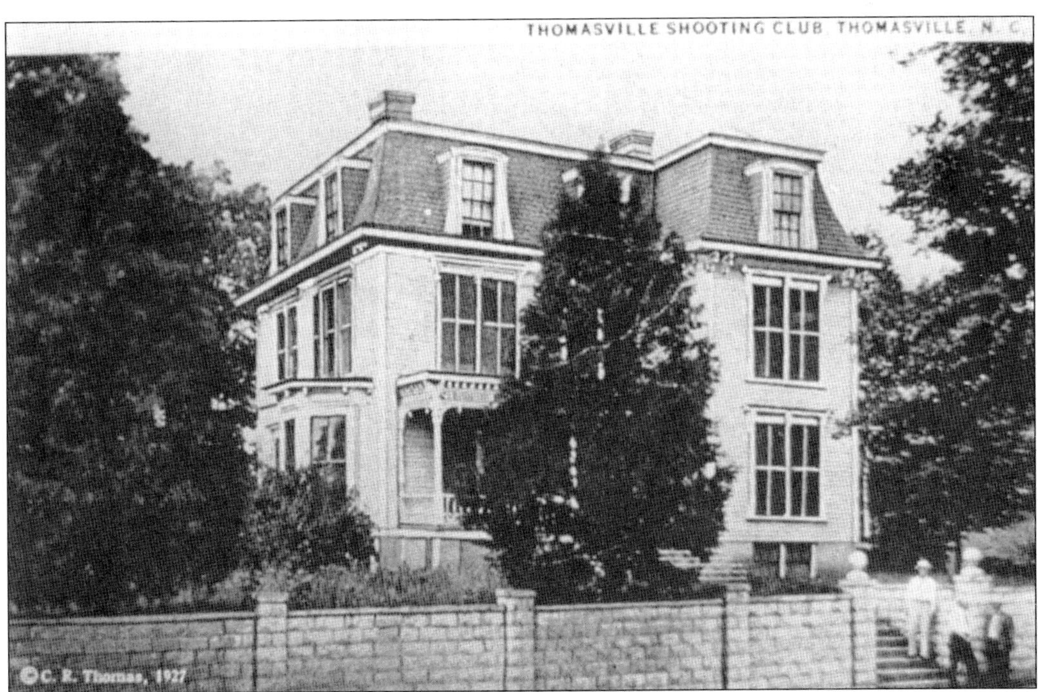

Thomasville Shooting Club, 1927. A previously untold chapter in Thomasville's history is that of the Thomasville Shooting Club, which was incorporated on April 13, 1894. George W. Davis, organizer of the club and Wall Street broker, came to Thomasville in the 1870s to hunt quail and woodcock. While interning at a New York hospital, a doctor told Davis, "You can't go off and shoot woodcock and still become a doctor." Davis left the medical profession that day. He organized a field trial club in the 1880s, which was later reorganized into the Thomasville Shooting Club. The lodge sat between present Winston and Trade Streets on West Main Street. The men on the steps are, from left to right, Archie Primm, C.R. Thomas, and C.L. Harris.

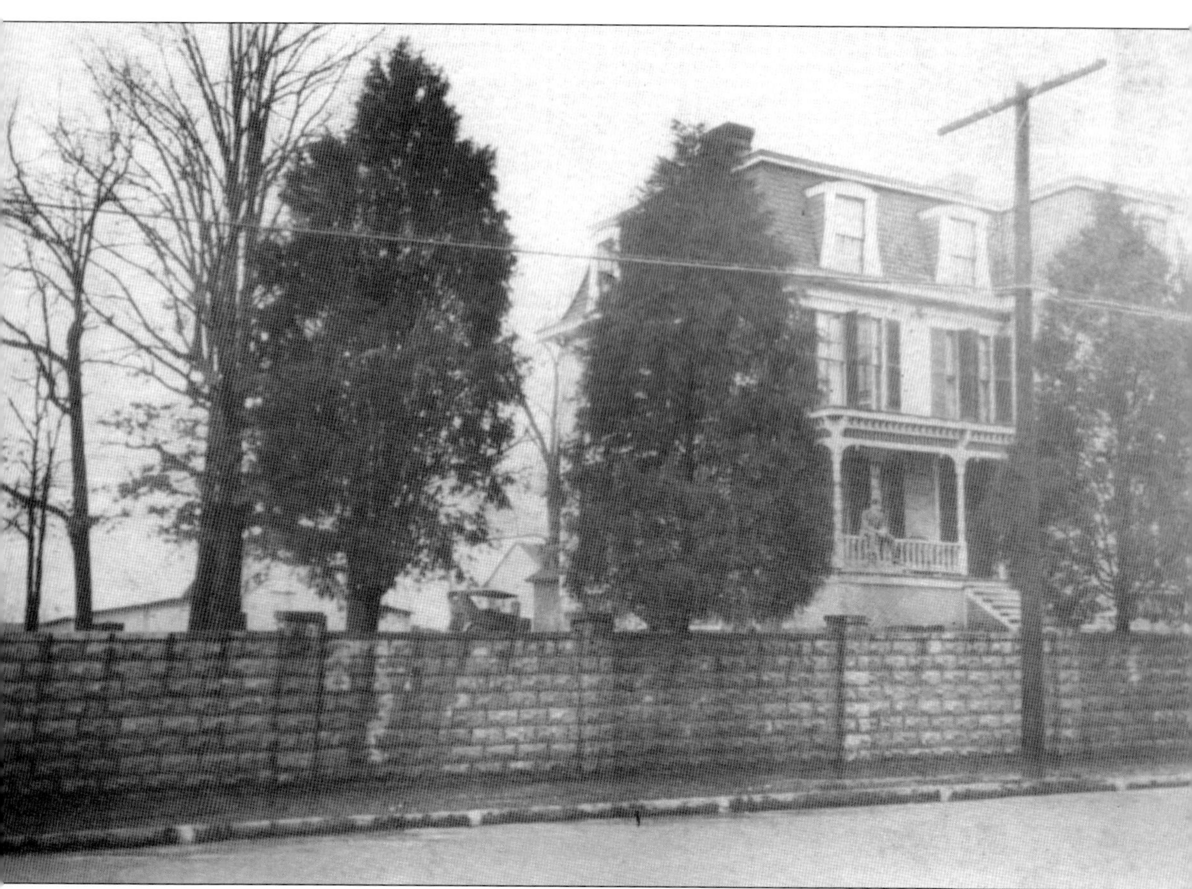

THE CLUBHOUSE. The lodge (a misnomer if ever there was one), which was built by Ped Thomas, son of John W. Thomas, was a three-and-a-half-story mansion with over 20 rooms. The first floor consisted of a large sitting room, small study, dining room, storage room, and at least one bedroom. The basement housed a complete kitchen with a commercial wood-burning cooking range, two pantries, a utility room, and storage space. More bedrooms were on the second and third (half-story) floors.

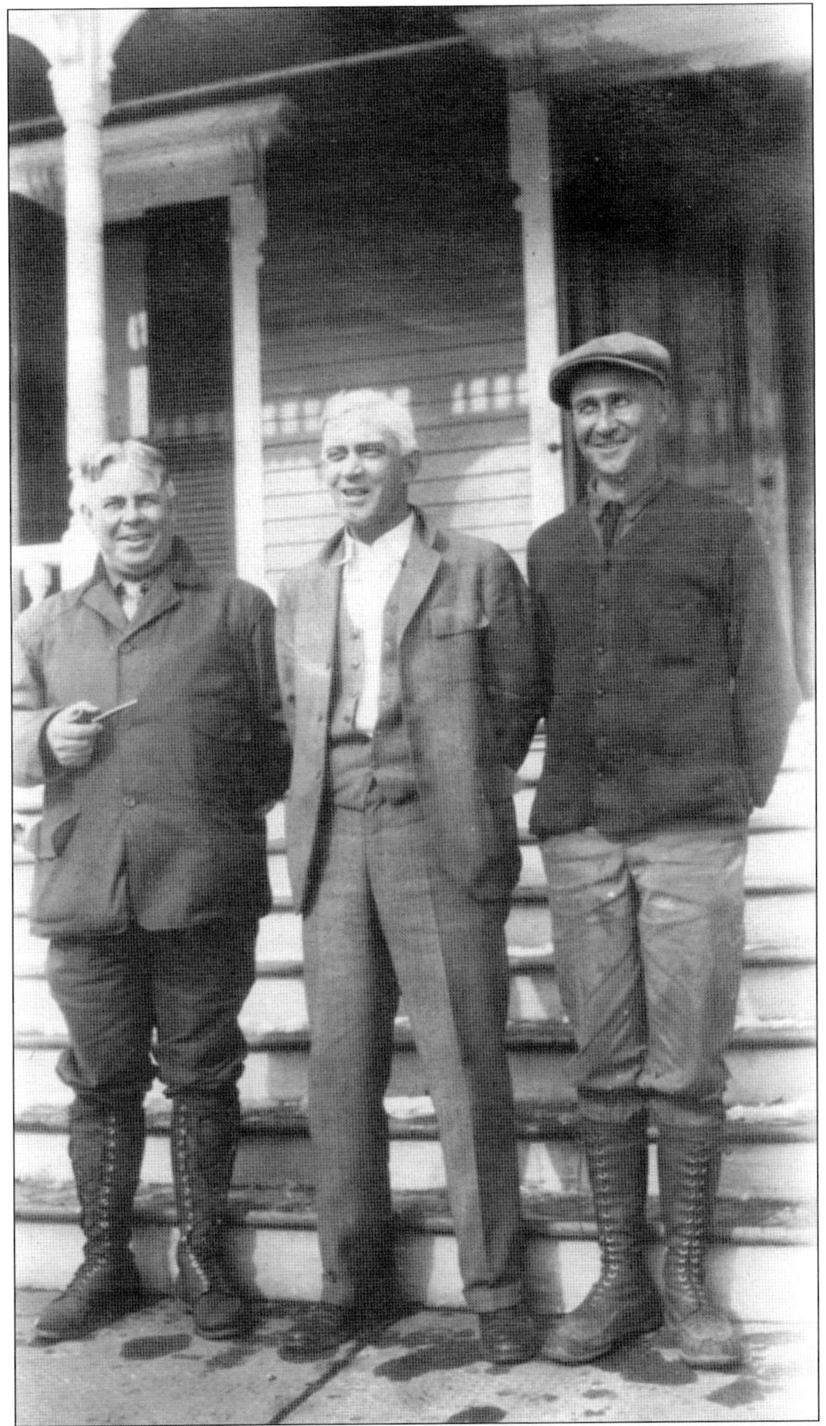

Thomasville Shooting Club Staff. Pictured here are lead hunting guide and dog trainer Everett Swaim Sr. (left), club manager Archie Primm (center), and guide John Workman. This photograph was taken in front of the front porch. After this house was sold in the 1940s, a small lodge was built just north of town on Lodge Drive.

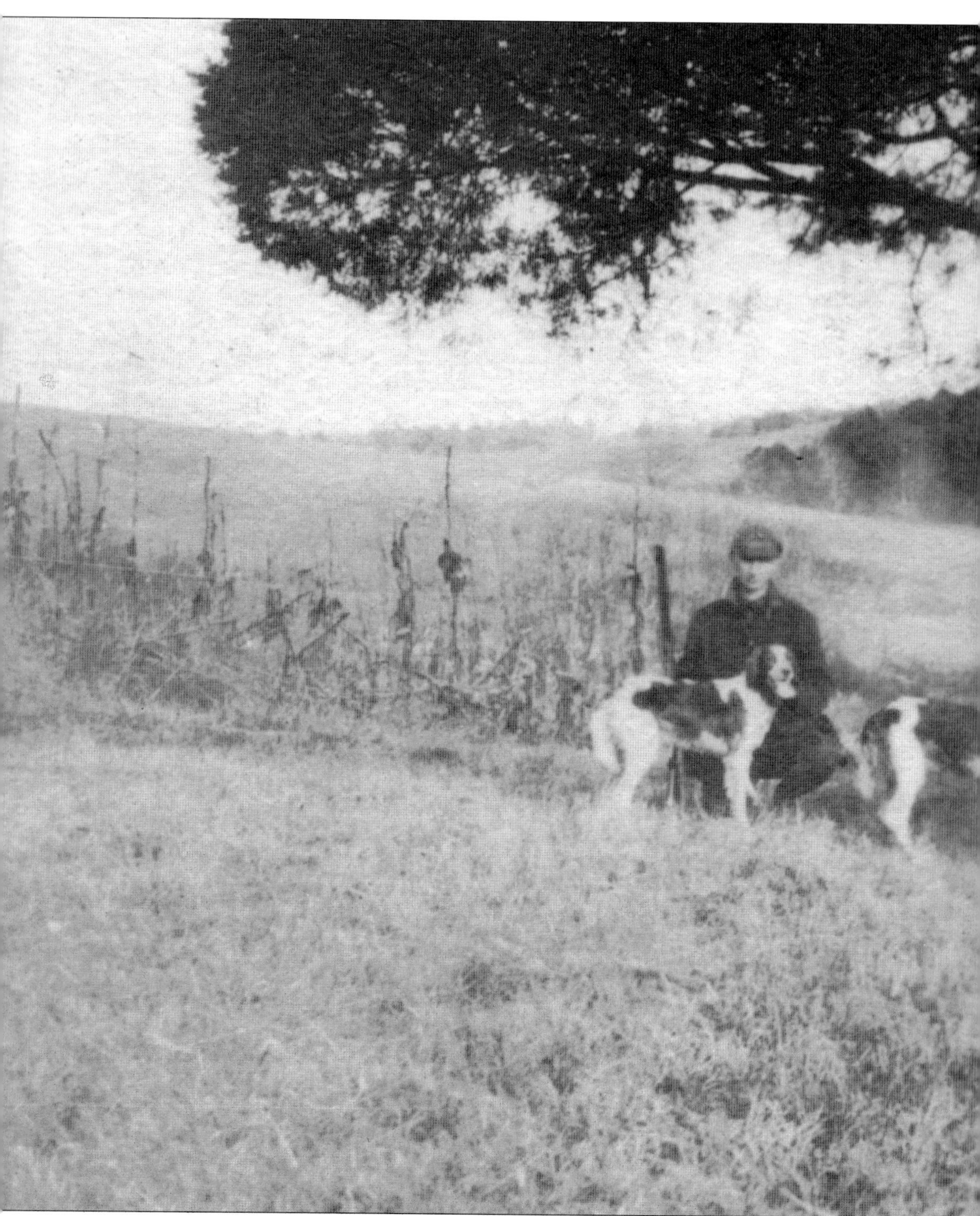

None Was Better to Be Had. Out in the countryside were thousands of acres of pastures, cornfields, and idle land covered with sedge and brush—the habitat of quail. Although the hunting here was good, club organizer George W. Davis made an extended trip through Virginia, South

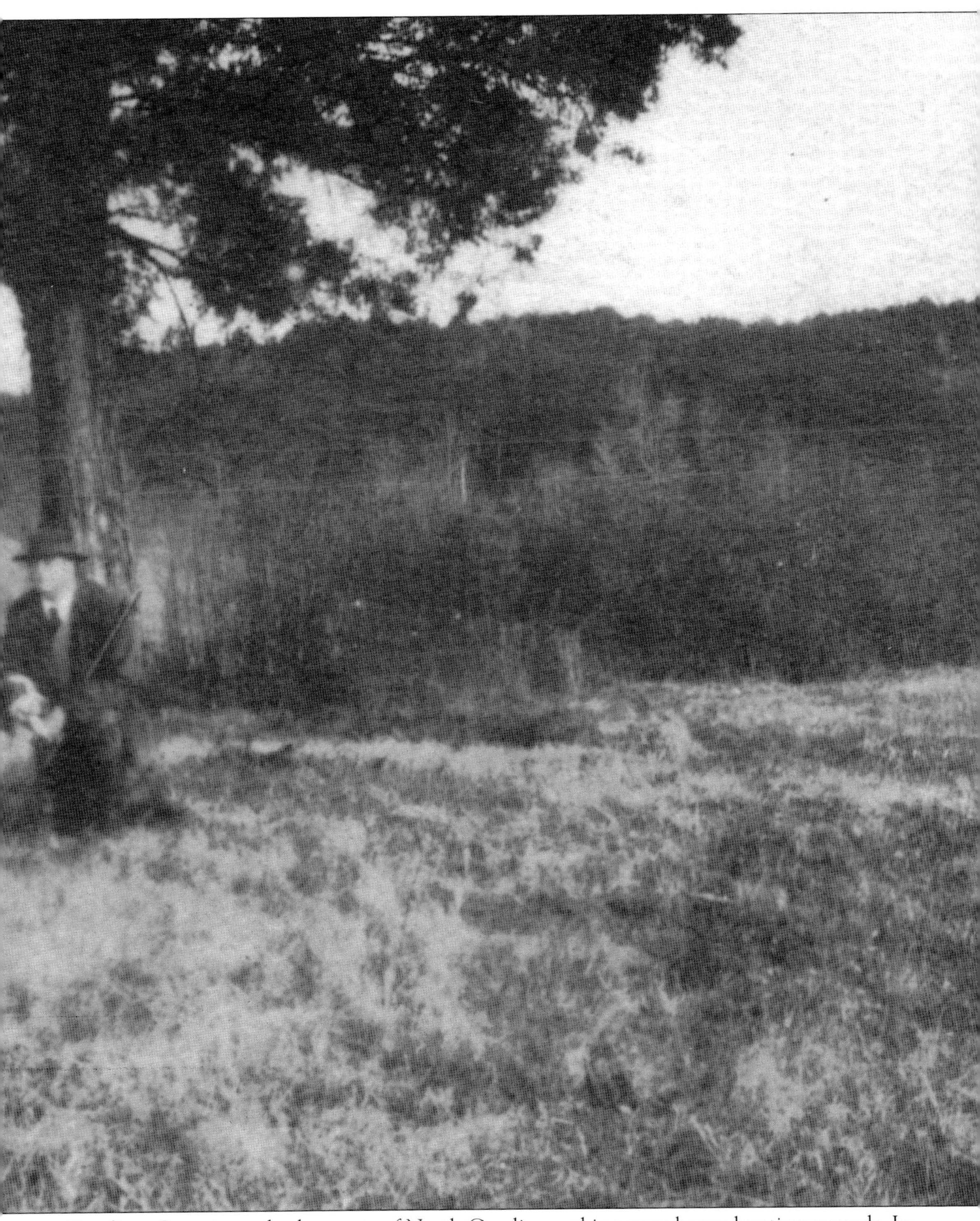

Carolina, Georgia, and other parts of North Carolina seeking even better hunting grounds. In the early 1890s, he decided he was wasting his time.

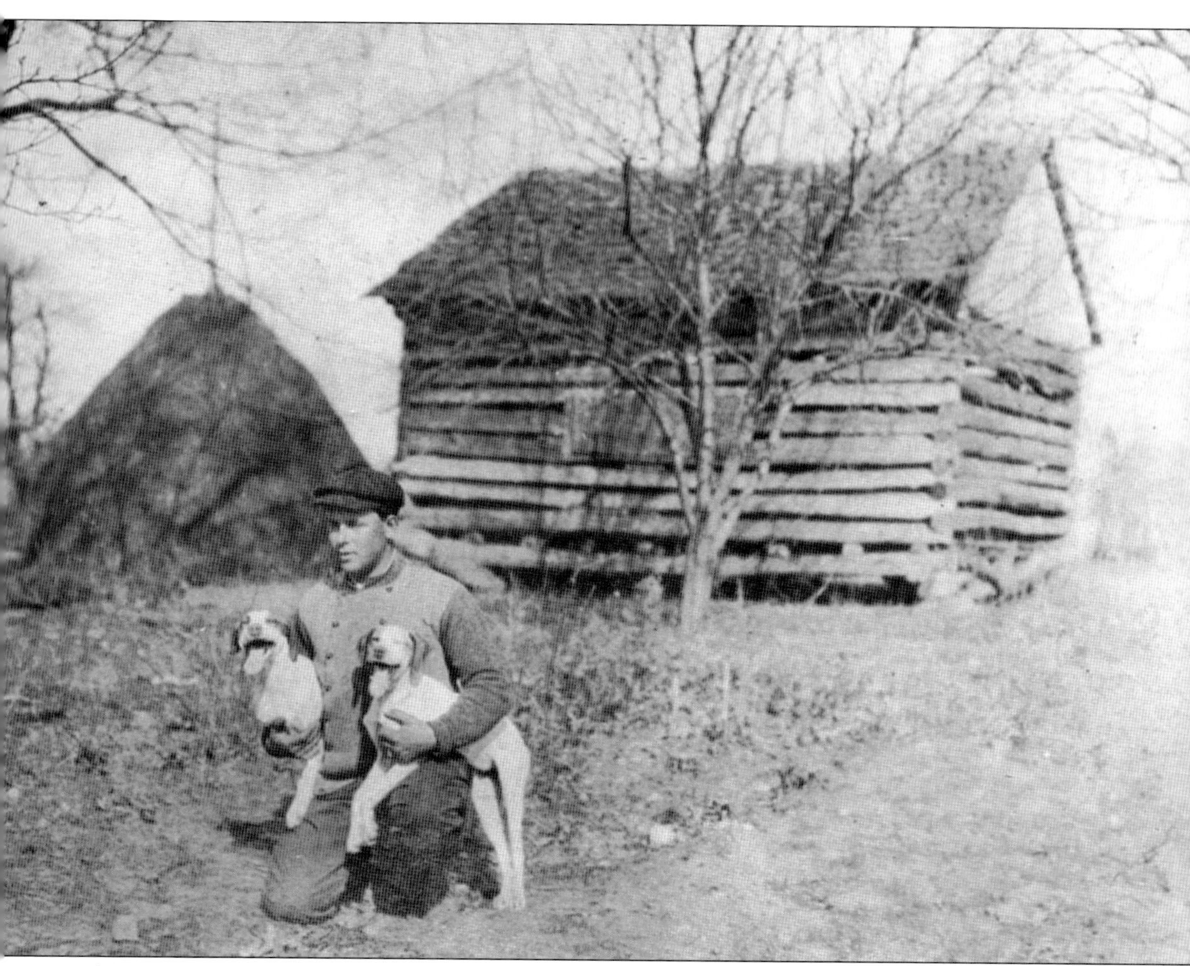

A Lifelong Devotion. George W. Davis hired Everett Swaim Sr. to take care of the club and care for and train the dogs. Swaim spent much of his time acquiring leases for hunting land—more than 60,000 acres in total. For 51 seasons, Swaim was credited as being the most outstanding guide in the country, and no one was as good as he. As demonstrated by his age in the photographs in this chapter, Swaim spent his life working for the club and catering to the needs of the members. Two of his children, Austin and Toland, were named after club members Austen Colgate and Dr. Robert Toland.

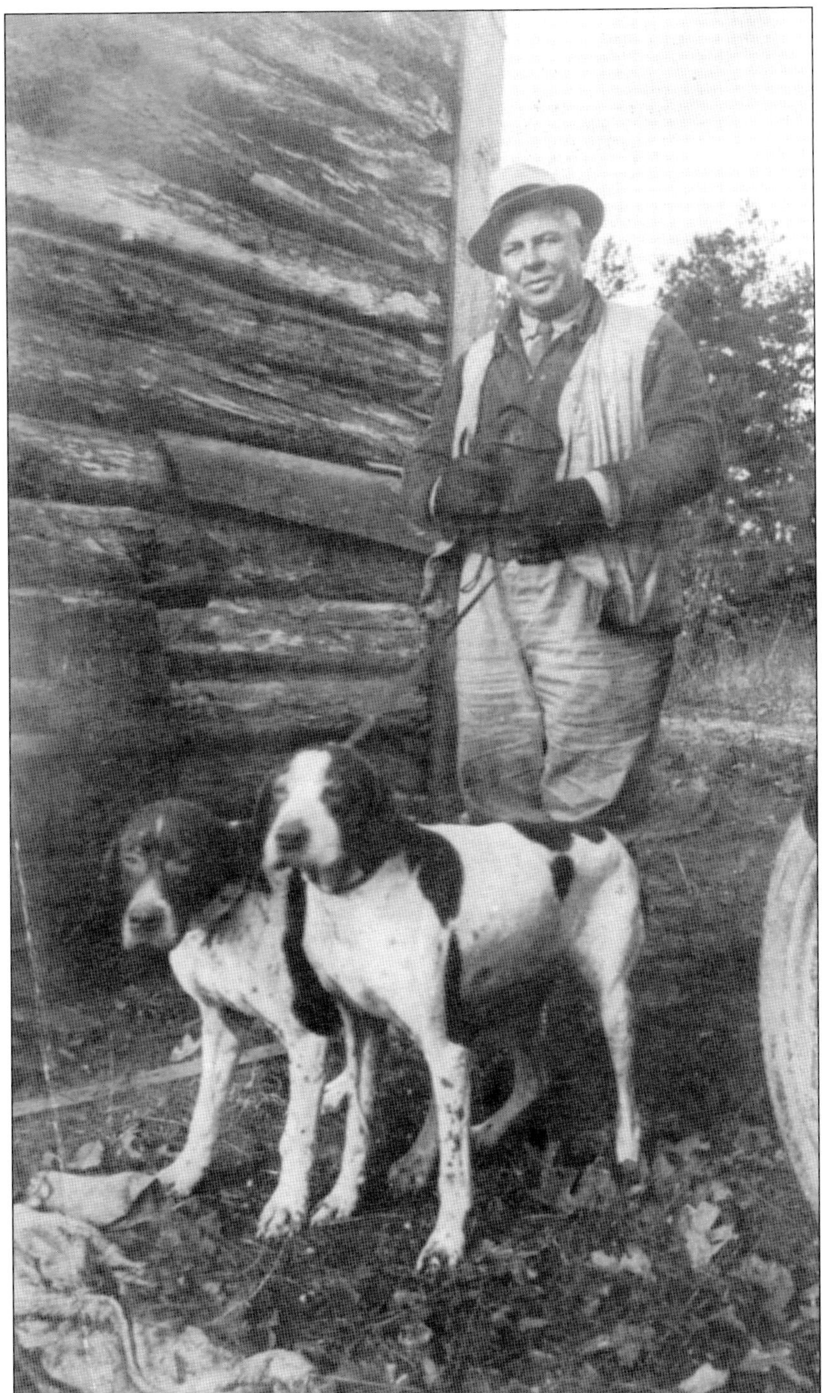

An Aging Guide. Everett Swaim Sr., known to many as "Father," was more than a tobacco farmer on the outskirts of town. Through his devotion to a small bird, he watched conservation come into effect and gain traction over the years. A man of deep belly laughs and the occasional strong drink, Swaim made sure those who came to Thomasville were shown the utmost respect and invited back to the small town.

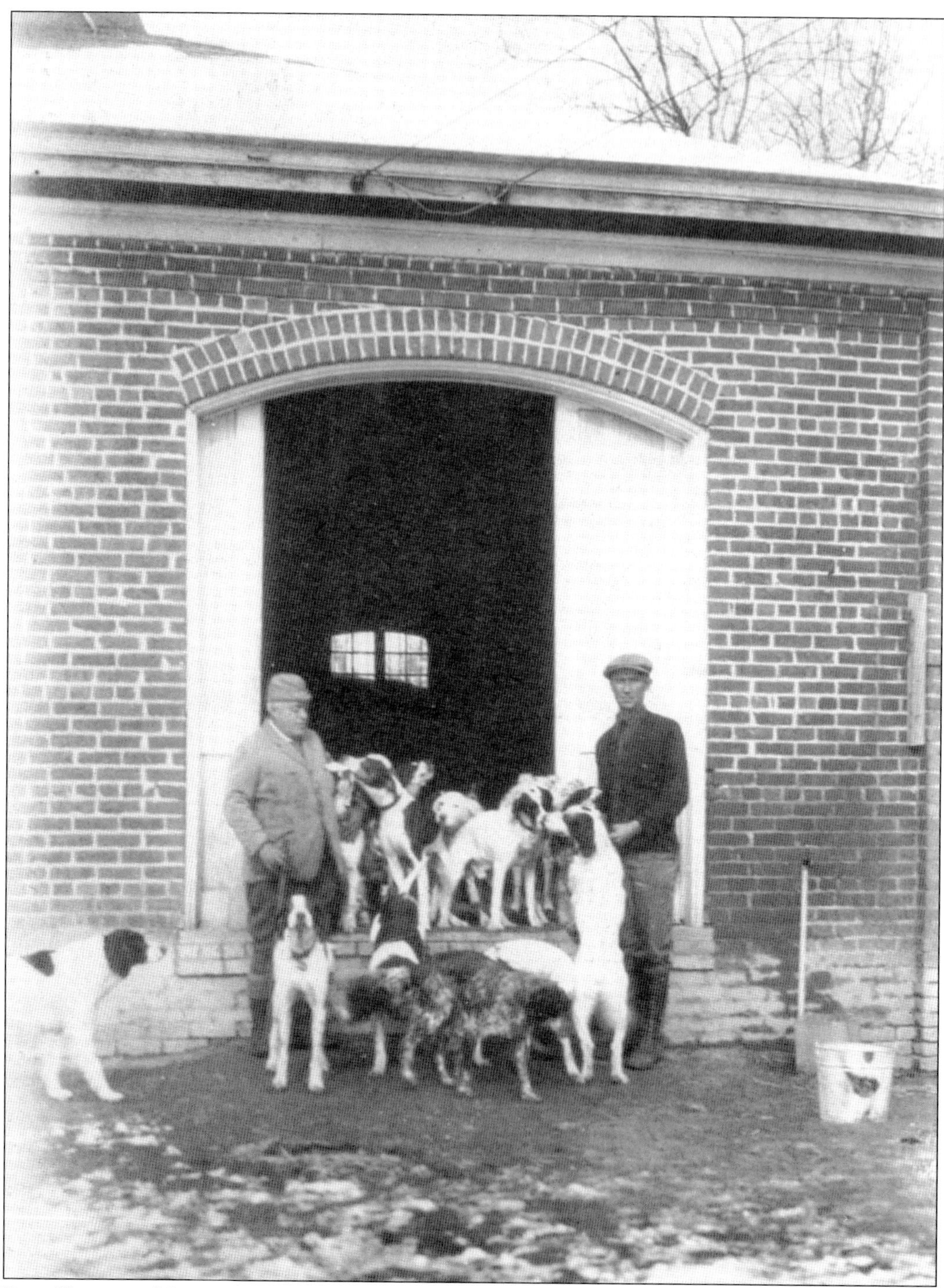

Dog Kennels. Hours spent training the bird dogs paid dividends in the field. The kennels were first located behind the clubhouse and later on the site of the old Dogwood Hosiery on Salem Street. Members would buy purebred English pointers and setters from England and have them shipped to Everett Swaim Sr. to be trained by hunting season. Dogs that did not train well were given to Swaim's children as pets or "taken care of."

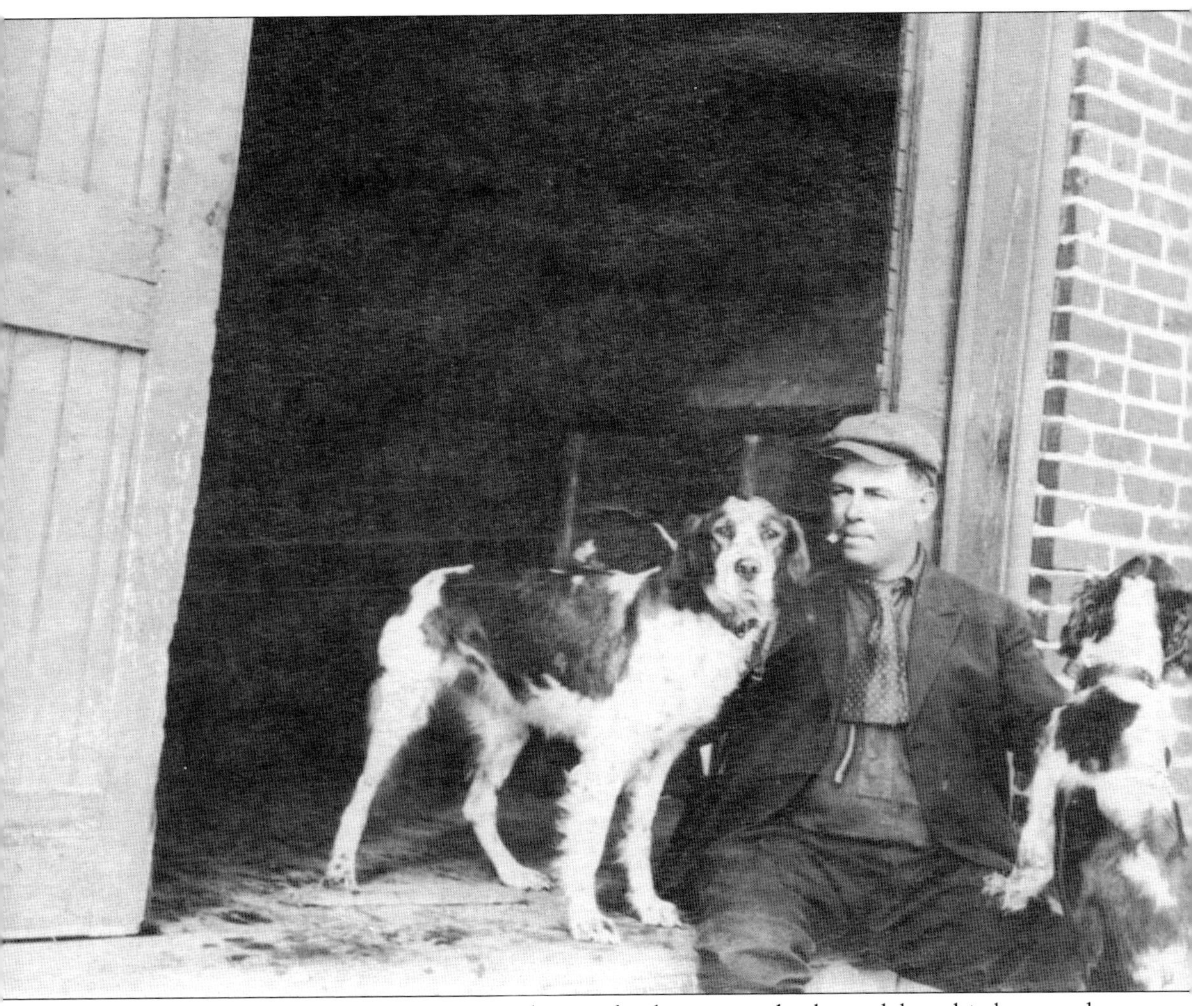

Man's Best Friend. Everett Swaim Sr. was known for the cigar on his lip and dog whistle around his neck. This photograph was taken on the grounds of the dog kennels, although Swaim had kennels on his farm to keep a closer watch on the mischievous dogs and pregnant females. Man's best friend proved most useful in locating the birds on hunting expeditions.

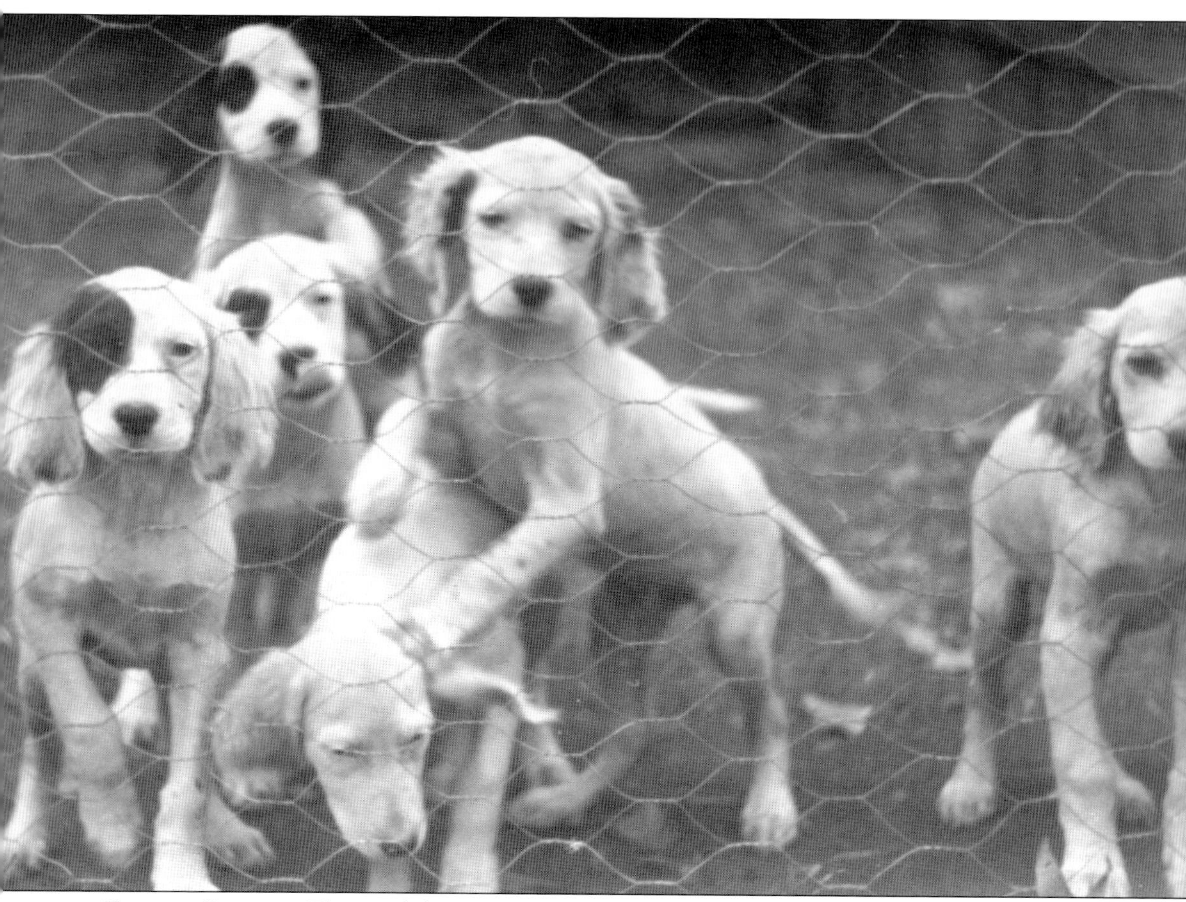

English Setters. The English setter is a sporting dog of sweet temper and showstopping good looks. Bred for the hills of England, setters fared well in the similar topography of Davidson County. Underneath the shaggy coat, which hunters would often clip, is a well-balanced hunter. The breed is wildly devoted, tenacious, and patient in the field.

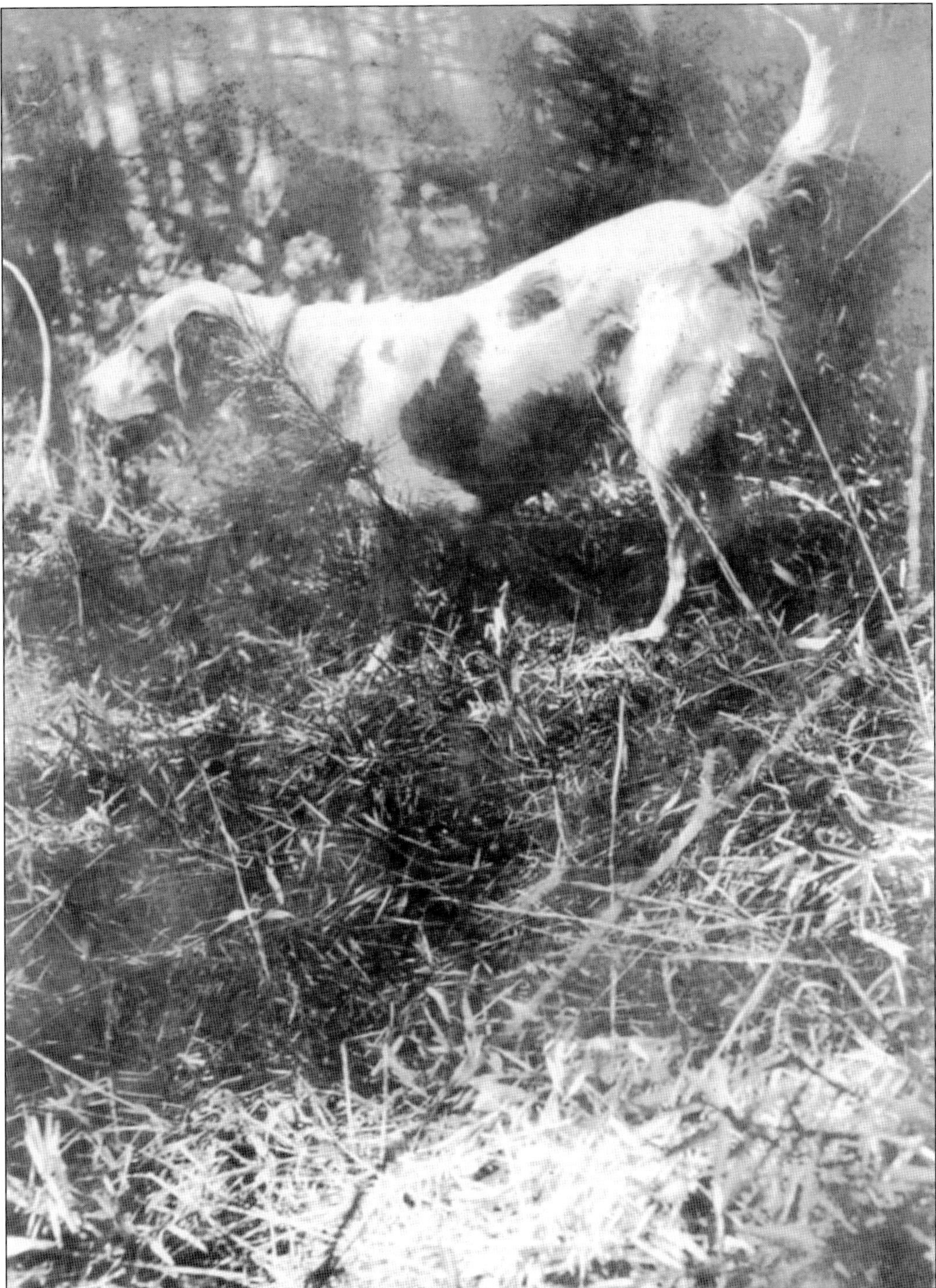

AMERICA'S OLDEST GUN DOG. These early European setters were used by hunters to locate and set game birds (hold them in place) while the hunters placed nets that would entrap the birds when they were flushed. When hunters began using firearms, selective breeding encouraged an upright point that shooters could easily see.

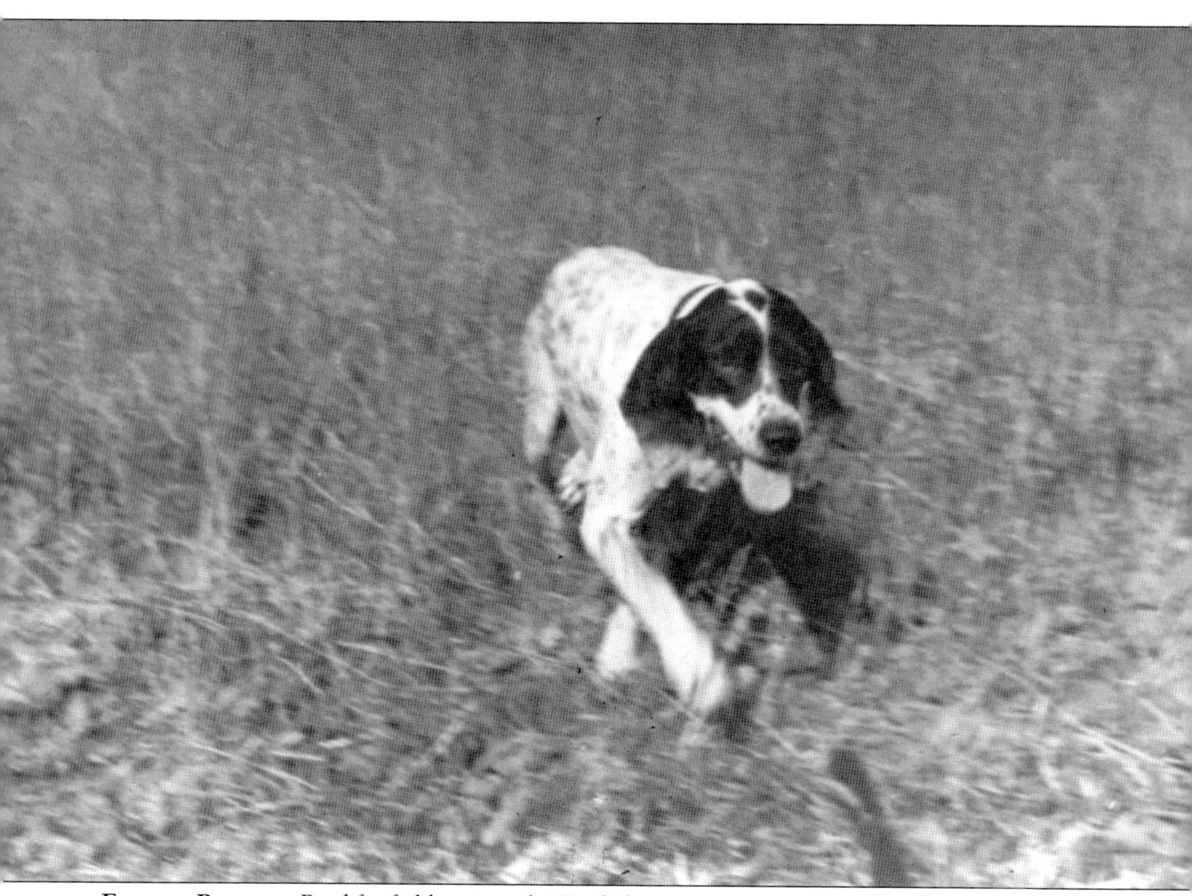

English Pointer. Bred for field action, the English pointer was—and still is—one of the hardest-working bird dogs. Its short coat and muscular body make it ideal for hunting in the sage fields of Davidson County. The breed is characterized by its high energy and undying loyalty. These even-tempered gun dogs find, point, and retrieve birds with utmost efficiency.

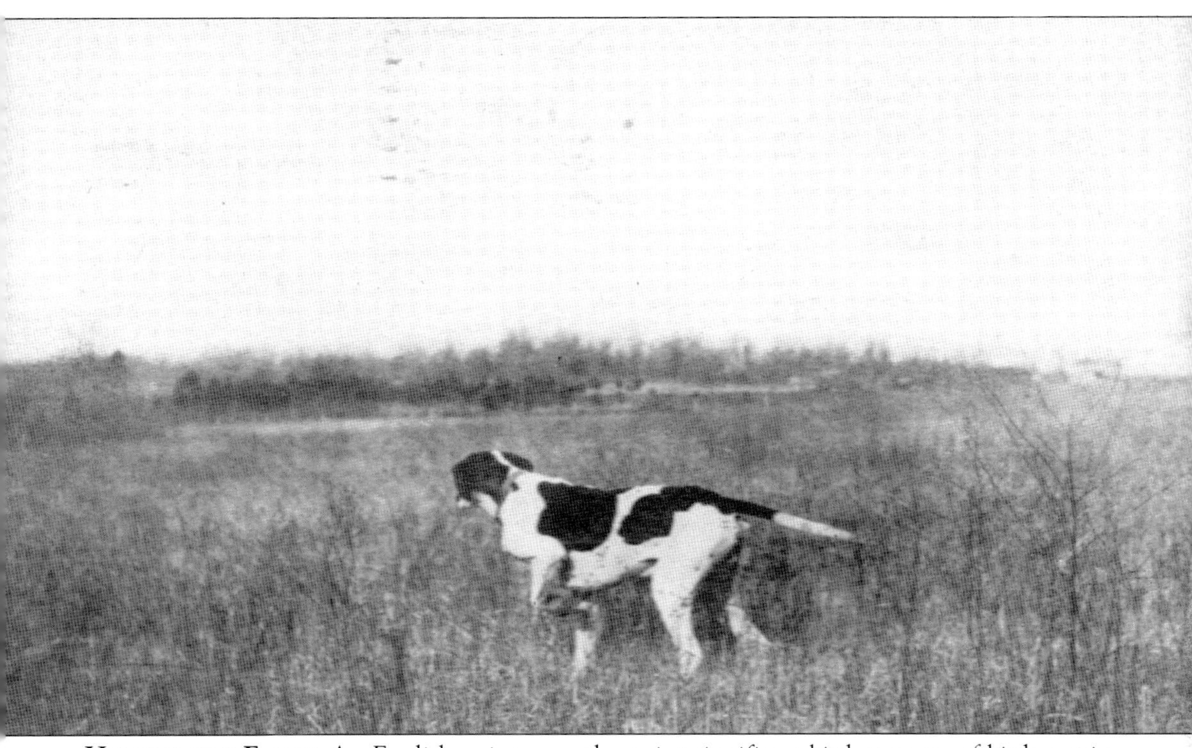

Holding the Front. An English pointer on the point signifies a bird or covey of birds out in front. Once it locates birds, the dog points at attention to alert its human companions. Once given the go-ahead, the dog would lunge forward to flush the bird(s) and hope to be rewarded with a retrieve.

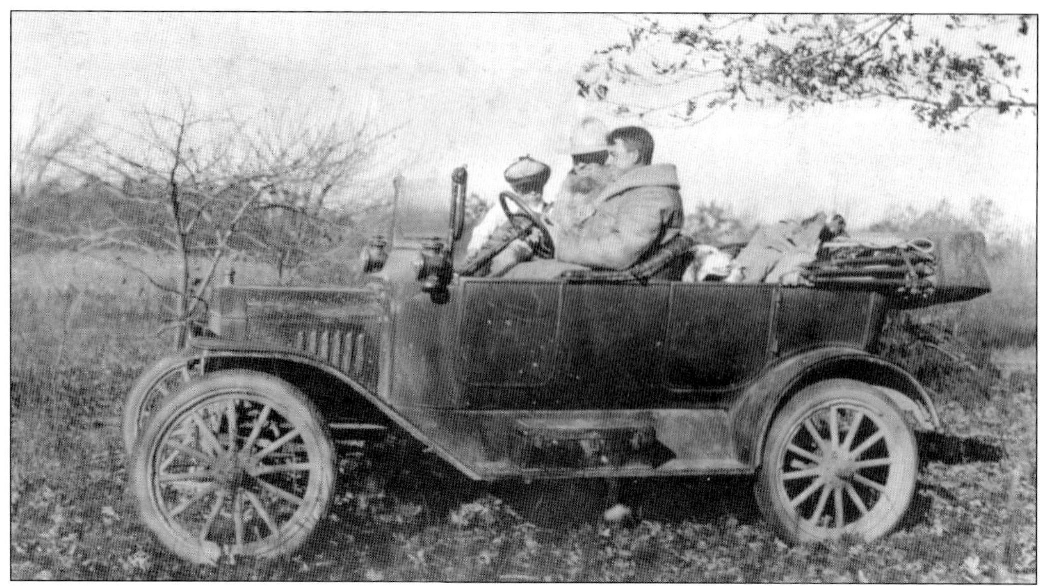

Modern Transportation. High-wheeled Harvester trucks were not very comfortable to a tired man on a cold, rainy evening. But club members often had the opportunity to warm themselves up by pushing these low-powered trucks, which had a hard time negotiating hills.

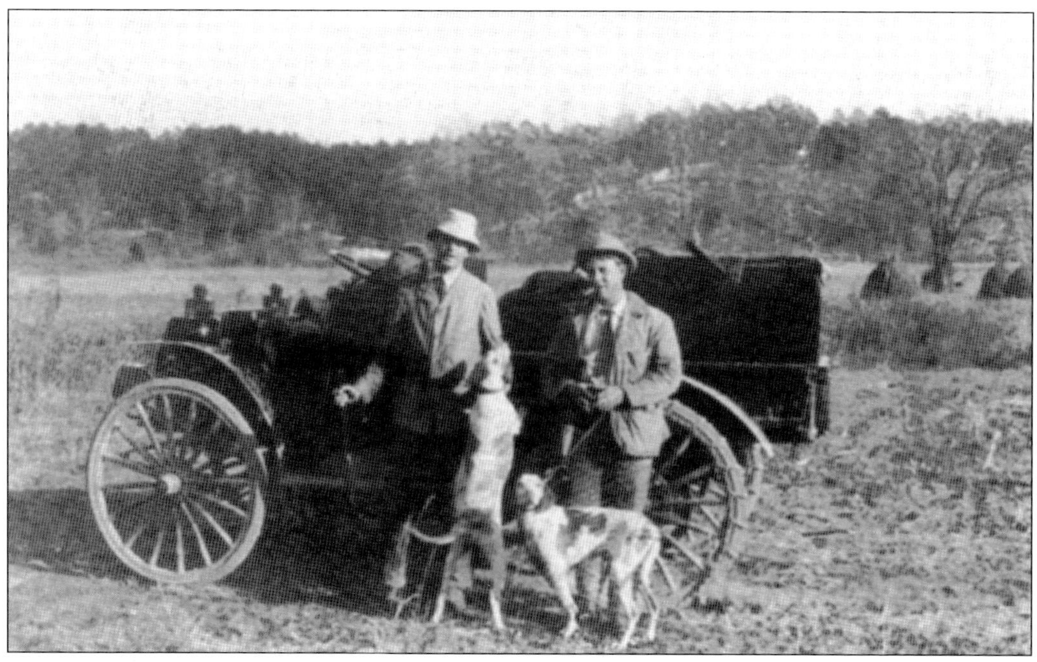

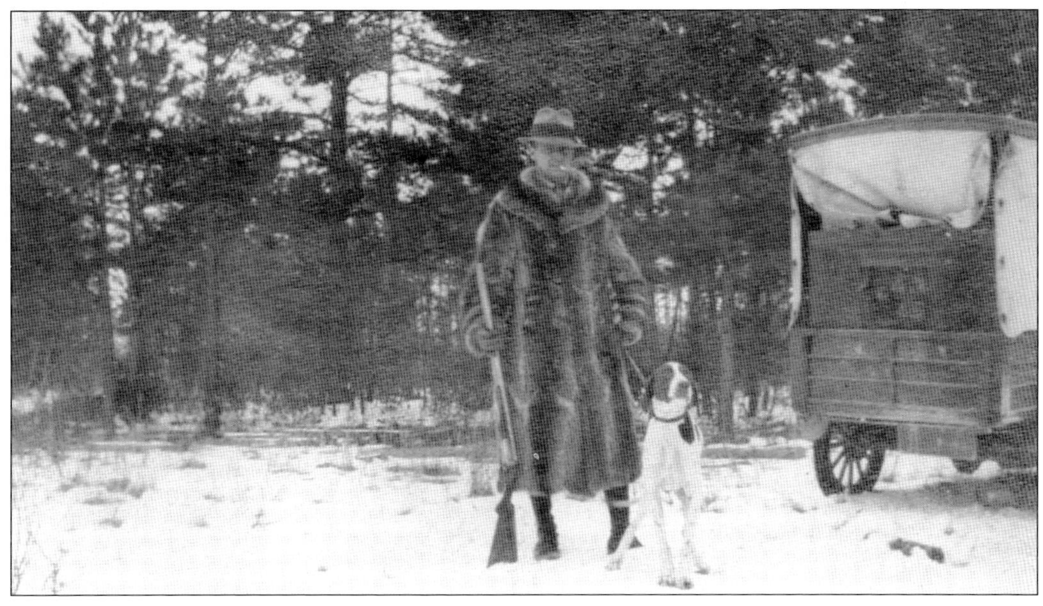

Dressed for Success. Thomasville was known far beyond the boundaries of Davidson County not for its culture or thriving businesses but for its quail. Untold thousands of dollars were spent on what boiled down to a dog pointing. The surety that there was a covey of quail underneath the dog's nose allowed the man with the expensive custom gun to try his luck and test his eye.

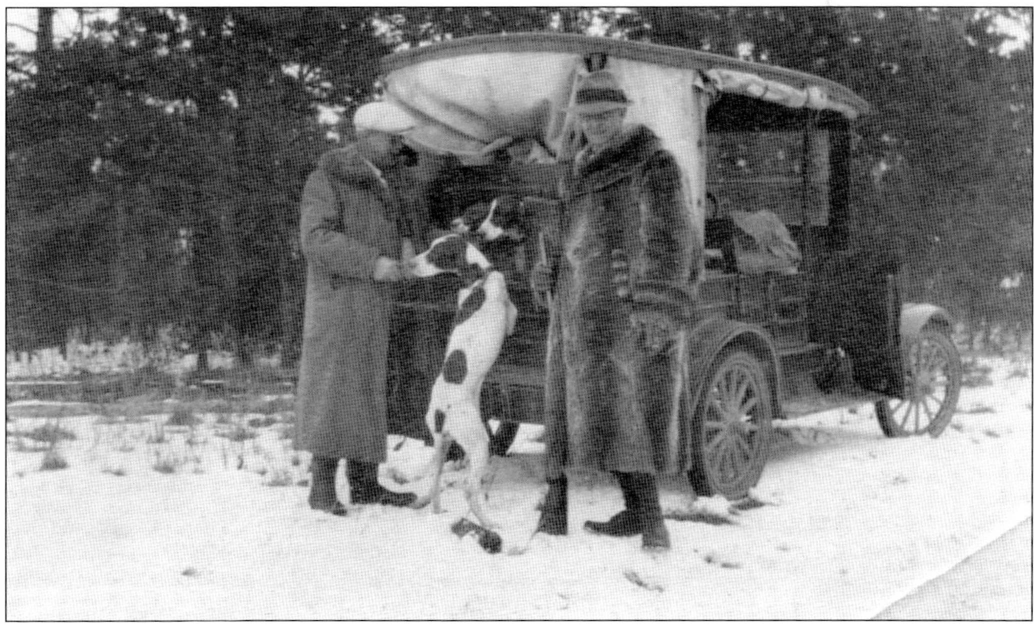

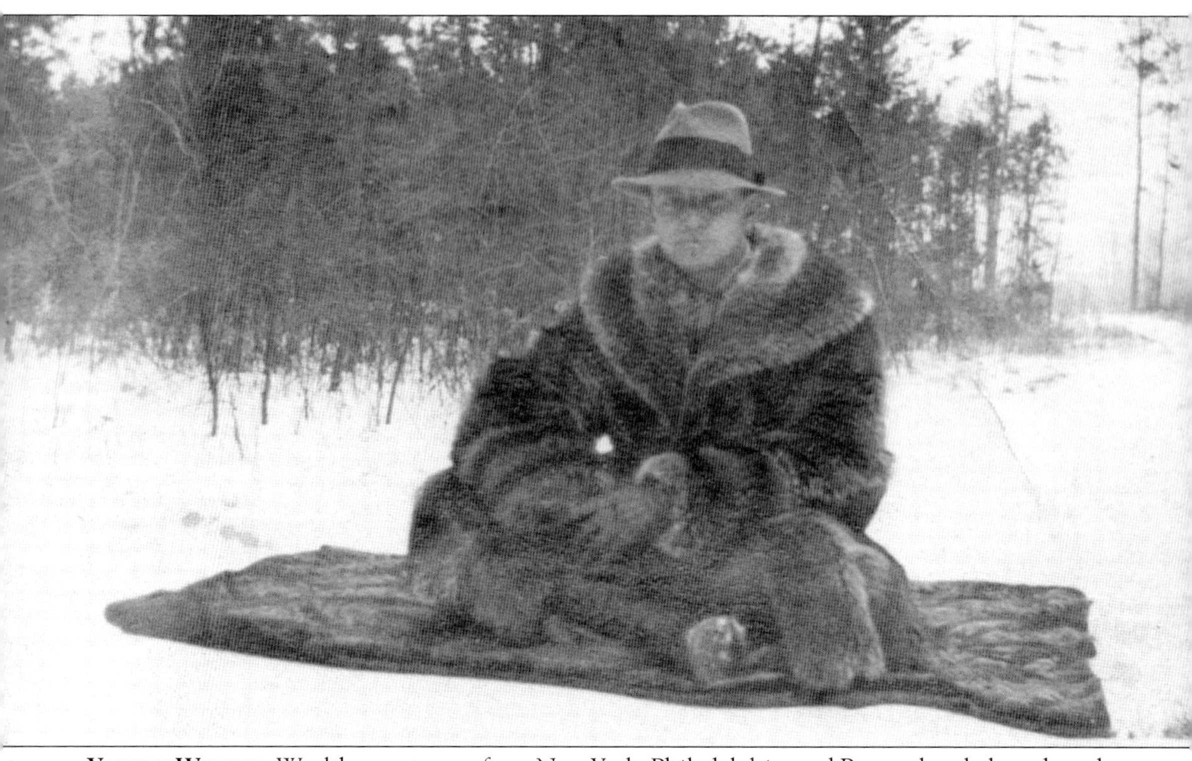

YANKEE WEALTH. Wealthy sportsmen from New York, Philadelphia, and Boston headed south each winter to shoot quail in Thomasville, a resort for shooting. Members would travel in their own personal Pullman cars and stay in town for much of the winter. Many of the telegrams between some of the country's most influential men read, "Will meet you in Thomasville."

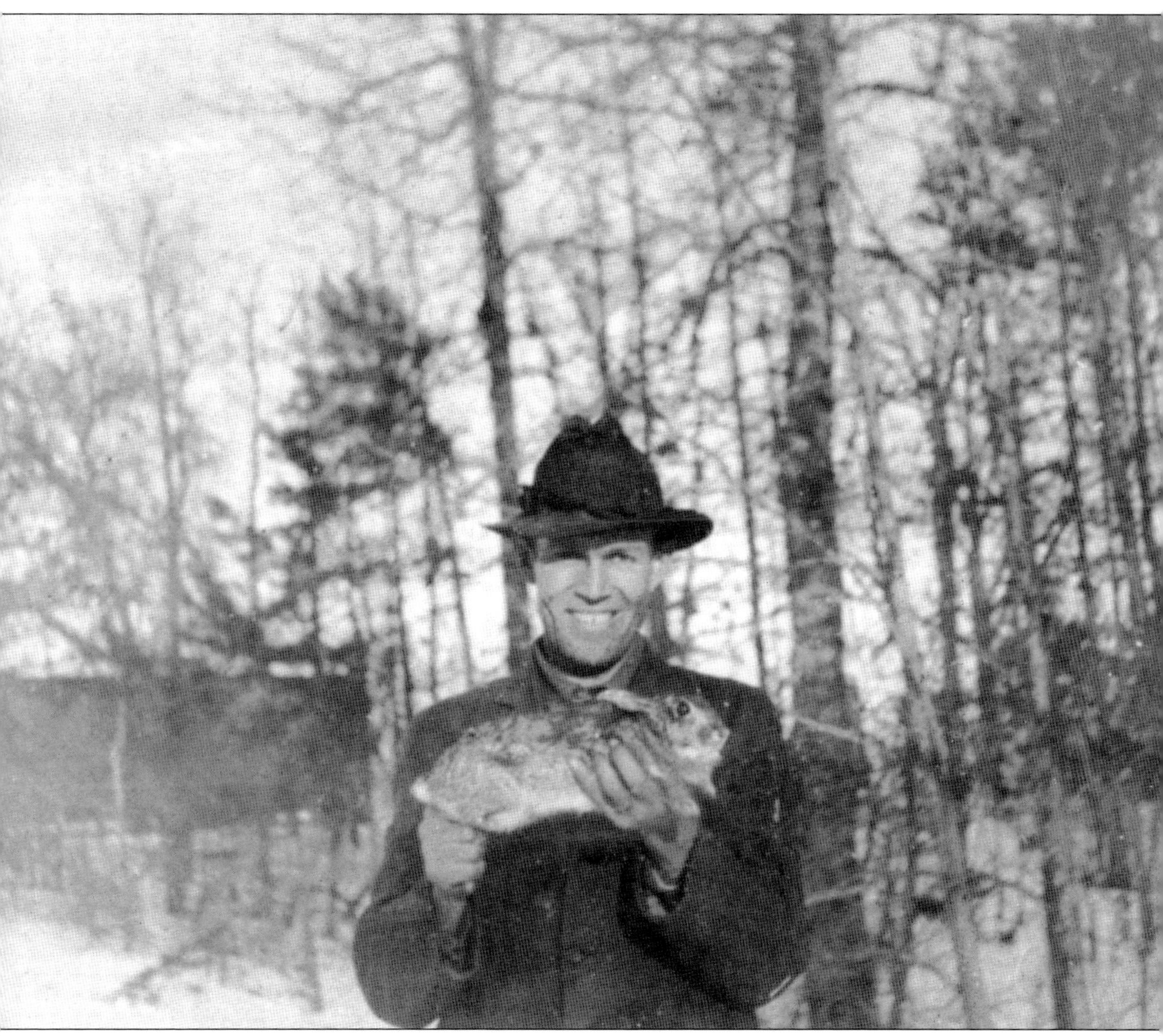

Toothy Grin for Small Game. Members of the club used mainly 16-, 28-, and 36-gauge guns for wing and small game shooting. Personally customized English double-barrel guns—Churchills, Greeners, and Purdeys—were favorites. This grin reveals a pleased hunter who decided to catch a rabbit barehanded rather than pepper it with shot.

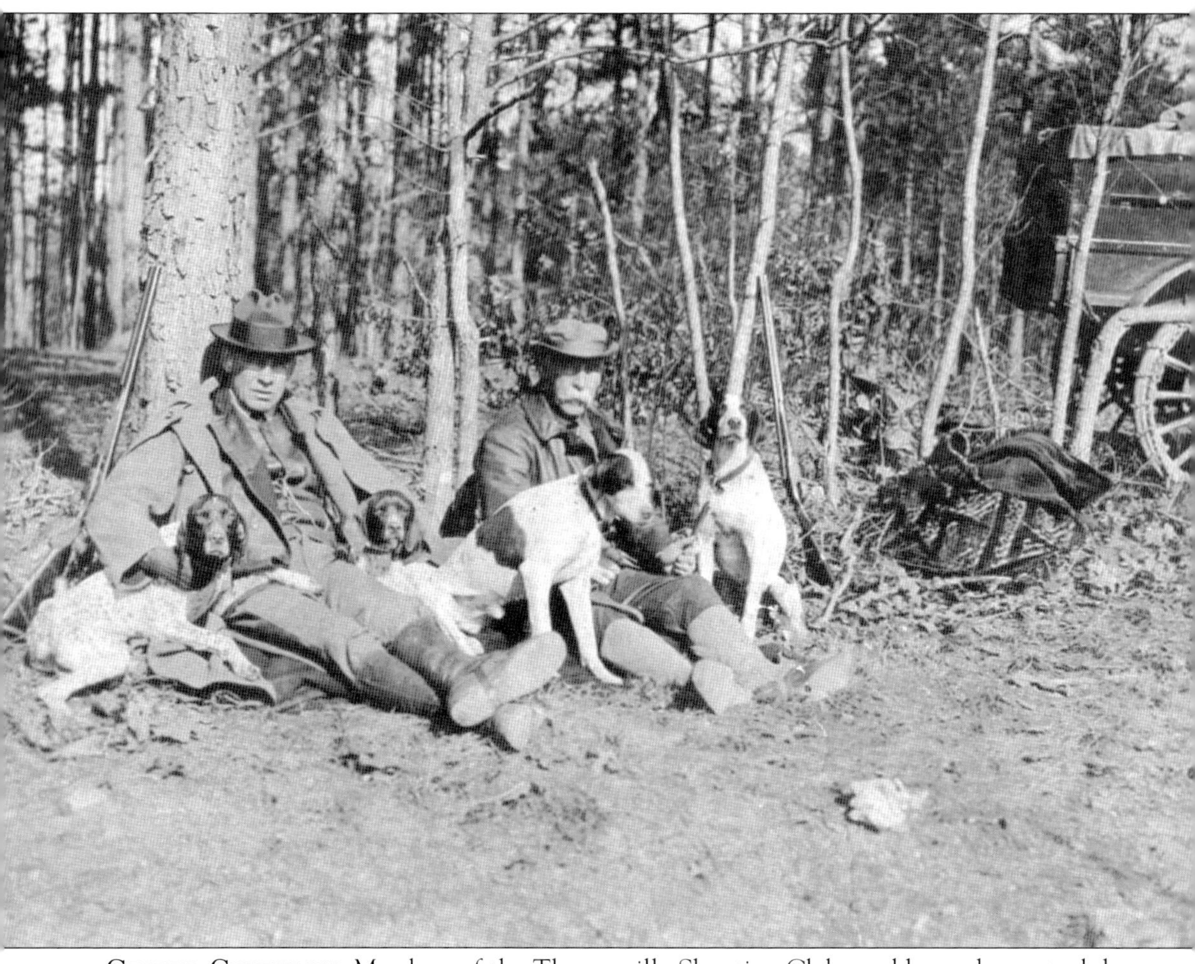

Genteel Gentlemen. Members of the Thomasville Shooting Club would spend a genteel day afield, with every outing treated as a special event. Here, two men pose with dogs and their trusty double-barrels resting on trees beside them.

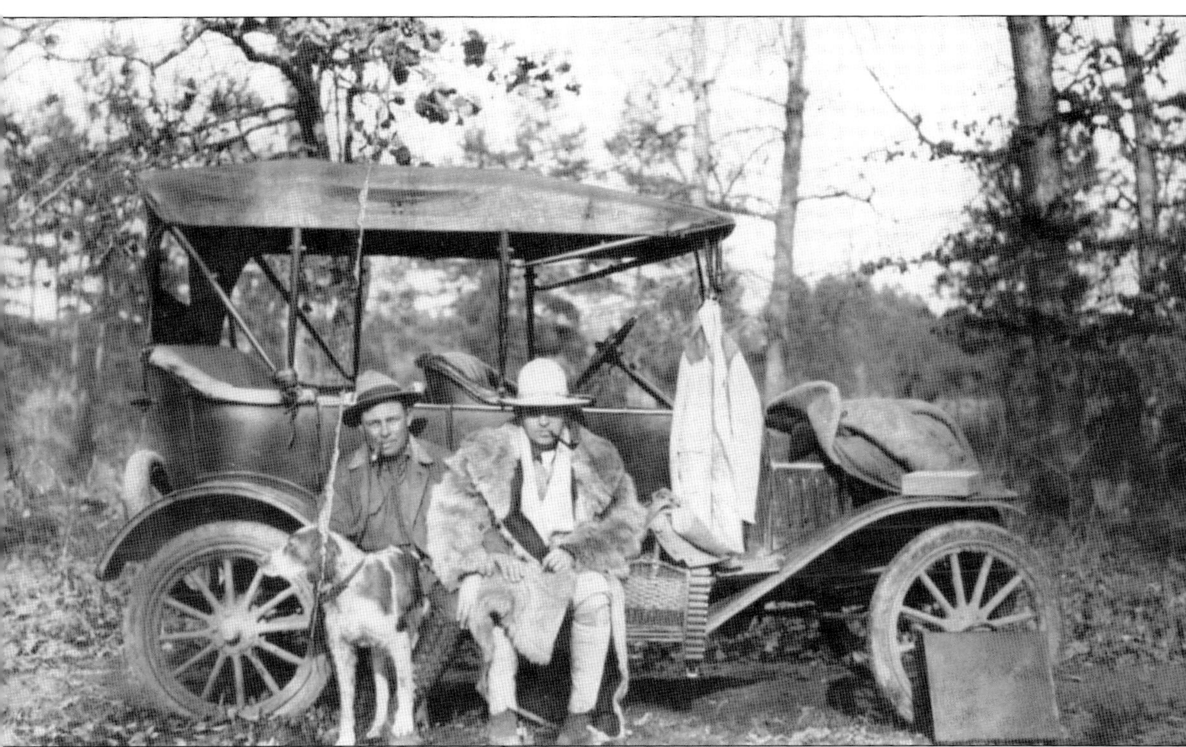

Opulent Sportsman. Prominent visitors came to what was once the quail capital of the South. Adm. Robert Peary, discoverer of the North Pole; Admiral Branson, commander of the North Atlantic Fleet; and evangelist Dwight Moody were notable guests. The grandson of the president of France tried quail for the first time in Thomasville. He remarked (in reference to the quail), "I have never seen anything in such a hell of a hurry in my life."

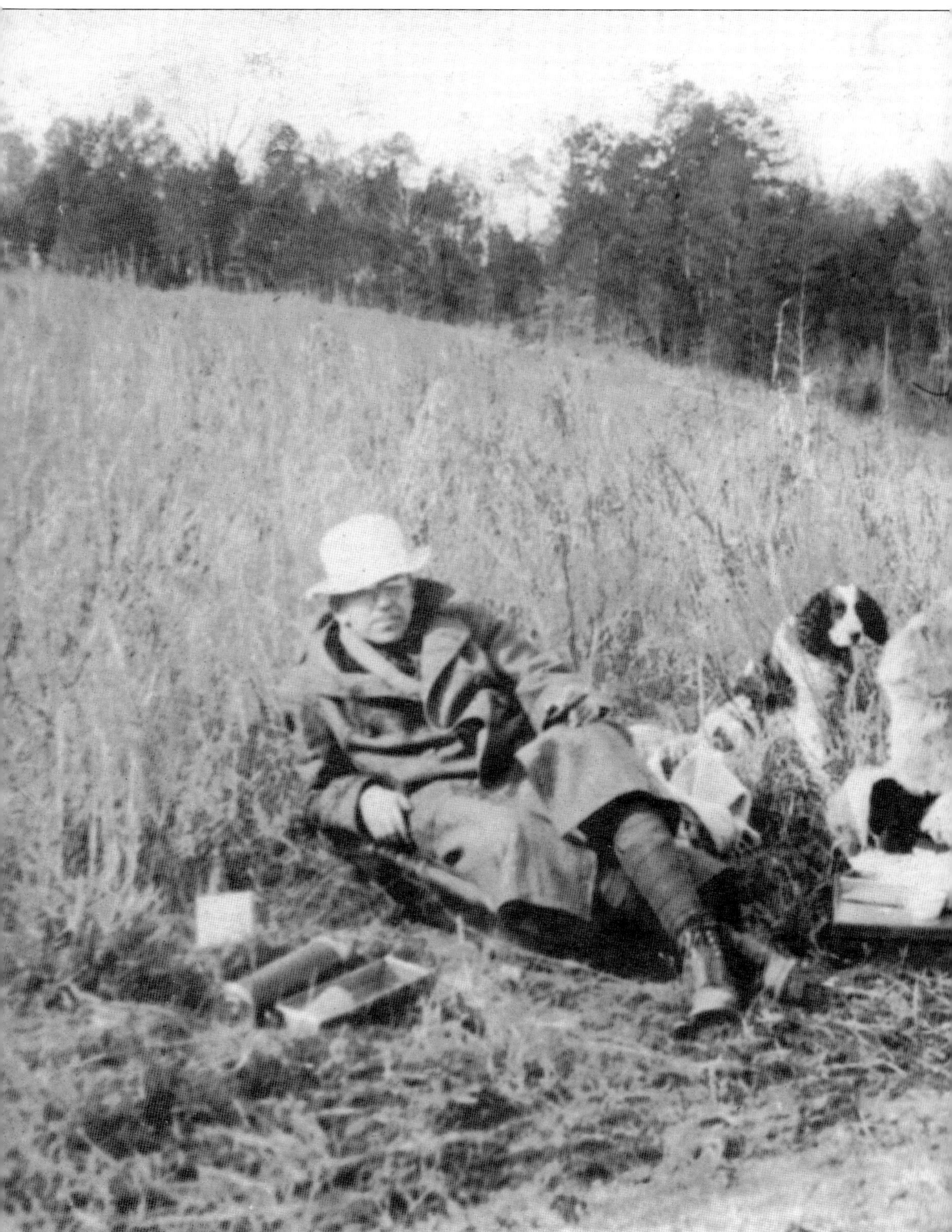

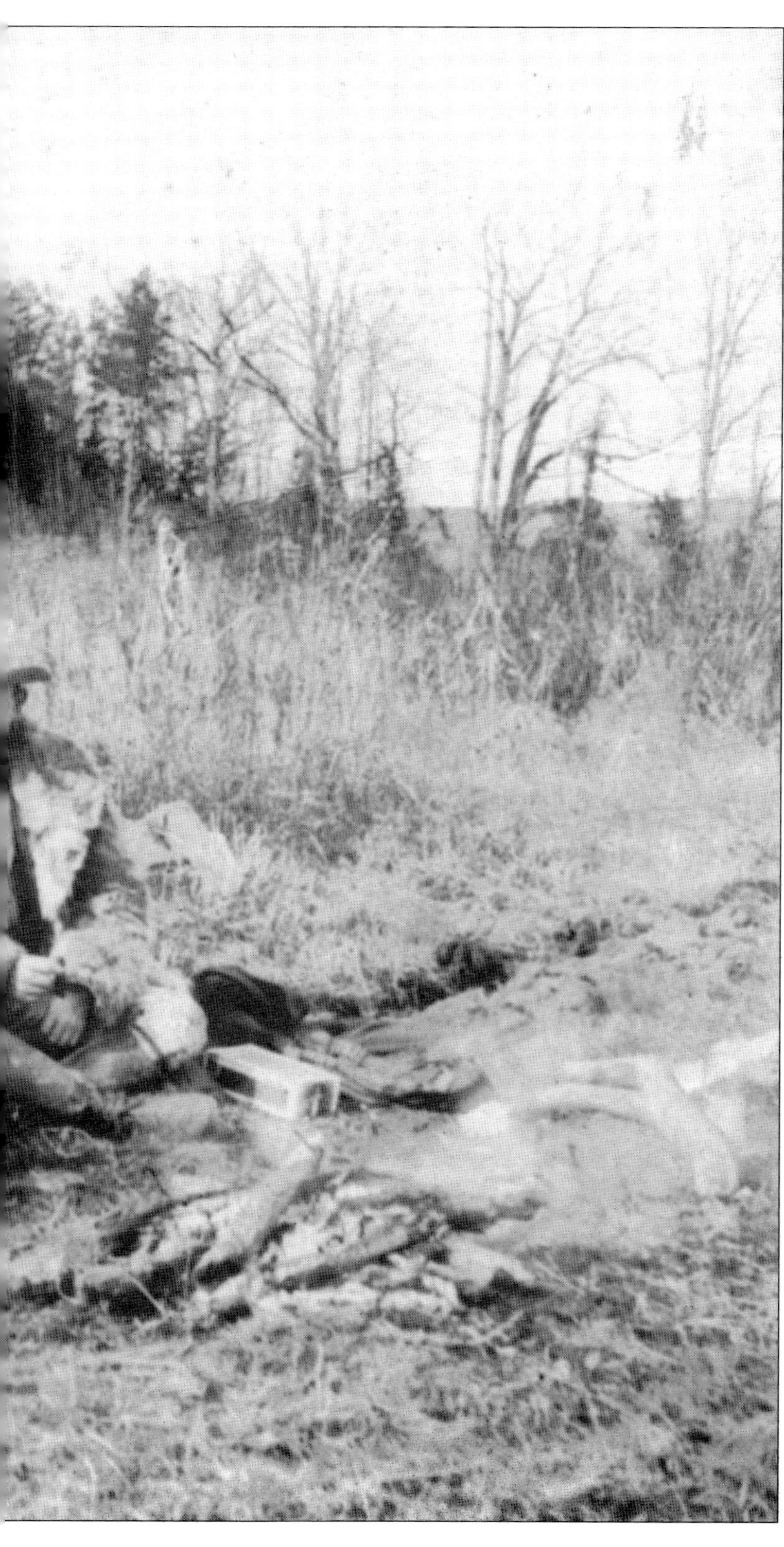

Field Lunch. Hunts usually consisted of two guns and a guide. Although some hunting was done on horseback, most was done from spring wagons and gigs or on foot. The hunters would ride a buggy to a likely spot, put down a brace of dogs, and walk in on foot. Hunting parties considered it bad shooting if less than 15 or 20 coveys were found in a day.

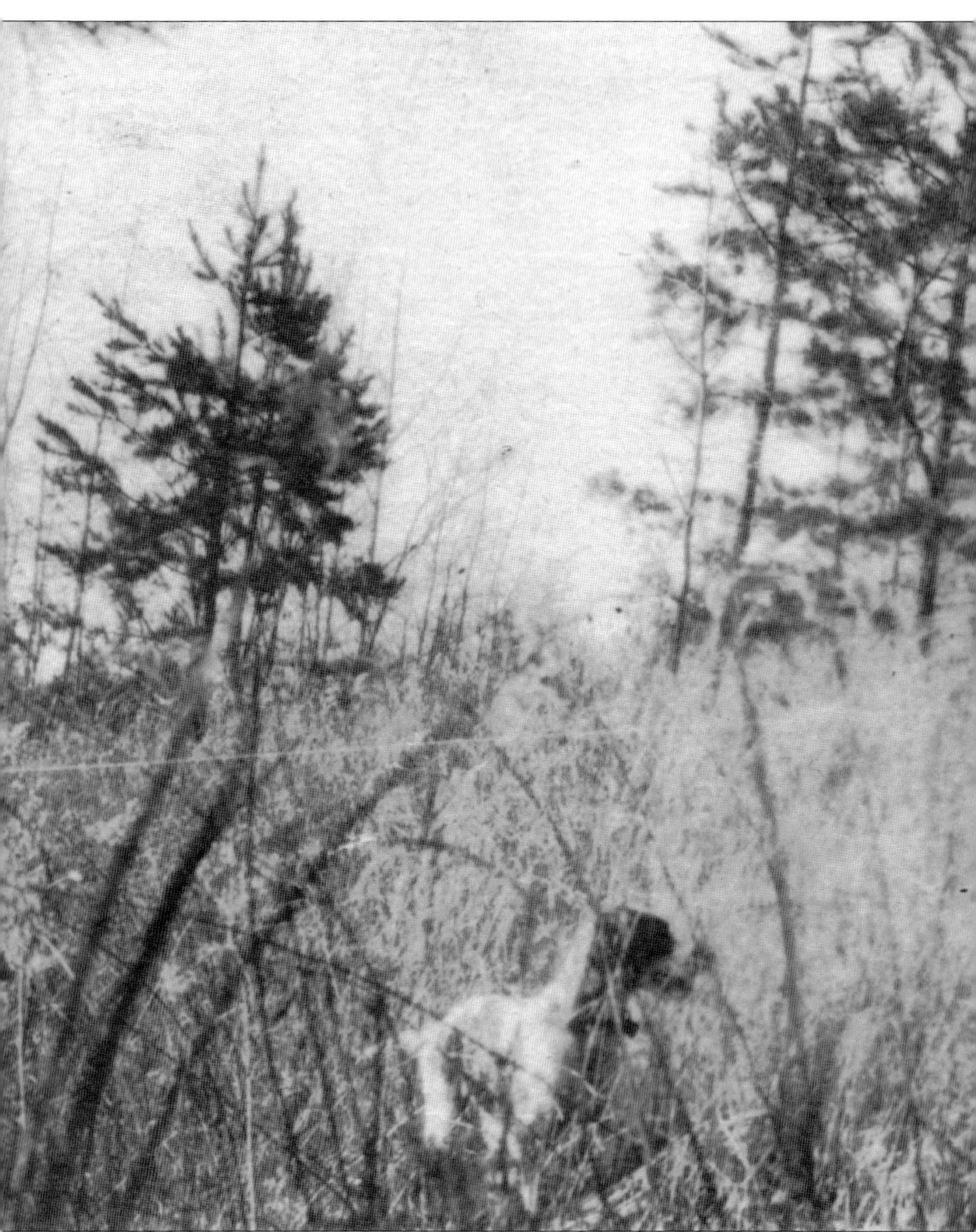

THE FLUSH. In organized excitement, a member moves toward a pointing dog. The dog then flushes the bird, and the smell of burnt powder fills the air. If the flush is successful, the dog retrieves

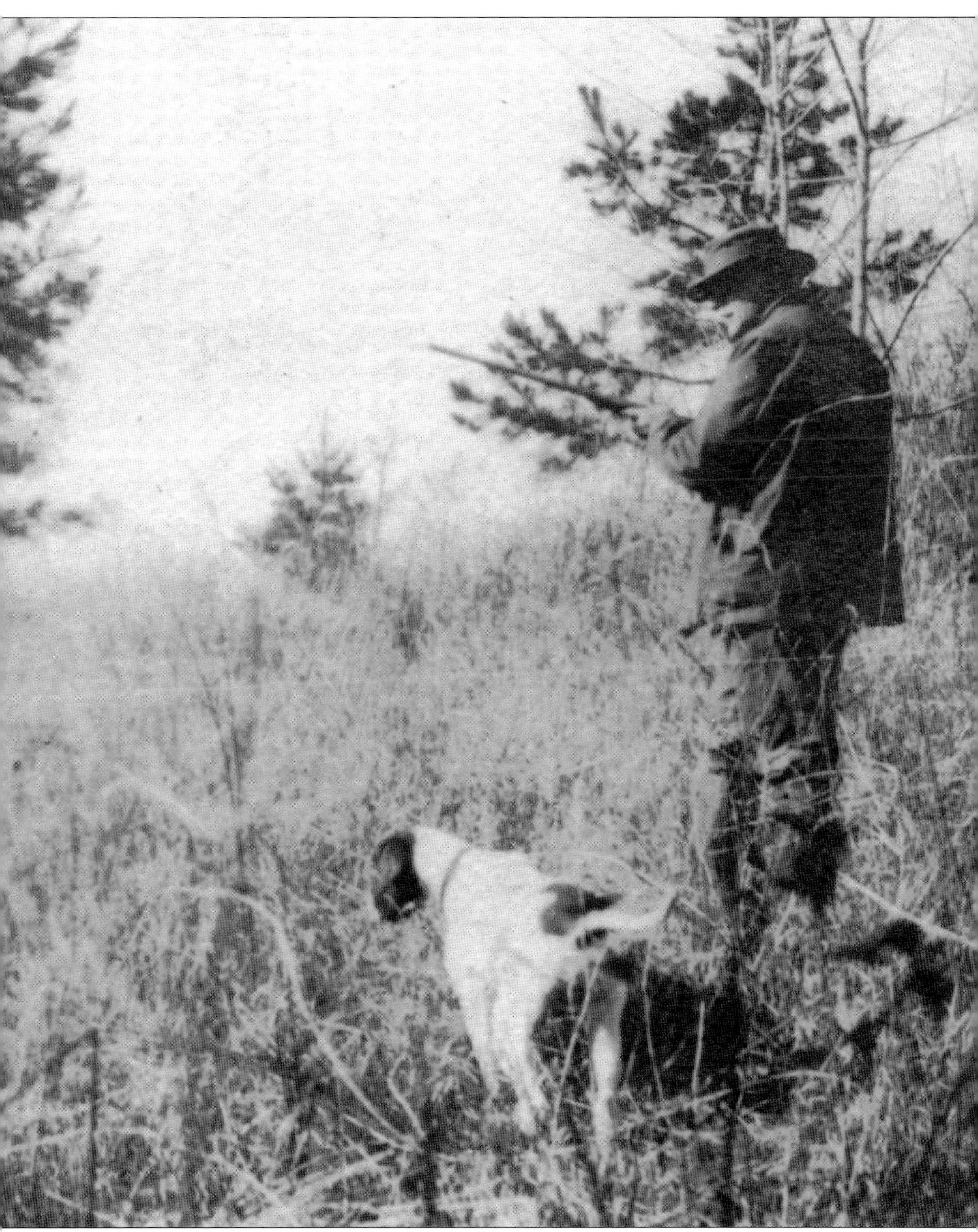

the downed bird(s); this scene plays on throughout the day. Only members of the club and their guests were allowed to hunt on the club's leased property.

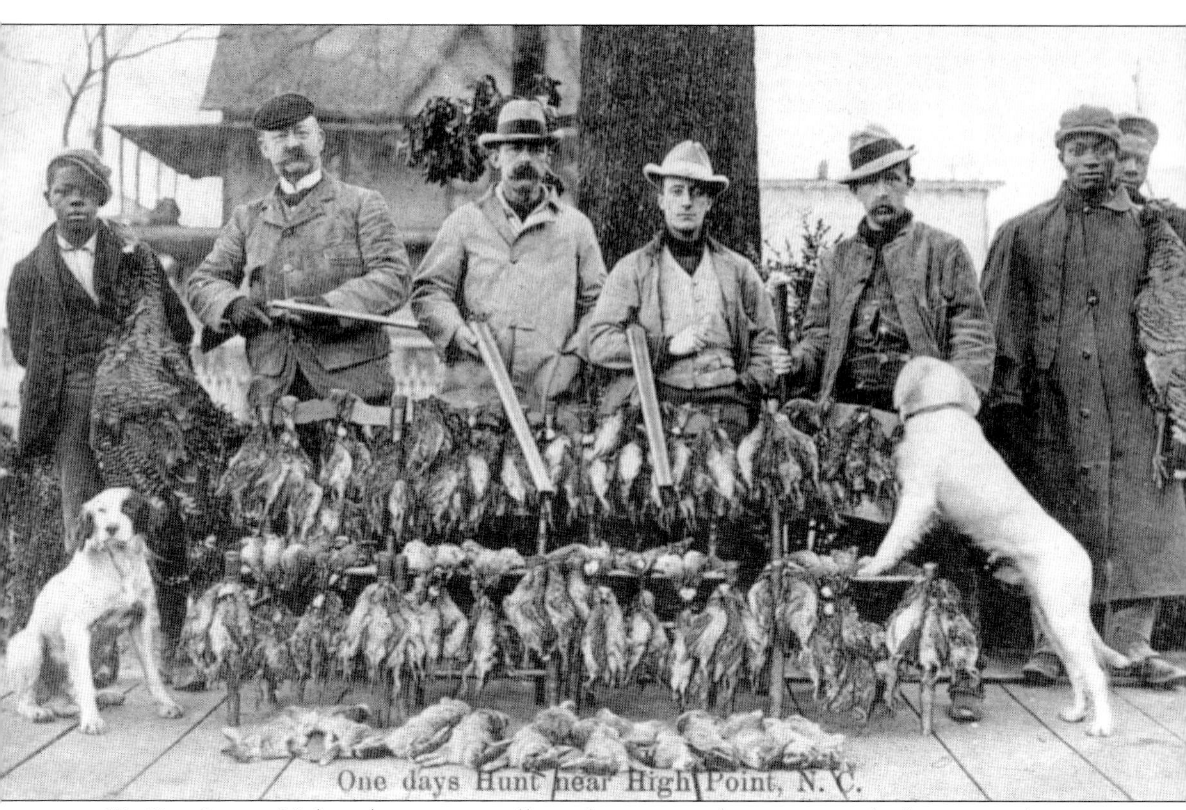

No Bag Limit. Unless they were intelligently instructed, it was easy for hunters to become a menace to game rather than a help—too often, conditions for game got out of balance. Unlike this neighboring hunt club, the Thomasville Shooting Club prided itself on early conservation techniques to preserve excellent quail-hunting for the future. Rural areas outside of town still hold a few small coveys of quail.

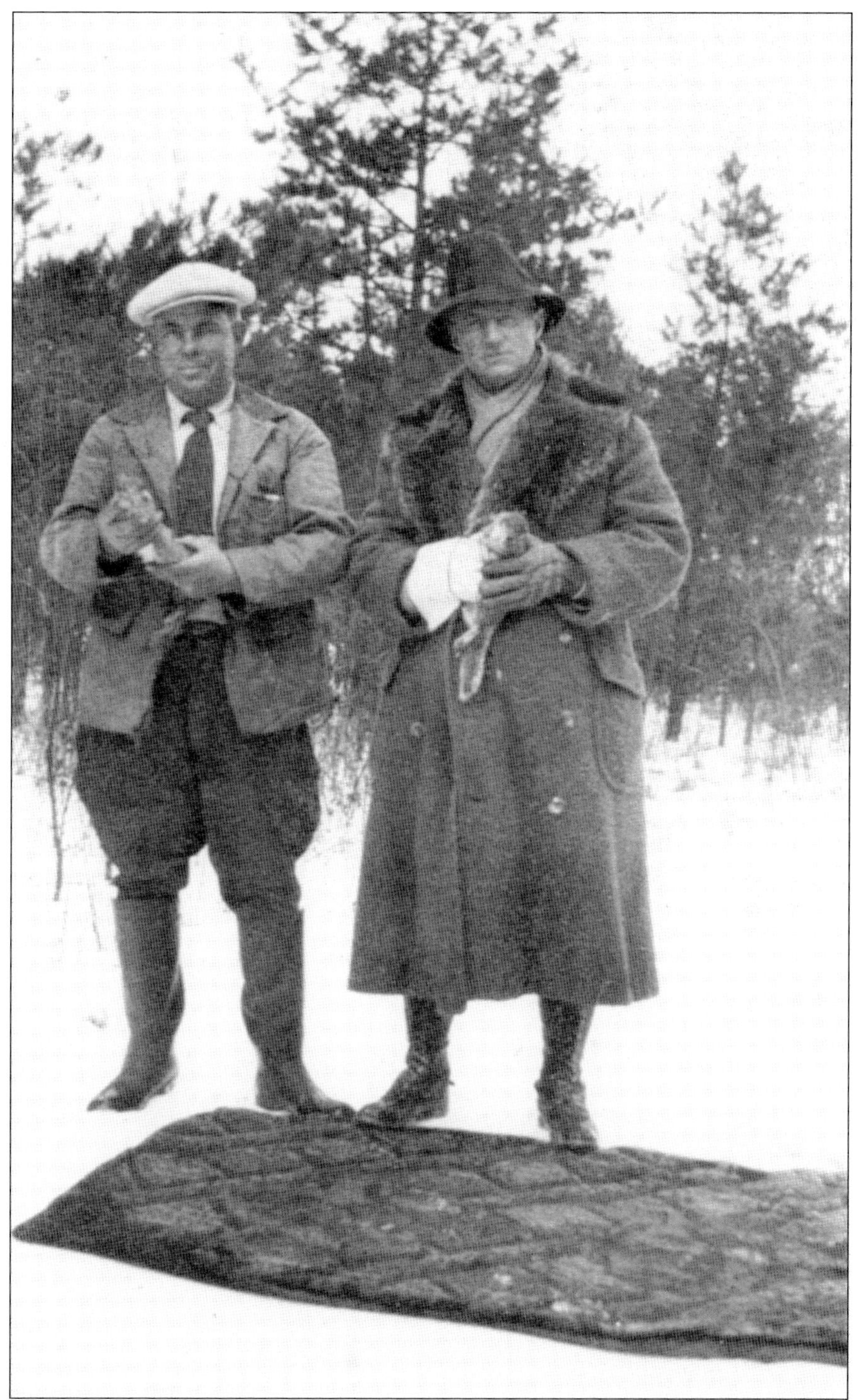

The Harvest. The later days of the Thomasville Shooting Club saw fewer wild coveys of quail due in part to farming improvements and lost habitat. Under the direction of club manager Archie Primm, Everett Swaim raised many a covey of quail and would then place them on the club's land for hunters to chase after the next day.

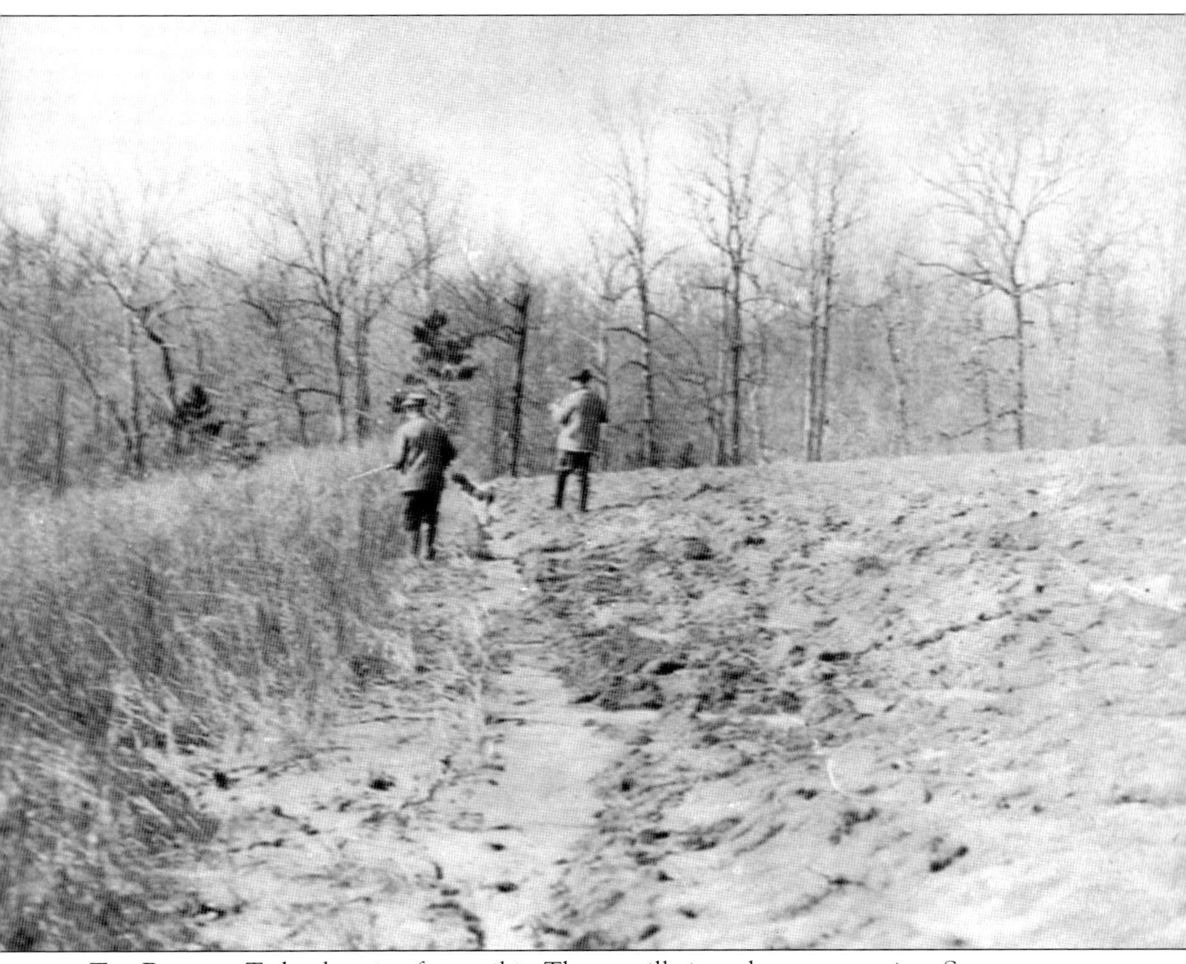

The Reality. Today, hunting for quail in Thomasville is no longer an option. Sure, a covey or two of birds exists somewhere nearby, but not in the numbers of the late 1800s and early 1900s. A big portion of the once-leased hunting grounds is now covered by Lake Tom-A-Lex, Thomasville's drinking-water reservoir.

Bibliography

Capel, Wint. *In Words & Pictures: Thomasville in the Nineteen Twenties*. Chapel Hill, NC: CapeCorp Press, 1999.

———. *The Good Doctor's Downfall*. Lincoln, NE: iUniverse Inc., 2004.

Davidson County Schools: A History 1843–1993. Clarksville, TN: Jostens Inc., 1993.

Hiatt, Cecil P. *High Point, Thomasville & Denton Railroad Company*. Winston-Salem, NC: National Railway Historical Society Inc., 2010.

Hill, Mary, and Wint Capel. *Thomasville, North Carolina, 1852–2002: A History of City Government*. Thomasville, NC: City of Thomasville, 2001.

Matthews, Mary Green, and M. Jewell Sink. *Pathfinders Past and Present: A History of Davidson County, North Carolina*. High Point, NC: Hall Printing Company, 1972.

———. *Wheels of Faith and Courage: A History of Thomasville, North Carolina*. High Point, NC: Hall Printing Company, 1952.

Touart, Paul Baker. *Building the Backcountry: An Architectural History Of Davidson County*. Charlotte, NC: Davidson County Historical Association, 1987.